Contents

D1362648

The child at work and play

Comparative approaches to childhood

The child in social time

Editor's Acknowledgements
My thanks are offered to Dave Walsh and Paul Filmer for their friendship, support and inspiration throughout this project, and also to Jane Jenks, Tony Seward and Maureen Hambrook for their comments on an earlier draft of the Introduction.

The Sociology of Childhood

ESSENTIAL READINGS

Edited by
Chris Jenks

Department of Sociology
University of London
Goldsmiths College

Batsford Academic and Educational Ltd

Selection and editorial matter
© C. Jenks 1982
First published 1982

All rights reserved. No part of this publication
may be reproduced, in any form or by any means,
without permission from the Publisher

Typeset in Hong Kong by Graphicraft Typesetters
and printed in Great Britain by Billing & Son Ltd. Worcester

for the publishers
Batsford Academic and Educational Ltd
an imprint of B.T. Batsford Ltd.
4 Fitzhardinge Street
London W1H OAH

British Library Cataloguing in Publication Data

The Sociology of childhood.
    1. Children – Addresses, essays, lectures
    I. Jenks, Chris
    305.2'3   HQ767.9

    ISBN 0-7134-3695-6
    ISBN 0-7134-3696-4 Pbk

We would not have our Guardians grow up among representations of moral deformity, as in some foul pasture where, day after day, feeding on every poisonous weed they would, little by little, gather insensibly a mass of corruption in their very souls. Rather we must seek out those craftsmen whose instinct guides them to whatsoever is lovely and gracious; so that our young men, dwelling in a wholesome climate, may drink in good from every quarter, whence, like a breeze bearing health from happy regions, some influence from noble works constantly falls upon eye and ear from childhood upward, and imperceptibly draws them into sympathy and harmony with the beauty of reason, whose impress they take. Hence, . . . the decisive importance of education in poetry and music: rhythm and harmony sink deep into the recesses of the soul and take the strongest hold there, bringing that grace of body and mind which is only to be found in one who is brought up in the right way. Moreover, a proper training in this kind makes a man quick to perceive any defects or ugliness in art or in nature. Such deformity will rightly disgust him. Approving all that is lovely, he will welcome it home with joy into his soul and, nourished thereby, grow into a man of noble spirit. All that is ugly and disgraceful he will rightly condemn and abhor while he is still too young to understand the reason; and when reason comes, he will greet her as a friend with whom his education has made him long familiar.

Plato, *The Republic*

1 Introduction: constituting the child
Chris Jenks

Just what, after all, are we to make of children? This question is not new; indeed, from the earliest Socratic dialogues onwards social theorists have systematically endeavoured to constitute a view of the child that is compatible with their particular visions of social life. Since that initial Hellenic desire to seek out the origins of virtue in order to instil rhythm and harmony into the souls of the young, up until our contemporary pragmatic concerns with the efficacy of specific child-rearing practices, after centuries of debate, we have still not achieved any consensus over the issue of childhood. What remains perpetually diffuse and ambiguous is the basic conceptualization of childhood as a social practice; it is unrealized as an emergent patterning of action.

Whether to regard children as pure, bestial, innocent, corrupt or even as we view our adult selves; whether they think and reason as we do, are immersed in a receding tide of inadequacy or are possessors of a clarity of vision which we have through experience lost; whether their forms of language, games and conventions are alternatives to our own, imitations or crude precursors of our own now outgrown, or simply transitory impenetrable trivia amusing to witness and recollect; whether they are constrained and we have achieved freedom, or we have assumed constraint and they are truly free -- all these considerations, and more, continue to exercise our theorizing about the child in social life.

A review of the multiplicity of perspectives that are and have been adopted in attempting to explain childhood reveals, at one level, a continuous paradox, albeit expressed in a variety of ways. Simply stated, the child is familiar to us and yet strange, he inhabits our world and yet seems to answer to another, he is essentially of ourselves and yet appears to display a different order of being: his serious purpose and our intentions towards him are meant to resolve that paradox by transforming him into an adult, like ourselves. This points to the necessity and contingency of the relationship between the child and the adult, both in theory and in commonsense. The difference between the two positions indicates the identity of each; the child cannot be imagined except in relation to a conception of the adult, but interestingly it becomes impossible to produce a well defined sense of the adult and his society without first positing the child. From this may be distilled two elements that appear common to all approaches to childhood. First, a belief that the child instances difference and particularity, and secondly, following from the former, a desire to account for the integration of that difference into a more broadly conceived sense of order and universality that comprises adult society.

Typically, however, the overwhelming irony of this kind of formulation is its failure to acknowledge that very paradox. The child side of the relationship is, within theory, recovered negatively. Such theories tend to be predicated upon a strong, but unexplicated, knowledge of the difference of childhood and they proceed to an overattentive elaboration of the processes of integration. It is as if the basic ontological questions, 'What is a child?', 'How is the child possible as such?', were, so to speak, answered in advance of the theorizing and then dismissed. To take an analogy, just as the early anthropologist, a self-styled civilized man, 'knew' the savage to be different to himself and thus worthy of study; so we also, as rational adults, recognize the child as different and in need of explanation. Both of these positions proceed from a pre-established but tacit ontological theory, a theory of what constitutes the difference of the Other, be it savage or child. It is these unstated modes of theorizing, these tacit commitments to difference, that give rise to the routine definition of the savage or the child as a 'natural' meaningful order of being. Such implicit theories serve to render the child-adult continuum as conventional for the modern social theorist, as the distinction between primitive and rational thought was for the early anthropologist. Such social hierarchies are taken for granted in our thinking because we do not examine the assumptions upon which they are based. These assumptions embody the values and interests of the theorist, which in turn generate normative models of the social world. In this way children and savages alike are excluded from the analysis or reimported as an afterthought. A major concern of this text is to encourage the reader to make a critical reconstruction of such sets of assumptions as they may be available, to different degrees, within the papers that follow. In this way the child might be recovered positively.

Within the terms of the analogy it may be observed that whereas the anthropologist had to travel to his savages across social space, the child as a phenomenon has been brought into recognition across social time. Both of these passages symbolize a searching for knowledge and both such processes are significant in fashioning their object; that is to say that they have succeeded in establishing different classifications and boundaries around their phenomena. The manner of gathering and the character of the distance are significant in the constitution of either savage or child. In the articles which follow, Ariés[1], DeMause and Coveney seek, in their different ways, to demonstrate the evolution of the image of childhood and its mode of recognition and reception through the historical process. Thus the child emerges in contemporary culture as a formal category and as a social status accompanied by programmes of care and schemes of education. Although such analysis ensures that the child be realized as the social construction of a particular historical context, it is his identity as a social status that determines his difference in the everyday world. The child status has its boundaries maintained through the crystallization of conventions into institutional forms like families, nurseries, clinics and schools, all agencies specifically designed to process the status as a uniform entity.

Just as the savage serves as the anthropologist's referrent for man's elementary forms of organization and primitve classifications, giving a sense of the primal state of human being in the historical-cultural process, so also the child is taken to display to adults their state of once untutored difference, but in a more collapsed form: a spectrum reduced from 'human history' to one of generations. This temporal dimension is explored later by both Mannheim and Hendricks and Hendricks. It might be suggested that in the child man can see his immediate past but also the immortality of his immanent future.

In the everyday world the category of childhood is concretely descriptive of a community which though relatively stable in its structure is by definition only fleeting in its particular membership. It further signifies a primary experience in the existential biography of each individual and thus inescapably derives its commonsense meanings and relevance not only from what it might now be as a social status but also from how all individuals, at some time, must have been. Perhaps because of this seemingly all-encompassing character of the phenomenon as a social status and because of the essentially personal character of its particular articulation, commonsense thinking and everyday language in contemporary society are rife with notions concerning childhood. Being a child, having been a child, having children and having to relate to children are all experiences which contrive to make the category available as 'normal' and 'natural'. Such understandings, within the collective awareness, are organized around the single most compelling metaphor of contemporary culture, that of 'growth'. Stemming from this, the physical signs of anatomical development are taken to be indications of a social transition, so that the realms of the social and the natural tend to be conflated.

What I seek to affirm in my theorizing, however, is that childhood is not a natural phenomenon and cannot properly be understood as such. The social transformation from child to adult does not follow directly from physical growth; the recognition of children by adults, and vice versa, is not singularly contingent upon physical difference; and neither is that form of difference an adequately intelligible basis for the relationship between the adult and the child. Childhood is to be understood as a social construct, it makes reference to a social status delineated by boundaries incorporated within the social structure and manifested through certain typical forms of conduct, all of which are essentially related to a particular cultural setting. The anthropologist would readily recognize the significance of such concepts within the social life of his savage; he would demonstrate that the variety and hierarchy of social statuses within the tribe are clearly prescribed by boundaries, which are, in turn, maintained through conventional practices deeply bound within ritual. Any transition from one status to another is never simply a matter of inevitable biological growth; it involves rites of passage and initiation, all of which are disruptive and painful. The fact of addressing the somewhat more diffuse boundaries that mark off childhood today, and the fact of considering such transition from within a secular society, are both no guarantee that the ritualism will be any less deep seated in its application nor indeed any less violent in its implications for the individual's consciousness.

The social propensity to routinize and naturalize childhood, both in commonsense and in theory, serves to conceal its import behind the cloak of the mundane; its significance and 'strangeness' as an historical and social phenomenon become obscured. Within everyday rhetoric childhood is taken for granted, it is regarded as necessary and inevitable, and thus as a normal part of life. This naturalism extends into the conventional language of the social sciences, particularly psychology, where childhood is addressed largely in terms of biological and cognitive development through the concept of 'maturation'. Independently, sociology has sought to understand the problem of cultural acquisition through theories of socialization. All of these ways of proceeding leave the child himself untheorized, they all contrive to gloss over the social experience of childhood. We might here concur with Hillman who states that much of what is said about children and childhood is not really about children and childhood at all. I will suggest that, in significant ways, the child within the social sciences is employed as a device through which to propound versions of social cohesion.

From within a variety of disciplines, perspectives and sets of interests childhood receives treatment as a stage, a structured becoming, never as a course of action nor a social practice. The kind of 'growth' metaphors that are used in discussion about children are all of the character of what is yet to be, yet which is also presupposed; thus childhood is spoken of as 'becoming', as a *tabula rasa*, as laying the foundations, taking on, growing up, preparation, inadequacy, inexperience, immaturity and so on. Such metaphors all seem to speak of a relation to an unexplicated but nevertheless firmly established, rational adult world. This world is not only assumed to be complete and static, but also desirable. It is a benevolent totality which extends a welcome to the child, it invites him to cast off the quality that ensures his difference and it encourages his acquiescence to the preponderance of the induction procedures that will guarantee his corporate identity.

For the anthropologist to proceed from such a position would be for him to invite the charge of ethnocentrism. If he were to suggest that the savage was in some way in his shadow, acting through delusion or operating with a proto-typical form of his own cultural devices then he would be working against a backdrop of his own social standards treated as necessarily preeminent and essentially morally superior. This intransigent encoding of his own cultural experience would thus become the central unexplored problem in the anthropologist's work, and his view of the savage would make direct reference to that analytic problem; in the same way any view of the child reflects a preferred, but unexplored, model of the social order.

In line with this form of ethnocentrism, socialization theories present the normative structure of the adult/parent world as their independent variable. Against the yardstick of this assumed consensual reality the child is judged to be more or less competent and consequently the continuous lived social practice of being a child in relation to a specific meaning structure is ignored. This unilateral manipulation of the child within socialization theories condemns him to be an absent presence, a nominal cipher without an active dimension.

Here again we witness the irony of my original formulation: that although lay members systematically manage to establish childhood as a social category in its own right, most social theories, through their emphasis on a taken for granted adult world, signally fail to constitute 'the child' as an ontology in its own right. The grounds of difference between children and adults are undisclosed; such theorizing is forgetful of its origins. The social practice emergent as childhood is, within socialization theories, without moment; it finds voice only as a distant echo of what it is yet to become.

Accounts of this nature begin from a specific and given model of structured human conduct and then seek to explain childhood as teleologically related to that preestablished end. In such a way socialization theories methodically fail to recognise or acknowlege their intentional character, which is the justification of particular social worlds. The interests and purposes within such worlds remain undisclosed. This crucial point is clearly expressed by O'Neill when he states that 'any theory of child socialization is implicitly a theory of a social reality if not a particular social order.'

It can now, perhaps, be seen that my analytic concern, stemming from the notion of childhood, has emerged from a more fundamental orientation towards the preservation of both social and sociological worlds. It is in this context that any analysis must attempt to open up the boundaries that have been placed around the experience of childhood, whether such boundaries are common-sensical, educational, psychological, medical or biological in type. In this way it becomes possible to actually topicalize 'the child' for social theory.

The constitution of the child presents a major problem within sociological formulations. Whenever a social world is assembled in theorizing it is traditionally populated by and articulated through 'normal', 'natural' and 'rational' models of human conduct. Within sociological worlds, the implicit view of man, however specific and insular it may be, is consistently based on the assumption of a kind of behavioural totality, a sense of completeness and arrival. The rational acting member of such worlds personifies adulthood. All action within sociological worlds, if it is to be intelligible, gravitates inevitably towards a universal yet covert specification of rule, the rule of the social system. Even deviant behaviour, in whatever concrete form, is managed in terms of its being either a negatively orientated or an unreasonably stigmatized expression of adult behaviour. What can be noted, however, is that the child, childhood, child behaviour and child's play cannot be viewed adequately through the same overall explanatory devices. Sociological worlds are constructed in terms of universal 'rational adults' yet our everyday experience as practical members of real social worlds abounds with children and the notions of difference and divergence that they represent.

In a strong sense the possibility of difference inherent in

childhood, considered either as a course of action or as a community, presents a potentially disintegrative threat to sociological worlds. Childhood constitutes a way of conduct that cannot properly be evaluated and routinely incorporated within the grammar of existing social systems. It is in this regard that theory moves to envelope the child within its own projections. Childhood is understood after the fact of successful social systems, it is treated as a residual category and incorporated through remedial theories of socialization.

As already stated, childhood receives treatment through its archetype image; it is conceptualized as a structured becoming, not as a social practice nor as a location of Self. This archetype of the child is sustained in language and within the language communities of the institutions and specialisms which serve to patrol the boundaries around childhood as a social status. These boundaries do not simply mark out the extent and compass of the child in society, they more deeply express the control component exercised in the framework of that social system and the interests that sustain its functioning. The image of the child, in language, presupposes and stands in relation to the 'interested' character of a structured adult world. The metaphoricity reveals the moral basis of such interests.

The empirical content of the child's difference has been explored within the body of the literature, for example in the work of the Opies. Such attempts to produce children as embodied and as occupying a world of their own making are, at that level, an important contribution. This kind of descriptive specification of the child's difference is, however, only a beginning; we need to look to the reasons for the child, the grounds for the image and the archetype in our languages.

The order of socialization theories so far discussed begins from a specific and given model of the social formation, which embodies the theorist's purpose, and relentlessly strives to subvert and restructure the child's potentially dangerous and disruptive difference into a form that equates with the unexplicated moral grounds of the initial theorizing. Such processing generates what Wrong (1961) has termed 'the oversocialised conception of man' and can be experienced in its finest form within the Social System of Parsons.

Parsons' work sets up a magnificent structure of social organization integrating action with constraint. This edifice operates at the levels of the economic, the political, the cultural, the interactional and the personal - it is thus intended to permeate and saturate all expressions of collective human experience. Parsons' Social System constitutes the oneness of the social world through two metaphors, firstly that of 'organicism' which speaks of the unspecific, the living and is concerned with content; secondly that of a 'system' which makes reference to the explicit, the dead and is concerned with form. Through the central concept of socialization Parsons commits a theoretic violence, particularly upon the child, through seeking to convert their worlds from content to form. It is as if societies are conceived of as living organisms but are everywhere becoming machines. To reinvoke my original terms, the Social System seeks to transform or integrate difference into communality.

Parsons' concerns are grounded in the Hobbesian problem of order; however, within the sociological tradition Hobbes' Leviathan, the monstrous form of the political state which provides for and symbolizes the unity of the people, is supplanted by the concept of 'society'. Society becomes the monitor for all order and it further inculcates a set of rules of conduct which are enforced less by individual will and political sovereignty than by society's own pre-existence. This supra-individual monolith remains the unquestioned basis for all theorizing within the order-based sociological tradition.

Simply stated, the Social System is evolved from the top downwards, from a presumption of central consensual values to the level of the individual personality. When Parsons speaks of the production of a general theory of action within the System, he is addressing the persistent translation of universal cultural values into particular social norms. That is, he is asking how do social actors routinely develop the social norms that inform their day to day conduct from the deeply embedded cultural sentiments inherent in the Social System; how does the collective consciousness become real in the minds of individual men?

It is the social norms that provide the rules by which the inter-action between Self and Other (or Ego and Alter in Parsons' terms) is governed. It is the persistent and necessary translation of cultural values into social norms that provides the dynamic within the System; it is as if the organism pulsates and its life blood circulates from the universalistic centre to the particularistic individual cells that comprise its mass. Social action conceived of in these terms is what Parsons refers to as 'instrumental activism'.

The social norms become both the means and ends of all action within the System. More than this they become the source of 'identity' between the actor and the System, and the social order itself resides in this identity between the actor and the System. The concept of identification is an important one to Parsons as it was to Freud before him. In Freud's theory of psychosexual development the narcissistic infant was thought capable of a primitive form of object-choice, called 'identification', in which he sought an object conceived of in his own image which he therefore desired as he loved himself. In Parsons' Social System the social norms are the source of this identity because they diminish the potential distinction between the self and the collectivity, by engendering a coinciding set of interests for both the self and the collectivity. It is through this basic identification that individuals become committed to the Social System, they can be claimed as members and their behaviours cohere. Social norms therefore establish the ground rules of social life and the System is stable when the norms are effective in governing interaction.

We may now look, in wider terms, at how the Social System is constructed and articulated, at how the living body is built up but through its functioning becomes a machine. In Parsons' world life passes into death at the hands of the theorist and socialization is the key to this mortification.

At the outset the System is confronted by the problem of order, but teleologically it is also defined by Parsons in terms of that very order. At the analytic level, order is sustained by two pervasive system tendencies (which are common to all systems). These tendencies are called 'functional prerequisites' and are the tendency to self maintenance and the tendency to boundary maintenance. The functional prerequisites refer to the inside and the outside respectively; the former to the System's capacity to sustain itself, maintain its own equilibrium, the internal homeostatic balance; the latter refers to the System's capacity to pronounce its difference, to demarcate its boundaries and thus to stand in a relation with its environment. These two functional prerequisites emerge from bio-systems theory; they are the point at which the metaphors of the systemic and the organic merge and thus the point at which the rule of analysis becomes the rule of nature.

A closer look at the actual framework of the System shows that it is further comprised of certain sub-systems. It is the functional interchange between these sub-systems which provides for the evolution of the overall System and its emergent qualities. Functional interchange between sub-systems is thus another sign of life within the machine. These sub-systems are concerned with the survival, maintenance and growth of the wider System. They are the 'physical sub-system', the 'cultural sub-system' and the 'personality sub-system'; it is the latter which is specifically concerned with problems of childhood and socialization.

The personality sub-system is presented with the unsocialized, highly differentiated child as its primary reality. The problem that the System addresses here is that of sustaining existing patterns of interaction by invoking the latent sociality within the child. It needs to ensure that the individual child is supplied with a suitable environment so that he shall be enabled to generate the appropriate capacities that are demanded by the adult System as a whole. This problem is to be handled by the family which stands as an affective repository within the total System. It is the family which is theoretically operative in carrying out the primary socialization of the child and of subsequently providing emotional support for all its members. Socialization can be regarded here as the building of the System's basic instrumental and expressive drives into the structure of individual personalities.

The psycho-analytic dimensions of Parsons' theorizing appear not simply through his selective use of Freudian categories, but rather through his need to penetrate inner selves. Essentially the Social System is dependent upon capturing total personalities, thus leaving no space for divergence, dissolution or difference. The System machine is fed by its compliant member personalities and must, perforce, consume children.

In one sense personality theory and the consequent specification of childhood are not very important to Parsons. His commitment is to the problem of the stability of complex social systems, so that actors come to be constructed in terms of features that are relevant to their functioning. It is their qualities as cogs in the machine that are to be stressed. The System seeks to undermine the autonomy of the Self and the expression of difference; following from such an aspiration the theory is characterized by a stable unitary isomorphism. This entails that all aspects of the social world, from total social systems, through sub-systems and particular institutions down to individual personalities, are viewed as formally analogous to each other. So personalities are microcosmically analogous to total social systems; they share the same form, content and patterning of responses.

With this isomorphism in mind we can proceed to the fundamental elements of the Parsonian personality theory, which he calls 'need dispositions'. These display two features; first, a kind of performance, an activity, and second a kind of sanction or satisfaction. Here then are the ingredients for a homeostatic balance between desire and satiation, as need dispositions all have built-in regulators; here at another level is the iron hand of coercion concealed in the velvet glove of normative constraint. The essential conceptual model remains of a naturalistic personality comprised of sets of need dispositions, the gratificaiton of which is neither wholly compatible nor entirely possible within the limitations imposed by the social structure. It begins to look as if we are witnessing an 'id' which needs to be contained by the 'super-ego' of the Social System, and this is precisely the case. The potentially overwhelming and yet expressive need dispositions have to be integrated, coordinated and modified by value standards and role expectations within the System.

As with Freud, the social bond is seen to reside in repression; the threat of infantile sexuality and the difference of childhood must be treated as pathological. In this way, given the integrity of a System contingent upon isomorphism, the socialization process or process of socio-libidinal castration serves to maintain both the inside and the outside within the requirements of order; that is, it maintains the personality system (and thus by implication the whole system) and also it optimizes the gratifications within the limits of the structure.

To return to the original point, Parsons, and the tradition of socialization theory that extends from his work, successfully abandons the child to the dictates of the Social System. The social practice of childhood is sublimated by the theorist's presumptive motives in sustaining integration and order at the analytic level. The child, like the deviant, signifies difference; in his unsocialized state he threatens to bring down social worlds and the threat can only be mollified within theory by treating the child through his archetype as a proto-adult, a potential and ultimate supplicant at the altar of the corporate rationality implicit within the Social System. The social practice of childhood is inevitably and necessarily displaced within the language of socialization. Thus, for example, Ritchie and Kollar (1964) state

The central concept in the sociological approach to childhood is socialisation. A synonym for this process may well be acculturation because this term implies that children acquire the culture of the human groupings in which they find themselves. Children are not to be viewed as individuals fully equipped to participate in a complex adult world, but as beings who have the potentials for being slowly brought into contact with human beings.

Such seemingly bland dehumanization is not uncommon within this form of reasoning. Conventional sociological worlds rest their orderliness upon a strong yet unexplicated theory of what everyone knows, that is, upon an ascriptive notion of competence on the part of their members. As a consequence of the adult member being considered naturally as mature, rational and competent, the child is viewed in juxtaposition as less than fully human, unfinished or incomplete. Such dichotomous discrimination in terms of socio-cognitive competence assumes its most explicit form in theories concerned with the learning process. It is in this context that the idea of becoming adult is taken to delineate a singular and highly specific mode of rationality. Although social theorists are aware that 'rationality' is a collective institution which addresses the relation between self and other, and despite the fact that their studies have shown them that rationality can neither dominate man nor be entirely free of his historical context; nevertheless, the irony persists, within theory, that particular versions of rationality are devised and manipulated in order to contrive the exclusion of certain groups. In learning theory it is the child who is so excluded.

At one level this exclusion also operates in the pedagogic theory and curriculum planning of the philosophers Hirst and Peters (1970). Their categories of understanding and their necessary precepts for the organization of knowledge all seem to legitimate and justify existing social orders; an elitist desire that attempts to pass as disinterested analysis. They put forward an educational programme which is described as being both 'rational' and 'liberal' in conception and is yet highly selective and thus exclusive in character.

More fundamentally the irony of exclusion through partial formulations of rationality is encountered in Piaget's theories of intelligence and child development. Piaget's work, his 'genetic epistemology', seeks to provide a description of the structuring of thought and finally the rational principle of nature itself; all through a theory of learning. As such Piaget's complete project stands as a contribution to philosophy also. Following in a neo-Kantian tradition his ideas endeavour to conciliate the divergent epistemologies of Empiricism and Rationalism; the former conceiving of reality as being available in the form of synthetic truths discoverable through direct experience, and the latter viewing reality analytically through the action of pure reason alone. Kant, in his time, had overcome this dichotomy through the invocation of 'synthetic *a priori* truths' that are the immanent conditions of understanding, not simply amenable to logical analysis. Piaget's categories of understanding in conceptual development may be treated as of the same order. His work meticulously constitutes a particular system of scientific rationality and presents it as both natural and universal.

Piaget's empirical studies on the development of thought and intelligence describe the inevitable and clearly defined stages of intellectual growth from sensory-motor intelligence, immediately succeeding birth, through pre-conceptual thought, intuitive thought and concrete operations up to the level of formal operations, for most people, in early adolescence. These stages are temporally ordered but also hierarchically arranged along a continuum from low status, infantile, 'figurative' thought to high status, adult, 'operative' intelligence. Figurative thought is instanced by particularistic activity, an inability to transfer experience and a highly concrete replication of object states; it is organized through affective responses in specific situations, the child is clearly dominated by objective structures. Operative intelligence, on the other hand, implies the informed cognitive manipulation and transformation of objects by the reflecting subject; it exemplifies logical process and freedom from domination by immediate experience.

Within this system each stage of intellectual growth is characterized by a specific 'schema' or well defined pattern and sequence of physical and mental actions governing the child's orientation to the world. The development and transition from figurative to operative thought, through the sequence of stages, depends upon a mastery and transcendence of the schemata at each stage. This implies a change in the child's relation to the world. This transition, the necessary passage through schemata, is what Piaget refers to as 'decentring' – it brings about a change from solipsistic subjectivism to a realistic objectivity, from affective response to cognitive evaluation, a movement from the disparate realm of value into the absolute realm of fact. The successful outcome of this developmental process may be typified as 'scientific rationality'. It is the stage at which the child, now adult, becomes at one with the logical structure of the cosmos: his matured thought gives him membership of the 'circle of science', the project of genetic epistemology has reached its fruition, it is complete. Concretely, scientific rationality is displayed through abstraction, generalization, logico-deductive process, mathematization and cognitive operations; at the analytic level, however, it reveals the intentional character of Piaget's theorizing and grounds his system in the same manner as did Parsons' transcendent 'cultural values'. Further, whereas socialization through identification provided the key to the dissolution of the child within the Social System, so also within Piaget's genetic epistemology the process of decentring can be exposed as the analytic device by and through which the child is wrenched from the possibility of difference within the realm of value and integrated into the consensus that comprises the tyrannical realm of fact. Scientific rationality or adult intelligence is thus the recognition of difference grounded in unquestioned collectivity – we are brought back to the irony contained within the original ontological question. The child is once more abandoned in theory. Real historically located children are subjected to the violence of a contemporary mode of scientific rationality which reproduces itself, at the expense of their difference, beyond the context of situated social life. The 'fact' of natural process overcomes the 'value' of real social worlds.

Piaget's developmental theory states that the dynamic of the decentring process is provided by the interplay between two fundamental, complementary processes, being 'assimilation' and 'accommodation'. The two processes concern the child's choice of and relation to that which is other than himself; assimilation concerns the absorption and integration of new object experiences into existing and previously organised schemata, and accommodation involves the modification of existing schemata or the construction of new schemata to encapsulate new and discordant object experiences. The processes are complementary in that accommodation generates new organizing principles to overcome the 'disequilibrium' produced by new experiences that cannot be readily assimilated. Within Piaget's demonstrations of adult scientific rationality, the child is deemed to have appropriately adapted to the environment when he has achieved a balance between accommodation and assimilation. Although from a critical analytic stance accommodation might be regarded as the source of the child's integration into the consensus reality, within the parameters of the original theory the process is treated as the locus of creativity and innovation – it is that aspect of the structuring of thought which is to be highly valued. In contradistinction Piaget treats children's play as non-serious, trivial activity in as much as it displays an emphasis of assimilation over accommodation. Play is merely diverting fun or fantasy, it deflects the child from his true logical purpose within the system of rationality; the criteria of play need not equate with the rigorous factual demands of reality. Treating play in this manner, from the perspective of the rational 'serious' adult, Piaget is specifically undervaluing what might stand as an important aspect of the expressive practice of the child and his world. Following Denzin and also Stone here I would suggest that play is indeed an important feature of the child's work as a social member and also of what Speier has termed the 'acquisition of interactional competencies'. Genetic epistemology pays insufficient attention to play in its urge to mathematize and thus formalize the 'rational' cognitive practices of collective adult individuals.

By treating the growth process of the child's cognition as impelled towards a prestated structure of adult rationality Piaget is driven to concur with Levy-Bruhl's notion of a 'primitive mentality' in relation to the 'pre-logical' thought of the child. Beyond this, because the rational development of the child's 'embryonic' mind is conceptualized as a natural process, the part played by language is also understated. It is treated as a symbolic vehicle which carries thought and assists the growth of concepts and a semiotic system, but which is insufficient in itself to bring about the mental operations which make concept formation possible. Language helps in the selection, storage and retrieval of information but it does not bring about the coordination of mental operations. This level of organization is conceptualized above language and in the domain of action; not action regarded as the performative conduct that generates social contexts, but rather a sense of action as rationally governed within the *a priori* strictures of an idealist metaphysics. Language for Piaget itemizes the world acting as a purely cognitive function. This is a position that Merleau-Ponty confounds in his work on the existential generation and use of language by children; an argument that serves to reunite the cognitive and the affective aspects of being which are so successfully sundered by Piaget.

At the outset of this Introduction I commented on the absence of any consensus view of the child within social theory. This is a deficiency which in the present state of theory it is neither possible nor indeed desirable to attempt to remedy in any definitive sense. Instead it has been my intention to show that it is the different manners in which theoretical commitments are grounded that gives rise to the diversity of views of childhood that are current at the present time. The collection of articles which follows will attest to this diversity and I trust that I have provided a starting point from which the reader may approach the evaluation of these available theories of childhood.

My critical appraisals of Parsons and Piaget were not random selections. They have been singled out for analysis because of the clarity and penetration of their work, because of the very significant influence that they have exercised on the social sciences in the areas of socialization theory and learning theory, and, particularly in the case of Piaget, because of the impact that his ideas have had upon the commonsense view of the child. They and the traditions of which they are a part have, to a large extent, captured and monopolized the child in social theory and in so doing they both exemplify the analytic point of this collection. The idea of childhood is not a natural but a social construct; as such its status is constituted in particular socially located forms of discourse. Whether the child is being considered in the commonsense world or in the disciplined world of specialisms, the meaningfulness of the child as a social being derives from its place, its purpose, within the theory. Social theory is not merely descriptive and certainly never disinterested, as will be apparent from the variety of perspectives gathered in this book. However, for the reader to approach that variety as if it added up to an eclectic overview or carefully comprised a wider image of the child would be to mistake my intention. The variety is gathered analytically around the central theme that the child is constituted purposively within theory; that is, the child is assembled intentionally to serve the purposes of supporting and perpetuating the fundamental grounds of and versions of man, action, order, language and rationality within particular theories. We are thus presented in what follows with different 'theoretical' children to serve the different theoretical models of social life from which they spring. In this sense the overall perspective in compiling this text has been phenomenological in character.

Naturally the reader will use this book as he wishes. My recommendation remains, however, that a sociology of childhood should emerge from the constitutive practices that provide for the child and the child-adult relationship. For the reader to engage in such analysis, as I have attempted with Parsons and Piaget, will demonstrate to him that he also is responsible for constituting the child, and that different images of the child are occasioned by the different theoretic social worlds that we inhabit. In this way the passage of our theorizing might emerge from the stenosis of the dominant 'natural' archetypes of childhood, being those of either the pathological or the schismatic. We need no longer abandon the child either to ignorance and secondary status or to radical difference and a bipartite world.

Note
1 All references in this chapter are to articles and extracts contained within the present volume, with the exception of:

HIRST, P.H. and PETERS, R.S. *The Logic of Education* Routledge & Kegan Paul, London, 1970.

RITCHIE, O.W. and KOLLAR, M.R. *The Sociology of Childhood* Appleton Century Crofts, New York, 1964.

WRONG, D. 'The Oversocialized Conception of Man in Modern Sociology' in *American Sociological Review* XXVI, April 1961.

An archaeology of childhood

Children have always been with us. However, the
manner of their recognition by adults and thus the
form of their relationship with adults has altered
from epoch to epoch. In this sense they cannot be
treated as invariant features of the social landscape.
Their location emerges from a set of social relations
of control, operating through hierarchy and based
on age. As a social category the child has come to
us through time and this passage has accompanied
changes in the economy, alterations in the structure
of the family, the transition to industrialization and
urbanization, and also man's search for a stronger
sense of identity within the contemporary division of
labour. Our uncovering of the historical strata upon
which children now stand will reveal that these
young people who populate our culture, with a
whole network of specialist public provision and
commercial enterprise dedicated to their presence,
were once the unacknowledged, abused and
exploited homunculi of the Middle Ages.

2 The discovery of childhood
Philippe Ariés

Antiquo-medieval speculation had bequeathed to posterity a copious terminology relating to the ages of life. In the sixteenth century, when it was proposed to translate the terminology into French, it was found that the French language, and consequently French usage, had not as many words at its disposal as had Latin or at least learned Latin. The 1556 translator of *Le Grand Propriétaire de toutes choses* makes no bones about recognizing the difficulty: 'It is more difficult in French than in Latin, for in Latin there are seven ages referred to by various names, of which there are only three in French: to wit, childhood, youth and old age.'

It will be noted that since youth signifies the prime of life, there is no room for adolescence. Until the eighteenth century, adolescence was confused with childhood. In school Latin the word *puer* and the word *adolescens* were used indiscriminately. Preserved in the Bibliothèque Nationale are the catalogues of the Jesuit College at Caen, a list of the pupils' names accompanied by comments. A boy of fifteen is described in these catalogues as *bonus puer*, while his young schoolmate of thirteen is called *optimus adolescens*. Baillet, in a book on infant prodigies, admitted that there were no terms in French to distinguish between *pueri* and *adolescentes*. There was virtually only one word in use: *enfant*.

At the end of the Middle Ages, the meaning of this word was particulary extensive. It could be applied to both the *putto* (in the sixteenth century the *putti* room, the bedchamber decorated with frescoes depicting naked children, was referred to as 'the children's room') and the adolescent, the big lad who was sometimes also a bad lad. The word *enfant* ('child') in the *Miracles de Notre-Dame* was used in the fourteenth and fifteenth centuries as a synonym of other words such as *valets, valeton, garcon, fils* ('valet', 'varlet', 'lad', 'son'):

Source: Philippe Ariés, *Centuries of Childhood*, tr. Robert Baldick, Jonathan Cape (1962), reprinted Penguin (1973).

'he was a *valeton*' would be translated today as 'he was a good-looking lad', but the same word could be used of both a young man ('a handsome *valeton*') and a child ('he was a *valeton*, so they loved him dearly . . . *li valez* grew up'). Only one word has kept this very ancient ambiguity down to our times, and that is the word *gars* ('lad'), which has passed straight from Old French into the popular modern idiom in which it is preserved. A strange child, this bad lad who was 'so perverse and wicked that he would not learn a trade or behave as was fitting in childhood . . . he kept company with greedy, idle folk who often started brawls in taverns and brothels, and he never came across a woman by herself without raping her'. Here is another child of fifteen: 'Although he was a fine, handsome son', he refused to go riding or to have anything to do with girls. His father thought that it was out of shyness: 'This is customary in children.' In fact, he was betrothed to the Virgin. His father forced him into marriage: 'The child became very angry and struck him hard.' He tried to make his escape and suffered mortal injuries by falling downstairs. The Virgin then came for him and said to him: 'Dear brother, behold your sweetheart.' And: 'At this the child heaved a sigh.' According to a sixteenth-century calendar of the ages, at twenty-four 'a child is strong and brave', and 'this is what becomes of children when they are eighteen.'

The same is true in the seventeenth century. The report of an episcopal inquiry of 1667 states that in one parish 'there is *un jeune enfans* ['a young child'] aged about fourteen who in the year or so he has been living in the aforementioned place has been teaching children of both sexes to read and write, by arrangement with the inhabitants of the aforementioned place'.

In the course of the seventeenth century a change took place by which the old usage was maintained in the more dependent classes of society, while a different usage appeared in the middle class, where the word 'child' was restricted to its modern meaning. The long duration of childhood as it appeared in the common idiom was due to the indifference with which strictly biological phenomena were regarded at the time: nobody would have thought of seeing the end of childhood in puberty. The idea of childhood was bound up with the idea of dependence: the words 'sons', 'varlets' and 'boys' were also words in the vocabulary of feudal subordination. One could leave childhood only by leaving the state of dependence, or at least the lower degrees of dependence. That is why the words associated with childhood would endure to indicate in a familiar style, in the spoken language, men of humble rank whose submission to others remained absolute - lackeys, for instance, journeymen and soldiers. A 'little boy' (*petit garcon*) was not necessarily a child but a young servant, just as today an employer or a foreman will say of a worker of twenty to twenty-five: 'He's a good lad.' Thus in 1549, one Baduel, the principal of a college, an educational establishment, wrote to the father of one of his young pupils about his outfit and attendants: 'A little boy is all that he will need for his personal service'.

At the beginning of the eighteenth century, Furetière's dictionary gave an explanation of the usage:

'Child' is also a term of friendship used to greet or flatter someone or to induce him to do something. Thus when one says to an aged person: 'Goodbye, good mother' ('so long, grandma,' in the modern idiom) she replies: 'Goodbye, my child' ('goodbye, lad'). Or she will say to a lackey: 'Child, go and get me this or that.' A master will say to his men when setting them to work: 'Come along, children, get to work.' A captain will say to his soldiers: 'Courage, children, stand fast.' Front-line troops, those most exposed to danger, were called 'the lost children'.

At the same time, but in families of gentle birth, where dependence was only a consequence of physical infirmity, the vocabulary of childhood tended rather to refer to the first age. Its use became increasingly frequent in the seventeenth century: the expression 'little child' (*petit enfant*) began to take on the meaning we give it. The older usage had preferred 'young child' (*jeune enfant*), and this expression had not been completely abandoned. La Fontaine used it, and again in 1714, in a translation of Erasmus, there was a reference to a 'a young girl' who was not yet five: 'I have a young girl who has scarcely begun to talk.' The word *petit* or 'little one' had also acquired a special meaning by the end of the sixteenth century: it referred to all the pupils of the 'little schools', even those who were no longer children. In England, the word 'petty' had the same meaning as in French, and a text of 1627 on the subject of school spoke of the *lyttle petties*, the smallest pupils.

It was above all with Port-Royal and with all the moral and pedagogic literature which drew its inspiration from Port-Royal (or which gave more general expression to a need for moral discipline which was widely felt and to which Port-Royal too bore witness), that the terms used to denote childhood became common and above all modern: Jacqueline Pascal's pupils at Port-Royal were divided into 'little ones', 'middle ones' and 'big ones'. 'With regard to the little children,' she wrote, 'they even more than all the others must be taught and fed if possible like little doves'. The regulations of the little schools at Port-Royal stated: 'They do not go to Mass every day, only the little ones.' People spoke in a new way of 'little souls' and 'little angels', expressions which foreshadowed the eighteenth century and Romanticism. In her tales, Mlle L'Héritier claimed to be addressing 'young minds', 'young people'. These pictures probably lead young people to reflections which perfect their reasoning. It can thus be seen that that seventeenth century which seemed to have scorned childhood, in fact brought into use expressions and phrases which remain to this day in our language. Under the word 'child' in his dictionary, Furetière quoted proverbs which are still familiar to us: 'He is a spoilt child, who has been allowed to misbehave without being punished. The fact is, there are no longer any children, for people are beginning to have reason and cunning at an early age.' 'Innocent as a new-born child.'

All the same, in its attempts to talk about little children, the French language of the seventeenth century was hampered by the lack of words to distinguish them from bigger ones. The same was true of English, where the word 'baby' was also applied to big children. Lily's Latin grammar in English, which was in use from the beginning of the sixteenth century until 1866, was intended for 'all lytell babes, all lytell chyldren'.

On the other hand there were in French some expressions which seem to refer to very little children. One of these was the word *poupart*. In one of the *Miracles de Notre-Dame* there was a 'little son' who wanted to feed a picture of the Infant Jesus. 'Tender-hearted Jesus, seeing the insistence and good will of the little child, spoke to him and said: "*Poupart*, weep no more, for in three days you shall eat with me."' But this *poupart* was not really what the French today would call a *bébé*: he was also referred to as a *clergeon* or 'little clerk', wore a surplice and served at Mass: 'Here there were also little children who had few letters and would rather have fed at their mother's breast than do divine service!' In the language of the seventeenth and eighteenth centuries the word *poupart* no longer denoted a child, but instead, in the form *poupon*, what the French today still call by the same name, but in the feminine: a *poupée*, or doll.

French was therefore reduced to borrowing from other idioms – either foreign languages or the slang used in school or trade – words to denote in French that little child in whom an interest was henceforth going to be taken. This was the case with the Italian *bambino* which became the French *bambin*. Mme de Sévigné also used in the same sense a form of the Provençal word *pitchoun*, which she had doubtless learnt in the course of one of her stays with the Grignans. Her cousin Coulanges, who did not like children but spoke of them a great deal, distrusted 'three-year-old *marmousets*', and old word which in the popular idiom would become *marmots*, 'brats with greasy chins who put a finger in every dish'. People also used slang terms from school Latin or from sporting and military academies: a little *frater*, a *cadet*, and, when there were several of them, a *populo* or *petit peuple*. Lastly the use of diminutives became quite common:

fanfan is to be found in the letters of Mme de Sévigné and those of Fénelon.

In time these words would come to denote a child who was still small but already beginning to find his feet. There would still remain a gap where a word was needed to denote a child in its first months of life; this gap would not be filled until the nineteenth century, when the French would borrow from the English the word 'baby', which in the sixteenth and seventeenth centuries had denoted children of school age. This borrowing was the last stage of the story: henceforth, with the French word *bébé*, the very little child had a name.

*   *   *

Medieval art until about the twelfth century did not know childhood or did not attempt to portray it. It is hard to believe that this neglect was due to incompetence or incapacity; it seems more probable that there was no place for childhood in the medieval world. An Ottonian miniature of the twelfth century provides us with a striking example of the deformation which an artist at that time would inflict on children's bodies. The subject is the scene in the Gospels in which Jesus asks that little children be allowed to come to Him. The Latin text is clear: *parvuli*. Yet the miniature has grouped around Jesus what are obviously eight men, without any of the characteristics of childhood; they have simply been depicted on a smaller scale. In a French miniature of the late eleventh century the three children brought to life by St Nicholas are also reduced to a smaller scale than the adults, without any other difference in expression or features. A painter would not even hesitate to give the naked body of a child, in the very few cases when it was exposed, the musculature of an adult: thus in a Psalter dating from the late twelfth or early thirteenth century, Ishmael, shortly after birth, has the abdominal and pectoral muscles of a man. The thirteenth century, although it showed more understanding in its presentation of childhood, remained faithful to this method. In St Louis's moralizing Bible, children are depicted more often, but they are still indicated only by their size. In an episode in the life of Jacob, Isaac is shown sitting between his two wives, surrounded by some fifteen little men who come up to the level of the grown-ups' waists: these are their children. When Job is rewarded for his faith and becomes rich once more, the illuminator depicts his good fortune by placing Job between an equal number of cattle on the left and children on the right: the traditional picture of fecundity inseparable from wealth. In another illustration in the Book of Job, some children are lined up in order of size.

In the thirteenth-century Gospel-book of the Sainte-Chapelle, in an illustration of the miracle of the loaves and fishes, Christ and one of the Apostles àre shown standing on either side of a little man who comes up to their waists: no doubt the child who carried the fishes. In the world of Romanesque formulas, right up to the end of the thirteenth century, there are no children characterized by a special expression but only men on a reduced scale. This refusal to accept child morphology in art is to be found too in most of the ancient civilizations. A fine Sardinian bronze of the ninth century BC shows a sort of Pietà: a mother holding in her arms the somewhat bulky body of her son. The catalogue tells us 'The little masculine figure could also be a child which, in accordance with the formula adopted in ancient times by other peoples, had been represented as an adult.' Everything in fact would seem to suggest that the realistic representation of children or the idealization of childhood, its grace and rounded charms, was confined to Greek art. Little Eroses proliferated in the Hellenistic period, but childhood disappeared from iconography together with the other Hellenistic themes, and Romanesque art returned to that rejection of the special features of childhood which had already characterized the periods of antiquity before Hellenism. This is no mere coincidence. Our starting-point in this study is a world of pictorial representation in which childhood is unknown; literary historians such as Mgr Calvé have made the same observation about the epic, in which child prodigies behave with the courage and physical strength of doughty warriors. This undoubtedly means that the men of the tenth and eleventh centuries did not dwell on the image of childhood, and that that image had neither interest nor even reality for them. It suggests too that in the realm of real life, and not simply in that of aesthetic transposition, childhood was a period of transition which passed quickly and which was just as quickly forgotten.

Such is our starting-point. How do we get from there to the little imps of Versailles, to the photographs of children of all ages in our family albums?

Around the thirteenth century, a few types of children are to be found which appear to be a little closer to the modern concept of childhood. There is the angel, depicted in the guise of a very young man, a young adolescent – a *clergeon*, as Père du Colombier remarks. But how old is this 'little clerk'? The *clergeons* were children of various ages who were trained to make the responses in church and who were destined for holy orders, seminarists of a sort in a period when there were no seminaries and when schooling in Latin, the only kind of schooling that existed, was reserved for future clerks. 'Here,' says one of the *Miracles de Notre-Dame*, 'there were little children who had few letters and would rather have fed at their mother's breast [but children were weaned very late at that time: Shakespeare's Juliet was still being breast-fed at three] than do divine service.' The angel of Reims, to take one example, is a big boy rather than a child, but the artists have stressed the round, pretty, and somewhat effeminate features of youths barely out of childhood. We have already come a long way from the small-scale adults of the Ottonian miniature. This type of adolescent angel was to become extremely common in the fourteenth century and was to last to the very end of the Italian *Quattrocento*: the angels of Fra Angelico, Botticelli and Ghirlandajo all belong to it.

The second type of child was to be the model and ancestor of all the little children in the history of art: the Infant Jesus, or the Infant Notre-Dame, for here childhood is linked to the mystery of motherhood and the Marian cult. To begin with, Jesus, like other children, is an adult on a reduced scale: a little God-priest in His majesty, depicted by Theotokos. The evolution towards a more realistic and more sentimental representation of childhood begins very early on in painting: in a miniature of the second half of the twelfth century, Jesus is shown wearing a thin, almost transparent shift and standing with His arms round His mother's neck, nestling against her, cheek to cheek. With the Virgin's motherhood, childhood enters the world of pictorial representation. In the thirteenth century it inspires other family scenes. In St Louis's moralizing Bible, there are various family scenes in which parents are shown surrounded by their children with the same tender respect as on the rood-screen at Chartres: thus in a picture of Moses and his family, husband and wife are holding hands while the children (little men) surrounding them are stretching out their hands towards their mother. These cases, however, remained rare: the touching idea of childhood remained limited to the Infant Jesus until the fourteenth century, when, as is well known, Italian art was to help to spread and develop it.

A third type of child appeared in the Gothic period: the naked child. The Infant Jesus was scarcely ever depicted naked. More often than not, like other children of His age, He was chastely wrapped in swaddling-clothes or clad in a shift or a dress. He would not be undressed until the end of the Middle Ages. Those few miniatures in the moralizing Bibles which depicted children showed them fully dressed, except in the case of the Innocents or the dead children whose mothers Solomon was judging. It was the allegory of death and the soul which was to introduce into the world of forms the picture of childish nudity. Already in the pre-Byzantine iconography of the fifth century, in which many features of the future Romanesque art made their appearance, the bodies of the dead were reduced in scale.

Corpses were smaller than living bodies. In the *Iliad* in the Ambrosian Library the dead in the battle scenes are half the size of the living. In French medieval art the soul was depicted as a little child who was naked and usually sexless. The Last Judgments lead the souls of the righteous to Abraham's bosom in this form. The dying man breathes the child out through his mouth in a symbolic representation of the soul's departure. This is also how the entry of the soul into the world is depicted, whether it is a case of a holy, miraculous conception – the Angel of the Annunciation presenting the Virgin with a naked child, Jesus's soul – or a case of a perfectly natural conception: a couple resting in bed apparently quite innocently, but something must have happened, for a naked child can be seen flying through the air and entering the woman's mouth – 'the creation of the human soul by natural means'.

In the course of the fourteenth and particularly the fifteenth century, these medieval types would develop further, but in the direction already indicated in the thirteenth century. We have already observed that the angel/altar-boy would go on playing its part without very much change, in the religious painting of the fifteenth century. On the other hand the theme of the Holy Childhood would never cease developing in both scope and variety from the fourteenth century on. Its popularity and fecundity bear witness to the progress, in the collective consciousness, of that idea of childhood which only a keen observer can distinguish in the thirteenth century and which did not exist at all in the eleventh century. In the group of Jesus and His mother, the artist would stress the graceful, affectionate, naive aspects of early childhood: the child seeking its mother's breast or getting ready to kiss or caress her, the child playing the traditional childhood games with fruit or a bird on a leash, the child eating its pap, the child being wrapped in its swaddling-clothes. Every gesture that could be observed – at least by somebody prepared to pay attention to them – would henceforth be reproduced in pictorial form. These features of sentimental realism would take a long time to extend beyond the frontiers of religious iconography, which is scarcely surprising when one remembers that this was also the case with landscape and genre painting. It remains none the less true that the group of Virgin and Child changed in character and became more and more profane: the picture of a scene of everyday life.

Timidly at first, then with increasing frequency, the painters of religious childhood went beyond that of Jesus. First of all they turned to the childhood of the Virgin, which inspired at least two new and popular themes; firstly the theme of the birth of the Virgin – people in St Anne's bedroom fussing over the new-born child, bathing her, wrapping her in swaddling-clothes and showing her to her mother, and then the theme of the Virgin's education – a reading lesson, with the Virgin following the words in a book held by St Anne. Then came other holy childhoods; those of St John, the Infant Jesus's playmate, St James, and the children of the holy women, Mary Zebedee and Mary Salome. A completely new iconography thus came into existence, presenting more and more scenes of childhood, and taking care to gather together in similar groups these holy children, with or without their mothers.

This iconography, which generally speaking started with the fourteenth century, coincided with a profusion of priors' tales and legends, such as those in the *Miracles de Notre-Dame*. It continued up to the seventeenth century and its development can be followed in painting, tapestry and sculpture. We shall in any case have occasion to return to it with regard to the religious practices of childhood.

From this religious iconography of childhood, a lay iconography eventually detached itself in the fifteenth and sixteenth centuries. This was not yet the portrayal of the child on its own. Genre painting was developing at this time by means of the transformation of a conventional allegorical iconography inspired by the antiquo-medieval concept of Nature: ages of life, seasons, senses, elements. Subject pictures and anecdotal paintings began to take the place of static representations of symbolic characters. Let us merely note here that the child became one of the characters most frequently found in these anecdotal paintings: the child with his family; the child with his playmates, who were often adults; the child in a crowd, but very definitely 'spot-lighted' in his mother's arms, or holding her hand or playing or even piddling; the child among the crowds watching miracles or martyrdoms, listening to sermons, or following liturgical rites such as presentations or circumcisions; the child serving as an apprentice to a goldsmith or a painter or some other craftsman; or the child at school, an old and popular theme which went back to the fourteenth century and would go on inspiring subject paintings up to the nineteenth century.

These subject paintings were not as a general rule devoted to the exclusive portrayal of childhood, but in a great many cases there were children among the characters depicted, both principal and secondary. And this suggests the ideas, first that children mingled with adults in everyday life, and any gathering for the purpose of work, relaxation or sport brought together both children and adults; and secondly, that painters were particularly fond of depicting childhood for its graceful or picturesque qualities (the taste for the picturesque anecdote developed in the fifteenth and sixteenth centuries and coincided with the appreciation of childhood's charms). They delighted in stressing the presence of a child in a group or a crowd. Of these two ideas one now strikes us as out of date, for today, as also towards the end of the nineteenth century, we tend to separate the world of children from that of adults; the other foreshadows the modern idea of childhood.

The origins of the themes of the angel, the holy childhoods, and their subsequent iconographical developments date as far back as the thirteenth century; two new types of child portrayal appeared in the fifteenth century: the portrait and the *putto*. The child, as we have seen, was not missing from the Middle Ages, at least from the thirteenth century on, but there was never a portrait of him, the portrait of a real child, as he was at a certain moment of his life.

$$* \qquad * \qquad *$$

In medieval society the idea of childhood did not exist; this is not to suggest that children were neglected, forsaken or despised. The idea of childhood is not to be confused with affection for children: it corresponds to an awareness of the particular nature of childhood, that particular nature which distinguishes the child from the adult, even the young adult. In medieval society, this awareness was lacking. That is why, as soon as the child could live without the constant solicitude of his mother, his nanny or his cradle-rocker, he belonged to adult society. That adult society now strikes us as rather puerile: no doubt this is largely a matter of its mental age, but it is also due to its physical age, because it was partly made up of children and youths. Language did not give the word 'child' the restricted meaning we give it today: people said 'child' much as we say 'lad' in everyday speech. The absence of definition extended to every sort of social activity: games, crafts, arms. There is not a single collective picture of the times in which children are not to be found, nestling singly or in pairs in the *trousse* hung round women's necks; or urinating in a corner, or playing their part in a traditional festival, or as apprentices in a workshop, or as pages serving a knight, etc.

The infant who was too fragile as yet to take part in the life of adults simply 'did not count': this is the expression used by Molière, who bears witness to the survival in the seventeenth century of a very old attitude of mind. Argan in *Le Malade Imaginaire* has two daughters, one of marriageable age and little Louison who is just beginning to talk and walk. It is generally known that he is threatening to put his elder daughter in a convent to stop her philandering. His brother asks him: 'How is it, Brother, that rich as you are and having only one daughter, *for I don't count the little one*, you can talk of putting her in a convent?' The little one did not count because she could disappear.

The quotation from Molière shows the continuance of the archaic attitude to childhood. But this survival, for all that it was stubborn, was precarious. From the fourteenth century on, there had been a tendency to express in art, iconography and religion (in the cult of the dead) the personality which children were seen to possess, and the poetic, familiar significance attributed to their special nature. We have followed the evolution of the *putto* and the child portrait. And we have seen that in the sixteenth and seventeenth centuries the child or infant – at least in the upper classes of society – was given a special costume which marked him out from the adults. This specialization of the dress of children and especially of little boys, in a society in which clothes and outward appearances had considerable importance, bears witness to the change which had taken place in the general attitude towards children: they counted much more than Argan's brother imagined. In fact, *Le malade imaginaire*, which seems as hard on little children as do certain remarks by La Fontaine, contains a whole conversation between Argan and little Louison: 'Look at me, will you!' 'What is it, papa?' 'Here!' 'What?' 'Haven't you anything to tell me?' 'If you wish, I can tell you, to amuse you, the story of the Ass's Skin, or else the fable of the Fox and the Crow which I was taught not so long ago.' A new concept of childhood had appeared, in which the child, on account of his sweetness, simplicity and drollery, became a source of amusement and relaxation for the adult.

To begin with, the attitude was held by women, women whose task it was to look after children – mothers and nannies. In the sixteenth-century edition of *Le Grand propriétaire de toutes choses* (1556) we are told about the nanny: 'She rejoices when the child is happy, and feels sorry for the child when he is ill; she picks him up when he falls, she binds him when he tosses about, and she washes and cleans him when he is dirty.' She brings the child up and teaches him to talk: 'She pronounces the words as if she had a stammer, to teach him to talk better and more rapidly . . . she carries him in her hands, then on her shoulder, then on her lap, to play with him when he cries; she chews the child's meat for him when he has no teeth so that he can swallow profitably and without danger; she plays with the child to make him sleep and she binds his limbs to keep them straight so that he has no stiffness in his body, and she bathes and anoints him to nourish his flesh . . .' Thomas More dwells on the subject of the schoolboy being sent to school by his mother: 'When the little boy will not rise in time for her, but lies still abed and slugg, and when he is up, weepeth because he hath lien so long, fearing to be beaten at school for his late coming thither, she telleth him then that it is but early days, and he shall come time enough, and biddeth him: "Go, good son, I warrant thee, I have sent to thy master myself, take thy bread and butter with thee, thou shalt not be beaten at all."' Thus she sends him off sufficiently reassured not to burst into tears at the idea of leaving her at home, but she does not get to the bottom of the trouble and the late arrival will be well and truly beaten when he gets to school.

Children's little antics must always have seemed touching to mothers, nannies and cradle-rockers, but their reactions formed part of the huge domain of unexpressed feelings. Henceforth people would no longer hesitate to recognize the pleasure they got from watching children's antics and 'coddling' them. We find Mme de Sévigné admitting, not without a certain affection, how much time she spends playing with her grand-daughter: 'I am reading the story of Christopher Columbus's discovery of the Indies, which is entertaining me greatly; but your daughter entertains me even more. I do so love her . . . she strokes your portrait and caresses it in such an amusing way that I have to kiss her straight away.' 'I have been playing with your daughter for an hour now; she is delightful.' And, as if she were afraid of some infection, she adds, with a levity which surprises us, for the death of a child is something serious for us and nothing to joke about: 'I do not want her to die.' For, as we have seen from Molière, this first appreciation of childhood went with a certain indifference, or rather with the indifference that was traditional.

The 'coddling' attitude towards children is even better known to us by the critical reactions it provoked at the end of the sixteenth century and particularly in the seventeenth century. Peevish persons found insufferable the attention paid to children. Montaigne bristles: 'I cannot abide that passion for caressing new-born children, which have neither mental activities nor recognizable bodily shape by which to make themselves lovable, and I have never willingly suffered them to be fed in my presence.' He cannot accept the idea of loving children 'for our amusement, like monkeys', or taking pleasure in their 'frolicking, games and infantile nonsense'.

Another example of this state of mind, a century later, is to be seen in Coulanges, Mme de Sévigné's cousin. He was obviously exasperated by the way his friends and relatives fussed over their children, for he composed a song dedicated to 'fathers of families', urging them not to spoil their offspring or allow them to eat with adults.

It is important to note that this feeling of exasperation was as novel as 'coddling', and even more foreign that 'coddling' to the indifferent attitude of people in the Middle Ages. It was precisely to the presence of children that Montaigne and Coulanges, like Mme de Sévigné, were hypersensitive; it should be pointed out that Montaigne and

Coulanges were more modern than Mme de Sévigné in so far as they considered it necessary to keep children apart from adults. They held that it was no longer desirable that children should mingle with adults, especially at table; no doubt because if they did they were 'spoiled' and became ill-mannered.

The seventeenth-century moralists and pedagogues shared the dislike felt by Montaigne and Coulanges for 'coddling'. Thus the austere Fleury, in his treatise on studies, speaks very much like Montaigne: 'When little children are caught in a trap, when they say something foolish, drawing a correct inference from an irrelevant principle which has been given to them, people burst out laughing, rejoice at having tricked them, or kiss and caress them as if they had worked out the correct answer. It is as if the poor children had been made only to amuse the adults, like little dogs or little monkeys.'

The author of Galatée, the manual of etiquette commonly used in the best colleges, those of the Jesuits, speaks like Coulanges: 'Those persons are greatly at fault who never talk of anything but their wives, their little children and their nannies. "My little son made me laugh so much! Just listen to this . . ."'

M. d'Argonne, in his treatise on education, L'Éducation de Monsieur de Moncade (1690), likewise complains that people take an interest in very small children only for the sake of their 'caresses' and 'antics'; too many parents 'value their children only in so far as they derive pleasure and entertainment from them'.

It is important to remember that at the end of the seventeenth century this 'coddling' was not practised only by people of quality, who, in fact, were beginning to disdain it. Its presence in the lower classes was noted and denounced. J.-B. de la Salle in his Conduite des écoles chrétiennes (1720) states that the children of the poor are particularly ill-mannered because 'they do just as they please, their parents paying no attention to them, even treating them in an idolatrous manner: what the children want, they want too.'

In the moralists and pedagogues of the seventeenth century, we see that fondness for childhood and its special nature no longer found expression in amusement and 'coddling', but in psychological interest and moral solicitude. The child was no longer regarded as amusing or agreeable: 'Every man must be conscious of that insipidity of childhood which disgusts the sane mind; that coarseness of youth which finds pleasure in scarcely anything but material objects and which is only a very crude sketch of the man of thought.' Thus Balthazar Gratien in El Discreto, a treatise on education published in 1646 which was still being translated into French in 1723. 'Only time can cure a person of childhood and youth, which are truly ages of imperfection in every respect.' To be understood, these opinions need to be put back in their temporal context and compared with the other texts of the period. They have been interpreted by some historians as showing ignorance of childhood, but in fact they mark the beginning of a serious and realistic concept of childhood. For they do not suggest that people should accept the levity of childhood: that was the old mistake. In order to correct the behaviour of children, people must first of all understand it, and the texts of the late sixteenth century and the seventeenth century are full of comments on child psychology. The authors show a great solicitude for children, who are seen as witnesses to baptismal innocence, comparable to the angels, and close to Christ who loved them. But this interest calls for the development in them of a faculty of reasoning which is still fragile, a determined attempt to turn them into thinking men and good Christians. The tone is sometimes grim, the emphasis being laid on strictness as opposed to the laxity and facility of contemporary manners; but this is not always the case. There is even humour in Jacqueline Pascal, and undisguised tenderness. In the texts published towards the end of the century, an attempt is made to reconcile sweetness and reason. Thus the Abbé Goussault, a counsellor at the High Court, writes (1693): 'Familiarizing oneself with one's children, getting them to talk about all manner of things, treating them as sensible people and winning them over with sweetness, is an infallible secret for doing what one wants with them. They are young plants which need tending and watering frequently: a few words of advice offered at the right moment, a few marks of friendship and affection given now and then, touch them and bind them. A few caresses, a few little presents, a few words of cordiality and trust make an impression on their minds, and they are few in number that resist these sweet and easy methods of making them persons of honour and probity.'

The first concept of childhood – characterized by 'coddling' – had made its appearance in the company of little children. The second, on the contrary, sprang from a source outside the family: churchmen or gentlemen of the robe, few in number before the sixteenth century, and a far greater number of moralists in the seventeenth century, eager to ensure disciplined, rational manners. They too had become alive to the formerly neglected phenomenon of childhood, but they were unwilling to regard children as charming toys, for they saw them as fragile creatures of God who needed to be both safeguarded and reformed. This concept in its turn passed into family life.

In the eighteenth century, we find those two elements in the family, together with a new element: concern about hygiene and physical health. Care of the body was not ignored by seventeenth-century moralists and pedagogues. People nursed the sick devotedly (at the same time taking every precaution to unmask malingerers), but any interest shown in healthy bodies had a moral purpose behind it: a delicate body encouraged luxury, sloth, concupiscence – all the vices in fact!

General de Martange's correspondence with his wife gives us some-idea of a family's private life and preoccupations about a century after Mme de Sévigné. Martange was born in 1722 and married in 1754. He shows great interest in everything concerning his children's life, from 'coddling' to education; he watches closely over their health and even their hygiene. Everything to do with children and family life has become a matter worthy of attention. Not only the child's future but his presence and his very existence are of concern: the child has taken a central place in the family.

3 The image of the child

Peter Coveney

Until the last decades of the eighteenth century the child did not exist as an important and continuous theme in English literature. Childhood as a major theme came with the generation of Blake and Wordsworth. There were of course children in English literature before the Romantics. They were the subject of innumerable Elizabethan lyrics; and through Dryden, Pope and Prior there had been a whole tradition of minor, complimentary verses addressed to young 'children of quality'. But in the Elizabethan drama, in the main body of Augustan verse, in the major eighteenth-century novel, the child is absent, or the occasion of a passing reference; at the most a subsidiary element in an adult world.

With Blake's *The Chimney Sweeper* and Wordsworth's Ode on *Intimations of Immortality from recollections of Early Childhood*, we are confronted with something essentially new, the phenomenon of major poets expressing something they considered of great significance through the image of the child. Blake's 'Innocence' and Wordsworth's 'natural piety' had their easily distinguishable ancestry. But the fact remains that within the course of a few decades the child emerges from comparative unimportance to become the focus of an unprecedented literary interest, and, in time, the central figure of an increasingly significant proportion of our literature. The appearance of the child was indeed simultaneous with the changes in sensibility and thought which came with the end of the eighteenth century. The simultaneity of the changes and the appearance is too exact to be coincidental. It seems inescapable that the appearance of the modern literary child was closely related to the revolution in sensibility which we call the 'romantic revival'. The creation of the romantic child came from deep within the whole genesis of our modern literary culture.

Source: Peter Coveney, *Poor Monkey*, Hutchinson (1957), reprinted as *The Image of Childhood*, Penguin (1967).

To suggest a relation between literature and society might seem to imply that too much, perhaps, is to be explained too easily by too little. But without proposing anything rigid, it is generally acceptable that some relation of cause and effect lay between Elizabethan England and the preoccupations of Shakespearian tragedy. The world of Shakespeare was confronted with the problem of social, and, more narrowly, political disintegration. The sense of cosmic strain and social disorder in Shakespeare derived in some way from the dissolution of medieval society that was in process, and the discoveries of the new cosmology. The tensions of Renaissance individualism were translated into the central interests of the drama. The recurrent theme of 'Rome' was natural to an age concerned with the appearance of the 'nation-state' and the loyalties of the 'citizens' and 'statesmen' who served it. It is this sort of relation between a society and its literature which lies between modern society and the theme of childhood in nineteenth- and twentieth-century literature. There is a similar relation between theme and context.

The end of the eighteenth century saw the origins of the spiritual crisis against which so much of our modern literature has been written. The securities of the eighteenth-century peace dissolved in the era of the Revolution. The social and political ferment which had ended with the middle of the seventeenth century was renewed. The social, political, and, more especially, the intellectual problems arising from the French and Industrial Revolutions found no resolution. In a rapidly dissolving culture, the problem of the nineteenth-century artist was essentially new and inevitably complicated. The long artistic alienation had begun. The concern of the modern European intellect has been, in part, the maintenance of individual integrity within the search for the security of universal order. At no time, except perhaps in the early decades of the seventeenth century, has that maintenance and search been so pressing in its demand as in the century of Darwin, Marx and Freud.

The society created by the industrial developments of the late eighteenth and nineteenth centuries was increasingly unconcerned with and often inimical to art. The frequent fate of the later nineteenth-century artist was not only to find himself alienated and bewildered, but confronted by the rapid disintegration of his audience. The actual contraction of his audience may be debated – it is after all difficult to be precisely statistical about these things – but the proportion of the literate public to whom the serious artist could expect to address himself certainly diminished. For even if there were at the end of the century as many readers responsive to the best creative work as at the beginning, there was a new literate public who were most certainly not. A new mass literature supplied the demands of uninformed literacy; and the relative influence of the mature creative voice was proportionally diminished. The central problem of any culture in process of rapid development lies in cultural transmission, and there was as we know in the nineteenth century a serious, some would say disastrous, discontinuity. Whereas, for a few decades in the middle of the century, the Victorian middle class produced and respected literary figures who were public figures in the way Addison and Johnson had been, James at the end of the century was successively reduced (and it was not *wholly* his fault) to a private world of increasing irrelevance. Art for Art's sake was the aggressive defence of an art on the run; the ivory tower the substitute, *faute de mieux*, for the wished-for arena. Dickens was the last English man of letters to have a really successful public voice – something, for all that might be said, Wells and Shaw never achieved. After him the moat between literature and the literate public widens; and the impact of literature upon the real flow of public affairs becomes sporadic and occasional.

In this context of isolation, alienation, doubt and intellectual conflict, it is not difficult to see the attraction of the child as a literary theme. The child could serve as a symbol of the artist's dissatisfaction with the society which was in process of such harsh development about him. In a world given increasingly to utilitarian values and the Machine, the child could become the symbol of Imagination and Sensibility, a symbol of Nature set against the forces abroad in society actively de-naturing humanity. Through the child the artist could express his awareness of the conflict between human Innocence and the cumulative pressures of social Experience. If the central problem of the artist was in fact one of adjustment, one can see the possibilities for identification between the artist and the consciousness of the child whose difficulty and chief source of pain often lie in adjustment and accommodation to environment. In childhood lay the perfect image of insecurity and isolation, of fear and bewilderment, of vulnerability and potential violation. Professor Empson has spoken of the 'tap-root' which the nineteenth-century artist frequently kept for reference to his childhood. For some authors, the 'tap-root' became, *in extremis*, an habitual means of escape, a way of withdrawal from spiritual and emotional confusion in a tired culture. In an age when it became increasingly difficult to grow up, to find valid bearings in an adult world, the temptation seems to have been for certain authors to take the line of least emotional resistance, and to regress, quite literally, into a world of fantasy and nostalgia for childhood. Over one line of art, distinguishable at the end of the century, lay the seductive shadow of Peter Pan. If neurosis is the result of a fixation of the personality at an infantile stage of emotional development, there would often seem a neurotic connexion between some modern authors and their exclusive preoccupations with children. There may indeed have been an element of neurosis, to a greater or lesser extent, in the majority of authors concerned with the theme of childhood in the nineteenth and twentieth centuries.

But morbid involvement is a charge which can only be levelled at comparatively few. Nostalgia and regressing impulse, which were, in this sense, an artistic condition of the age, did not consume the genius of Blake, Wordsworth, Dickens and Mark Twain – though with Dickens and Mark Twain they were powerful and corrosive influences. The importance is that for them the child became a symbol of the greatest significance for the subjective investigation of the Self, and an expression of their romantic protest against the Experience of society. The nineteenth-century interest in the child was in fact no esoteric interest of minor writers existing on the eccentric peripheries of literature. The child lies at the heart of *The Prelude*, *Hard Times*, *Dombey and Son* and *Huckleberry Finn* – works which in any evaluation have undeniable significance as serious, one might say perhaps, adult art. To compare their strength with the sentimentalities of *David Copperfield* or *Peter Pan* is to see the extremes of interest to which the child could be put. Frequently, indeed, as in the case of Dickens, there was an amazing inconsistency within the work of the same author. The child is now a symbol of growth and development, and now a symbol of retreat into personal regression and self-pity. Increasingly isolated, and without the securities of a widely-accepted culture, the nineteenth-century artist was, it seems, impelled towards the subjective investigations and involvements which became the *raison*, and in some cases, the strength of his art. But, and the case of Wordsworth is specially relevant, with some the reference of their subjective interest is always towards outward development. The child became for Wordsworth the basis of a whole philosophy of human nature. For Dickens an interest in the child nourished the growth of a moral interest which he dramatized through the medium of his greatest fiction. The history of the child in nineteenth-century literature does in fact display both the weakness and the strength of all romantic art; how close together the morbid introversion and the objective awareness lay.

The concept of the child's nature which informed the work of Blake, Wordsworth and Dickens was of original innocence. Stemming most forcefully from Rousseau, and in contradiction to the long Christian tradition of original sin, it was this which gave the weight and edge to the general commentary of these authors as they expressed it through the symbol of the innocent child. But it was a symbol susceptible to continuous deterioration. The instrument became blunt through over-assertion and special pleading. The symbol which had such strength and richness in the poetry of Blake and some parts of the novels of Dickens became in time the static and moribund child-figure of the popular Victorian imagination; a residue only of a literary theme almost entirely evacuated of the significance it had earlier borne. The romantic assertion of innocence created a concept of the child's essential nature which for religious or psychological reasons might be considered either morally debilitating or emotionally false. It was against this conventionally innocent child that a revolution was effected at the turn of the nineteenth century. Just as the eighteenth century had turned from the Christian doctrine of original sin to the cult of original virtue in the child, so the nineteenth century turned from the assumption of original innocence to the scientific investigation of the infant and child consciousness. Literature, however, did not discover the child through the medium of psycho-analysis. The influence of Freud was to redirect, clarify, sometimes enrich (and in part, perhaps, explain) an interest which was already very clearly there. And in this the continuity of nineteenth-century interests becomes strikingly plain. The Romantic sensibility had often concerned itself with childhood as an agent in the quest for psychological insight and awareness. In the greatest authors, in Wordsworth and Dickens, say, subjective preoccupations had been balanced, if sometimes precariously, with the objective interests characteristic of a great literature. For them, childhood became part of the objective 'wisdom' which, through the power of their creative intelligence, they sought to convey. A major concern of Freudian analysis was to increase awareness of the child and objective appreciation of the importance of the childhood consciousness to the development of the adult mind. In this sense, it is not preposterous to suggest that across the century Wordsworth's *Prelude* and Freud's Essay on Infantile Sexuality may be said to join hands.

It is not easy to define the precise relationship between psycho-analysis and modern literature; but there can be no doubt that Freud's theories concerning human personality and motive, and especially his emphasis on the importance of the child's consciousness in the formation of adult personality, created an intellectual climate within which many authors have, if not always consciously, developed. Freud was a powerful agent in the ventilation of the sentimental atmosphere which had grown up around the Victorian child; a solvent too of the religious savagery towards the child, such as Butler described in his *Way of All Flesh*. Idealization of the child's nature and cruelty towards the 'children of Satan' existed side by side in nineteenth-century society - a phenomenon which justifies, perhaps, considerable investigation.

Cause and effect are difficult, however, to distinguish in the subtle field of artistic choice. Subjective and social factors are not easy to distinguish in discussing why any author should write about the particular themes he chooses. Less precise still may be the influence of intellectual ideas in directing the interests and motives of creative literature. Even so, the frequency of the treatment of childhood in modern literature suggests the presence of common and objective factors predisposing so many authors to their choice. A theme ceases to be personal or eccentric when it becomes the serious and deliberate choice of so many over so long a time. It becomes reasonable to speak in terms of a literary phenomenon, and, it is remarkable, a phenomenon of our own culture, as distinct from every other before it. It is not only a matter of literature influenced by the intellectual climate created by the theories of Rousseau in the eighteenth and Freud in the twentieth century, but that so many authors should find the child so congenial an image, either of growth or regression, of potency or regret. From the last decades of the eighteenth century, the symbol of the child accumulated about itself a variety of responses, but among them one can always make the distinction between those authors who went to the child to express their involvement with life, and those who retreated towards the symbol from 'life's decay' - to use Lewis Carroll's expression. In writing of childhood, we find that in a very exact and significant sense the modern author is writing of life. In the literature of the child in the nineteenth and twentieth centuries we have a reflection of the situation of certain artists in modern times; their response, at a deep and significant level, to the condition in which they found themselves; and, if their feelings could achieve the projection, the condition in which they found humanity. Considering the nature of that condition, it is perhaps not remarkable that through writing of childhood there should be those who wanted to go back to the beginning to begin again, and others who wanted just to go back.

4 The evolution of childhood

Lloyd DeMause

The history of childhood is a nightmare from which we have only
recently begun to awaken. The further back in history one goes, the
lower the level of child care, and the more likely children are to be
killed, abandoned, beaten, terrorized, and sexually abused. It is our
task here to see how much of this childhood history can be
recaptured from the evidence that remains to us.

That this pattern has not previously been noticed by historians is
because serious history has long been considered a record of public
not private events. Historians have concentrated so much on the
noisy sandbox of history, with its fantastic castles and magnificent
battles, that they have generally ignored what is going on in the
homes around the playground. And where historians usually look to
the sandbox battles of yesterday for the causes of those today, we
instead ask how each generation of parents and children creates
those issues which are later acted out in the arena of public life.

At first glance, this lack of interest in the lives of children seems
odd. Historians have been traditionally committed to explaining
continuity and change over time, and ever since Plato it has been
known that childhood is a key to this understanding. The importance
of parent-child relations for social change was hardly discovered by
Freud; St. Augustine's cry, 'Give me other mothers and I will give you
another world,' has been echoed by major thinkers for fifteen
centuries without affecting historical writing. Since Freud, of course,
our view of childhood has acquired a new dimension, and in the past
half century the study of childhood has become routine for the
psychologist, the sociologist, and the anthropologist. It is only
beginning for the historian. Such determined avoidance requires an
explanation.

Historians usually blame the paucity of the sources for the lack of
serious study of childhood in the past. Peter Laslett wonders why the

Source: Lloyd DeMause, *The History of Childhood*, Souvenir Press (1974).

'crowds and crowds of little children are strangely missing from the written record.... There is something mysterious about the silence of all these multitudes of babes in arms, toddlers and adolescents in the statements men made at the time about their own experience.... We cannot say whether fathers helped in the tending of infants.... Nothing can as yet be said on what is called by the psychologists toilet training.... It is in fact an effort of mind to remember all the time that children were always present in such numbers in the traditional world, nearly half the whole community living in a condition of semi-obliteration.' As the family sociologist James Bossard puts it: 'Unfortunately, the history of childhood has never been written, and there is some doubt whether it ever can be written [because] of the dearth of historical data bearing on childhood.'

The 'psychogenic theory of history' outlined in my project proposal began with a comprehensive theory of historical change. It posited that the central force for change in history is neither technology nor economics, but the 'psychogenic' changes in personality occurring because of successive generations of parent-child interactions. This theory involved several hypotheses, each subject to proof or disproof by empirical historical evidence:

1 That the evolution of parent-child relations constitutes an independent source of historical change. The origin of this evolution lies in the ability of successive generations of parents to regress to the psychic age of their children and work through the anxieties of that age in a better manner the second time they encounter them than they did during their own childhood. The process is similar to that of psychoanalysis, which also involves regression and a second chance to fact childhood anxieties.

2 That this 'generational pressure' for psychic change is not only spontaneous, originating in the adult's need to regress and in the child's striving for relationship, but also occurs independent of social and technological change. It therefore can be found even in periods of social and technological stagnation.

3 That the history of childhood is a series of closer approaches between adult and child, with each closing of psychic distance producing fresh anxiety. The reduction of this adult anxiety is the main source of the child-rearing practices of each age.

4 That the obverse of the hypothesis that history involves a general improvement in child care is that the further back one goes in history, the less effective parents are in meeting the developing needs of the child. This would indicate, for instance, that if today in

America there are less than a million abused children, there would be a point back in history where most children were what we would now consider abused.

5 That because psychic structure must always be passed from generation to generation through the narrow funnel of childhood, a society's child-rearing practices are not just one item in a list of cultural traits. They are the very condition for the transmission and development of all other cultural elements, and place definite limits on what can be achieved in all other spheres of history. Specific childhood experiences must occur to sustain specific cultural traits, and once these experiences no longer occur the trait disappears.

Psychological principles of childhood history: projective and reversal reactions

In studying childhood over many generations, it is most important to concentrate on those moments which most affect the psyche of the next generation: primarily, this means what happens when an adult is face to face with a child who needs something. The adult has, I believe, three major reactions available: (1) He can use the child as a vehicle for projection of the contents of his own unconscious (projective reaction); (2) he can use the child as a substitute for an adult figure important in his own childhood (reversal reaction); or (3) he can empathize with the child's needs and act to satisfy them (empathic reaction).

The projective reaction is, of course, familiar to psychoanalysts under terms which range from 'projection' to 'projective identification,' a more concrete, intrusive form of voiding feelings into others. The psychoanalyst, for instance, is thoroughly familiar with being used as a 'toilet-lap' for the massive projections of the patient. It is this condition of being used as a vehicle for projections which is usual for children in the past.

Likewise, the reversal reaction is familiar to students of battering parents. Children exist only to satisfy parental needs, and it is always the failure of the child-as-parent to give love which triggers the actual battering. As one battering mother put it: 'I have never felt loved all my life. When the baby was born, I thought he would love me. When he cried, it meant he didn't love me. So I hit him'.

The third term, empathic reaction, is used here in a more limited sense than the dictionary definition. It is the adult's ability to regress to the level of a child's need and correctly identify it without an admixture of the adult's own projections. The adult must then be able to maintain enough distance from the need to be able to satisfy it. It is an ability identical to the use of the psychoanalyst's unconscious called 'free-floating attention,' or, as Theodor Reik terms it, 'listening with the third ear.'

Projective and reversal reactions often occurred simultaneously in parents in the past, producing an effect which I call the 'double image,' where the child was seen as both full of the adult's projected desires, hostilities and sexual thoughts, and at the same moment as a mother or father figure. That is, it is *both* bad *and* loving. Furthermore, the further back in history one goes, the more 'concretization' or reification one finds of these projective and reversal reactions, producing progressively more bizarre attitudes toward children, similar to those of contemporary parents of battered and schizophrenic children.

The first illustration of these closely interlocking concepts which we will examine is in an adult-child scene from the past. The year is 1739; the boy, Nicolas, is four years old. The incident is one he remembers and has had confirmed by his mother. His grandfather, who has been rather attentive to him the past few days, decides he has to 'test' him and says, 'Nicolas, my son, you have many faults, and these grieve your mother. She is my daughter and has always obliged me; obey me too and correct these, or I will whip you like a dog which is being trained.' Nicolas, angry at the betrayal 'from one who has been so kind to me,' throws his toys into the fire. The grandfather seems pleased.

'Nicolas . . . I said that to test you. Did you really think that a grandpapa, who had been so kind to you yesterday and the day before, could treat you like a dog today? I thought you were intelligent . . .' 'I am not a beast like a dog.' 'No, but you are not as clever as I thought, or you would have understood that I was only teasing. It was just a joke . . . Come to me.' I threw myself into his arms. 'That is not all,' he continued, 'I want to see you friends with your mother; you have grieved, deeply grieved her . . . Nicolas, your father loves you; do you love him?' 'Yes, grandpapa!' 'Suppose he were in danger and to save him it was necessary to put your hand in the fire, would you do it? Would you put it . . . there, if it was necessary?' 'Yes grandpapa.' 'And for me?' 'For you? . . . yes, yes.' 'And for your mother?' 'For mamma? Both of them, both of them!' 'We shall see if you are telling the truth, for your mother is in great need of your little help! If you love her, you must prove it.' I made no answer; but, putting together all that had been said, I went to the fireplace and, while they were making signs to each other, put my right hand into the fire. The pain drew a deep sigh from me.

Nicolas Restif de la Bretonne, *Monsieur Nicolas; or, The Human Heart Unveiled.*

What makes this sort of scene so typical of adult-child interaction in the past is the existence of so many contradictory attitudes on the adult's part without the least resolution. The child is loved and hated, rewarded and punished, bad and loving, all at once. That this puts the child in a 'double bind' of conflicting signals (which Bateson and others believe underlie schizophrenia), goes without saying. But the conflicting signals themselves come from adults who are striving to demonstrate that the child is both very bad (projective reaction) and very loving (reversal reaction). It is the child's function to reduce the adult's pressing anxieties; the child acts as the adult's defense.

Infanticide and death wishes toward children

In a pair of books rich in clinical documentation, the psychoanalyst Joseph Rheingold examined the death wishes of mothers toward their children, and found that they are not only far more widespread than is commonly realized, but also that they stem from a powerful attempt to 'undo' motherhood in order to escape the punishment they imagine their own mothers will wreak upon them. Rheingold shows us mothers giving birth and begging their own mothers not to kill them, and traces the origin of both infanticidal wishes and post-partum depression states as not due to hostility toward the child itself, but rather to the need to sacrifice the child to propitiate their own mothers. Hospital staffs are well aware of these widespread infanticidal wishes, and often allow no contact between the mother and child for some time. Rheingold's findings, seconded by Block, Zilboorg, and others, are complex and have far-reaching implications; here we can only point out that filicidal impulses of contemporary mothers are enormously widespread, with fantasies of stabbing, mutilation, abuse, decapitation, and strangulation common in mothers in psychoanalysis. I believe that the further back in history one goes, the more filicidal impulses are acted out by parents.

The history of infanticide in the West has yet to be written, and I shall not attempt it here. But enough is already known to establish that, contrary to the usual assumption that it is an Eastern rather than a Western problem, infanticide of both legitimate and illegitimate children was a regular practice of antiquity, that the killing of legitimate children was only slowly reduced during the Middle Ages, and that illegitimate children continued regularly to be killed right up into the nineteenth century.

Abandonment, nursing and swaddling

Although there were many exceptions to the general pattern, up to about the eighteenth century, the average child of wealthy parents spent his earliest years in the home of a wet-nurse, returned home to the care of other servants, and was sent out to service, apprenticeship, or school by age seven, so that the amount of time parents of means actually spent raising their children was minimal.

The effects of these and other institutionalized abandonments by parents on the child have rarely been discussed.

The most extreme and oldest form of abandonment is the outright sale of children. Child sale was legal in Babylonian times, and may have been quite common among many nations in antiquity. Although Solon tried to restrict the right of child sale by parents in Athens, it is unclear how effective the law was. Herodas showed a beating scene where a boy was told 'you're a bad boy, Kottalos, so bad that none could find a good word for you even were he selling you.' The church tried for centuries to stamp out child sale. Theodore, Archbishop of Canterbury in the seventh century, ruled a man might not sell his son into slavery after the age of seven. If Giraldus Cambrensis is to be believed, in the twelfth century the English had been selling their children to the Irish for slaves, and the Norman invasion was a punishment from God for this slave traffic. In many areas, child sale continued sporadically into modern times, not being outlawed in Russia, for instance, until the nineteenth century.

Another abandonment practice was the use of children as political hostages and security for debts, which also went back to Babylonian times. Sidney Painter describes its medieval version, in which it was 'quite customary to give young children as hostages to guarantee an agreement, and equally so to make them suffer for their parents' bad faith. When Eustace de Breteuil, the husband of a natural daughter of Henry I, put out the eyes of the son of one of his vassals, the king allowed the enraged father to mutilate in the same way Eustace's daughter whom Henry held as hostage.' Similarly, John Marshall gave up his son William to King Stephen, saying he 'cared little if William were hanged, for he had the anvils and hammers with which to forge still better sons,' and Francis I, when taken prisoner by Charles V, exchanged his young sons for his own freedom, then promptly broke the bargain so that they were thrown in jail. Indeed, it was often hard to distinguish the practice of sending one's children to serve as pages or servants in another noble household from the use of children as hostages.

Similar abandonment motives were behind the custom of fosterage, which was common among all classes of Welsh, Anglo-Saxons, and Scandinavians, wherein an infant was sent to another family to be reared to age 17, and then returned to the parents. This continued in Ireland until the seventeenth century, and the English often sent their children to be fostered by the Irish in medieval times. Actually, this was just an extreme version of the medieval practice of sending noble children at the age of seven or earlier into the homes of others or to monasteries as servants, pages, ladies-in-waiting, oblates, or clerks, practices still common in early modern times. As with the equivalent lower class practice of apprenticeship, the whole subject of the child as laborer in the homes of others is so vast and so poorly studied that it unfortunately cannot be much examined here, despite its obvious importance in the lives of children in the past.

Besides institutionalized abandonment practices, the informal abandoning of young children to other people by their parents occurred quite often right up to the nineteenth century. The parents gave every kind of rationalization for giving their children away: 'to learn to speak' (Disraeli), 'to cure timidness' (Clara Barton), for 'health' (Edmund Burke, Mrs. Sherwood's daughter), or as payment for medical services rendered (patients of Jerome Cardan and William Douglas). Sometimes they admitted it was simply because they were not wanted (Richard Baxter, Johannes Butzbach, Richard Savage, Swift, Yeats, Augustus Hare, and so on). Mrs. Hare's mother expresses the general casualness of these abandonments: 'Yes, certainly, the baby shall be sent as soon as it is weaned; and, if anyone else would like one, would you kindly recollect that we have others.' Boys were of course preferred; one eighteenth-century woman wrote her brother asking for his next child: 'If it is a boy, I claim it; if a girl, I will be content to stay for the next.'

Tying the child up in various restraint devices was a near-universal practice. Swaddling was the central fact of the infant's earliest years. As we have noted, restraints were thought necessary because the child was so full of dangerous adult projections that if it were left free it would scratch its eyes out, tear its ears off, break its legs, distort its bones, be terrified by the sight of its own limbs, and even crawl about on all fours like an animal. Traditional swaddling is much the same in every country and age; it 'consists in entirely depriving the child of the use of its limbs, by enveloping them in an endless length bandage, so as to not unaptly resemble billets of wood; and by which, the skin is sometimes excoriated; the flesh compressed, almost to gangrene; the circulation nearly arrested; and the child without the slightest power of motion. Its little waist is surrounded by stays . . . Its head is compressed into the form the fancy of the midwife might suggest; and its shape maintained by properly adjusted pressure . . .'

Swaddling was often so complicated it took up to two hours to dress an infant. Its convenience to adults was enormous – they rarely had to pay any attention to infants once they were tied up. As a recent medical study of swaddling has shown, swaddled infants are extremely passive, their hearts slow down, they cry less, they sleep far more, and in general they are so withdrawn and inert that the doctors who did the study wondered if swaddling shouldn't be tried again. The historical sources confirm this picture; doctors since antiquity agreed that 'wakefulness does not happen to children naturally nor from habit, i.e. customarily, for they always sleep,' and children were described as being laid for hours behind the hot oven, hung on pegs on the wall, placed in tubs, and in general, 'left, like a parcel, in every convenient corner.' Almost all nations swaddled. Even in ancient Egypt, where it is claimed children were not swaddled because paintings showed them naked, swaddling may have been practiced, for Hippocrates said the Egyptians swaddle, and occasional figurines showed swaddling clothes. Those few areas where swaddling was not used, such as in ancient Sparta and in the Scottish highlands, were also areas of the most severe hardening practices, as though the only possible choice were between tight swaddling or being carried about naked and made to run in the snow without clothes. Swaddling was so taken for granted that the evidence for length of swaddling is quite spotty prior to early modern times. Soranus says the Romans unswaddled at from 40 to 60 days; hopefully, this is more accurate than Plato's 'two years.' Tight swaddling, often including strapping to carrying-boards, continued throughout the Middle Ages, but I have not yet been able to find out for how many months. The few source references in the sixteenth and seventeenth century, plus a study of the art of the period, suggest a pattern of total swaddling in those centuries for between one to four months; then the arms were left free and the body and legs remained swaddled for between six to nine months. The English led the way in ending swaddling, as they did in ending outside wet-nursing. Swaddling in England and America was on its way out by the end of the eighteenth century, and in France and Germany by the nineteenth century.

Once the infant was released from its swaddling bands, physical restraints of all kinds continued, varying by country and period. Children were sometimes tied to chairs to prevent their crawling. Right into the nineteenth century leading strings were tied to the child's clothes to control it and swing it about. Corsets and stays made of bone, wood, or iron were often used for both sexes. Children were sometimes strapped into backboards and their feet put in stocks while they studied, and iron collars and other devices were used to 'improve posture,' like the one Francis Kemble described: 'a hideous engine of torture of the backboard species, made of steel covered with red morocco, which consisted of a flat piece placed on my back, and strapped down to my waist with a belt and secured at the top by two epaulets strapped over my shoulders. From the middle of this there rose a steel rod or spine, with a steel collar which encircled my throat and fastened behind.' These devices seemed to be more commonly used in the sixteenth to nineteenth centuries than in medieval times, but this could be due to the paucity of earlier sources. Two practices, however, were probably common to every country since antiquity. The first is the general scantiness of dress for 'hardening' purposes; the second is the use of stool-like devices which were supposed to assist walking, but in fact were used to prevent crawling, which was considered animal-like.

Periodization of modes of parent-child relations

Since some people still kill, beat, and sexually abuse children, any attempt to periodize modes of child rearing must first admit that psychogenic evolution proceeds at different rates in different family lines, and that many parents appear to be 'stuck' in earlier historical modes. There are also class and area differences which are important, especially since modern times, when the upper classes stopped sending their infants to wet-nurses and began bringing them up themselves. The periodization below should be thought of as a designation of the modes of parent-child relations which were exhibited by the psychogenically most advanced part of the population in the most advanced countries, and the dates given are the first in which I found examples of that mode in the sources. The series of six modes represents a continuous sequence of closer approaches between parent and child as generation after generation of parents slowly overcame their anxieties and began to develop the capacity to identify and satisfy the needs of their children. I also believe the series provides a meaningful taxology of contemporary child-rearing modes.

1 *Infanticidal Mode (Antiquity to Fourth Century A.D.).* The image of Medea hovers over childhood in antiquity, for myth here only reflects reality. Some facts are more important than others, and when parents routinely resolved their anxieties about taking care of children by killing them, it affected the surviving children profoundly. For those who were allowed to grow up, the projective reaction was paramount, and the concreteness of reversal was evident in the widespread sodomizing of the child.

2 *Abandonment Mode (Fourth to Thirteenth Century A.D.).* Once parents began to accept the child as having a soul, the only way they could escape the dangers of their own projections was by abandonment, whether to the wet nurse, to the monastery or nunnery, to foster families, to the homes of other nobles as servants or hostages, or by severe emotional abandonment at home. The symbol of this mode might be Griselda, who so willingly abandoned her children to prove her love for her husband. Or perhaps it would be

any of those pictures so popular up to the thirteenth century of a rigid Mary stiffly holding the infant Jesus. Projection continued to be massive, since the child was still full of evil and needed always to be beaten, but as the reduction in child sodomizing shows, reversal diminished considerably.

3 *Ambivalent Mode (Fourteenth to Seventeenth Centuries)*. Because the child, when it was allowed to enter into the parents' emotional life, was still a container for dangerous projections, it was their task to mold it into shape. From Dominici to Locke there was no image more popular than that of the physical molding of children, who were seen as soft wax, plaster, or clay to be beaten into shape. Enormous ambivalence marks this mode. The beginning of the period is approximately the fourteenth century, which shows an increase in the number of child instruction manuals, the expansion of the cults of Mary and the infant Jesus, and the proliferation in art of the 'close-mother image.'

4 *Intrusive Mode (Eighteenth Century)*. A tremendous reduction in projection and the virtual disappearance of reversal was the accomplishment of the great transition for parent-child relations which appeared in the eighteenth century. The child was no longer so full of dangerous projections, and rather than just examine its insides with an enema, the parents approached even closer and attempted to conquer its mind, in order to control its insides, its anger, its needs, its masturbation, its very will. The child raised by intrusive parents was nursed by the mother, not swaddled, not given regular enemas, toilet trained early, prayed with but not played with, hit but not regularly whipped, punished for masturbation, and made to obey promptly with threats and guilt as often as with other methods of punishment. The child was so much less threatening that true empathy was possible, and pediatrics was born, which along with the general improvement in level of care by parents reduced infant mortality and provided the basic for the demographic transition of the eighteenth century.

5 *Socialization Mode (Nineteenth to Mid-twentieth Centuries)*. As projections continued to diminish, the raising of a child became less a process of conquering its will than of training it, guiding it into proper paths, teaching it to conform, socializing it. The socializing mode is still thought of by most people as the only model within which discussion of child care can proceed, and it has been the source of all twentieth-century psychological models, from Freud's 'channeling of impulses' to Skinner's behaviorism. It is most particularly the model of sociological functionalism. Also, in the nineteenth century, the father for the first time begins to take more

than an occasional interest in the child, training it, and sometimes even relieving the mother of child-care chores.

6 *Helping Mode (Begins Mid-twentieth Century)*. The helping mode involves the proposition that the child knows better than the parent what it needs at each stage of its life, and fully involves both parents in the child's life as they work to empathize with and fulfill its expanding and particular needs. There is no attempt at all to discipline or form 'habits.' Children are neither struck nor scolded, and are apologized to if yelled at under stress. The helping mode involves an enormous amount of time, energy, and discussion on the part of both parents, especially in the first six years, for helping a young child reach its daily goals means continually responding to it, playing with it, tolerating its regressions, being its servant rather than the other way around, interpreting its emotional conflicts, and providing the objects specific to its evolving interests. Few parents have yet consistently attempted this kind of child care. From the four books which describe children brought up according to the helping mode, it is evident that it results in a child who is gentle, sincere, never depressed, never imitative or group-oriented, strong-willed, and unintimidated by authority.

Psychogenic theory: a new paradigm for history

Psychogenic theory can, I think, provide a genuinely new paradigm for the study of history. It reverses the usual '*mind as tabula rasa*,' and instead considers the '*world as tabula rasa*,' with each generation born into a world of meaningless objects which are invested with meaning only if the child receives a certain kind of care. As soon as the mode of care changes for enough children, all the books and artifacts in the world are brushed aside as irrelevant to the purposes of the new generation, and society begins to move in unpredictable directions. How historical change is connected with changing child-care modes we have yet to spell out.

If the measure of a theory's vitality is its ability to generate interesting problems, childhood history and psychogenic theory should have an exciting future. There is still a lot to learn about what growing up in the past was really like. One of our first tasks will be to investigate why childhood evolution proceeds at different rates in different countries and different class and family lines. Yet we already know enough to be able for the first time to answer some major questions on value and behavior change in Western history. First to benefit from the theory will be the history of witchcraft, magic, religious movements, and other irrational mass phenomena. Beyond this, psychogenic theory should eventually contribute to our understanding of why social organization, political form, and technology change in specific times and directions and not in others. Perhaps the addition of the childhood parameter to history may even end the historian's century-long Durkheimian flight from psychology, and encourage us to resume the task of constructing a scientific history of human nature which was envisioned so long ago by John Stuart Mill as a 'theory of the causes which determine the type of character belonging to a people or to an age.'

The child as emergent being

Far from conceiving of children as beings in stasis or as comprised of the constraints and expectations imposed by the world that surrounds them, we might rather address their quality of emergence. The child, as the person, can be regarded as project, as imbued with the essentials of choice, creativity and self-determination. In this way we may explore the existential potentiality of each individual forging his identity within the structured context of collective life. Rather than assuming the old order through strict determinism, children actively establish new orders of relevance and relation, they are the key to the future, not the replication of the past - they are 'ideal'.

5 The child's relations with others

Maurice Merleau-Ponty

I pass to the fact that appeared to me to be worthy of mention by way of introduction to this course: the relation that can be established between the development of intelligence (in particular, the acquisition of language) and the configuration of the individual's affective environment.

I call your attention to a short article by Francois Rostand entitled 'Grammaire et affectivité.'[1] Rostand begins by remarking that from the start there is a correlation between the age at which the child is most dependent on his parents (i.e., about two years) and the age at which he begins to learn language. There is a period when the child is 'sensitive' with regard to language, when he is capable of learning to speak. It has been shown that if the child up to two years of age does not have a linguistic model to imitate, if he does not find himself in an environment in which people are speaking, he will never speak as do those who have learned language during the period in question. This is the case with those children who are called 'savages,' who have been raised by animals or far from contact with speaking subjects. In no case have these subjects ever learned to speak with the linguistic perfection that is found among ordinary subjects. Deaf children whose retraining has been delayed and who consequently have not learned to speak during the 'sensitive' period never speak their language in exactly the same way as do those who can hear. One can show, in fact, that in their syntax or their morphology there exist, after retraining, some very odd peculiarities: for example, the absence or rarity of the passive voice in verbs. This allows us to presume that there will be a profound link between the acquisition of language (which would seem to be a strictly intellectual operation) and the child's place in the family environment. It is this relation that Rostand seeks to define exactly.

Source: Maurice Merleau-Ponty, *The Primacy of Perception*, Paris, Gallimard (1964). English translation published by Northwestern University Press.

It is a commonplace that the child's acquisition of language is also correlated with his relation to his mother. Children who have been suddenly and forcibly separated from their mothers always show signs of a linguistic regression. At bottom, it is not only the word 'mama' that is the child's first; it is the entire language which is, so to speak, maternal.

The acquisition of language might be a phenomenon of the same kind as the relation to the mother. Just as the maternal relation is (as the psychoanalysts say) a relation of *identification*, in which the subject projects on his mother what he himself experiences and assimilates the attitudes of his mother, so one could say that the acquisition of language is itself a phenomenon of identification. To learn to speak is to learn to play a series of *roles*, to assume a series of conducts or linguistic gestures.

Rostand mentions an observation made by Dr. Dolto-Marette in a case of jealousy in a child. The younger of two children shows jealousy when his new brother is born. During the first days of the newborn child's life, he identifies with it, carrying himself as though he himself were the newborn baby. There is a striking regression in language as well as in character. In the following days one notices in him a change of attitude. The subject identifies himself with his older brother and overcomes his jealousy; he adopts all the characteristics of the eldest, including an attitude toward the new baby that is identical to what, until now, had been his older brother's attitude toward him. Thanks to a fortunate circumstance his jealousy is overcome. By chance, just as the baby is born, a fourth child comes to stay in the family. This fourth child is bigger than all three brothers in the family. The presence of a child who is older than the eldest brother robs the latter of his status as the 'absolute eldest.' The eldest is now no longer 'absolutely big,' since there are others who are bigger than he is. The fourth child aids in the middle brother's transition and assimilation of the role of the eldest.

It is in this way that a case of neurotic stuttering is cured and a marked linguistic progress realized from day to day. The subject acquires the use of the simple past tense, the imperfect, the simple future, and the future with the verb *to go* ('I am *going* to leave'). Coming back to this observation, Rostand interprets it in the following fashion: The jealousy that invades the subject when he confirms the arrival of a new brother is essentially a refusal to change his situation. The newcomer is an intruder and is going to confiscate to his own advantage the place in the family that was held until now by our jealous subject. It is in the phase of the 'surpassing' of jealousy that one notices the appearance of a link between the affective phenomenon and the linguistic phenomenon: jealousy is overcome thanks to the constitution of a scheme of past-present-future. In effect, jealousy in this subject consists in a rigid attachment to his present – that is, to the situation of the 'latest born' which was hitherto his own. He considered the present to be absolute. Now, on the contrary, one can say that from the moment when he consents to be no longer the latest born, to become in relation to the new baby what his elder brother had until then been in relation to him, he replaces his attitude of 'my place has been taken' with another, whose schema might be somewhat like this: 'I *have been* the youngest, but I *am* the youngest no longer, and I *will become* the biggest.' One sees that there is a solidarity between the acquisition of this temporal structure, which gives a meaning to the corresponding linguistic instruments, and the situation of a jealousy that is overcome. For the subject the situation of jealousy is the occasion both for restructuring his relations with the others he lives with and at the same time for acquiring new dimensions of existence (past, present, and future) with a supple play among them.

Speaking Piaget's language, one might say that the whole problem of overcoming jealousy is a problem of 'de-centering.' Until now the subject has been centered on himself, centered on the situation of the latest born that he has occupied. In order to accept the birth of a new child, he must de-center himself. But the de-centering involved here is not, as it was for Piaget, a primarily intellectual operation, a phenomenon of pure knowledge. It is a matter of a lived de-centering, aroused by the situation of the child inside the family constellation.

One might even say that what the child learns, in solving the problem of jealousy, is to relativize his notions. He must relativize the notions of the youngest and the eldest: he is no longer *the* youngest; it is the new child who assumes this role. He thus must come to distinguish the absolute 'youngest' from the relative 'youngest' which he now becomes. And in the same way he must learn to become the eldest in relation to the newborn child, whereas until now the notion of 'eldest' had only an absolute meaning.

In Piaget's language, the child must learn to think in terms of reciprocity. Rostand himself cites Piaget's terms. But these terms take on a new meaning from the fact that training in reciprocity, relativity, and de-centering occurs here not by intellectual acts of 'grouping' but by operations within the vital order, by the manner in which the child restores [*réétablit*] his relations with others.

To this preliminary observation Rostand adds the following personal one: He noticed in a little girl of thirty-five months an interesting linguistic phenomenon that followed a frightening emotional experience (an encounter, while walking alone, with a big dog). Two months later this experience seemed to bear fruit. There was an abrupt acquisition of certain modes of expression (in particular, the imperfect tense of verbs) which until then the child had not used.

This step occurred at the birth of a younger brother. What we have to understand is the exact relation between this linguistic phenomenon, the birth of the younger brother, and the emotional experience of two months earlier.

The child had come across a dog who was nursing its young. At the time she encountered the dog, she knew already from her parents that she was going to have a little brother or sister in about two months. Meeting the dog which was nursing its litter was not an indifferent experience for the child; it was a visible symbol of something analogous that was about to happen in her own world. The pattern about to the realized two months later in the child's environment (parents, little girl, little brother) was already prefigured by the pattern (big dog; me, the little girl; the little dogs). The sight of the dogs was of paramount significance by virtue of its relation to the situation in which the child was about to find herself.

In order for her to accept the birth of a younger brother, what was basically necessary was a change of attitude. Whereas the little girl had been, until then, the object of all attention and of all caresses, she now had to accept the fact that some of this attention and these caresses would be transferred to another, and to associate herself with this attitude. She had to pass from an ingratiating [*captative*] attitude (i.e., one in which the child receives without giving) to a selfless [*oblative*], quasi-maternal attitude toward the child about to be born. It was necessary for her to accept a relative abandonment, to turn and confront a life that would henceforth be *her* life, that would no longer be supported, as it had been until then, by the exclusive attention of her parents. In short, the girl had to adopt an active attitude, whereas until then, her attitude had been passive.

The linguistic phenomenon that emerges at this same time can be understood in this perspective. I said earlier that the imperfect tense appeared in the child's language after the birth of her brother. More important, however, was the emergence of four verbs in the future tense; there was also a great increase in the use of 'me' and 'I.' If the future is a time of aggressiveness, a time when projects are envisioned, when one takes a stand in the face of what is to come and, instead of allowing it to come, moves actively toward it – then how was it made possible by the new situation of the little girl? The answer is that this was precisely the attitude demanded of the child by the birth of her brother. The acquisition of 'me' and 'I' presented no problems; it indicated that the subject adopted a more personal attitude and lived to a relatively greater degree by herself. Finally, the acquisition of the imperfect tense at the birth of her little brother indicated that the child was becoming capable of understanding that the present changes into the past. The imperfect is a former present which, moreover, is still referred to as present, unlike the past definite. The imperfect is 'still there.' The acquisition of the imperfect thus presupposes a concrete grasp of the movement from present to past which the child, on her part, was just in the process of achieving in her relations with her family. The fact is, all the verbs she used in the imperfect after the birth of her brother had to do with the baby. The baby *is* what the elder sister *used to be* in the world of the family.

To be sure, emotion plays a role only to the extent that it gives the subject the occasion to re-structure her relations with her human environment, and not at all simply as emotion. If the problem had not been resolved, if the subject had shown herself incapable of overcoming her jealousy or her uneasiness, nothing good would have come from the experience. Inversely, there can be cases in which the subject progresses in language without apparent emotion. In such cases, however, linguistic progress always has an interrupted character; the acquisition of the modes of expression always represents a sort of crisis, in which a whole realm of expression is annexed in a single stroke.

In sum, the intellectual elaboration of our experience of the world is constantly supported by the affective elaboration of our inter-human relations. The use of certain linguistic tools is mastered in the play of forces that constitute the subject's relations to his human surroundings, The linguistic usage achieved by the child depends strictly on the 'position' (in psychoanalytic terms) that is taken by the child at every moment in the play of forces in his family and his human environment.

Here again it is not a question of a causal analysis. There is no question of saying that the linguistic progress is *explained* by the affective progress, in the sense in which expansion is explained by heat. One might reply that the affective progress itself is also a function of the intellectual progress and that the entire intellectual development makes possible a certain affective progress. And this would also be true.

What we are seeking here is not a causal explanation, any more than before. My effort is to show the solidarity and unity of the two phenomena, not to reduce the one to the other, as is traditionally done by both empiricist and intellectualist psychologists. The child's experience of the constellation of his own family does more than impress on him certain relations between one human being and another. At the same time that the child is assuming and forming his family relations, an entire form of thinking arises in him. It is a whole usage of language as well as a way of perceiving the world.

The problem of the child's perception of others: the theoretical problem

Before studying the different relations established between the child and his parents, his peers, other children, brothers, sisters, or strangers, before undertaking a description and analysis of these different relations, a question of principle arises: How and under what conditions does the child come into contact with others? What is the nature of the child's relations with others? How are such relations possible from the day of birth on?

Classical psychology approached this problem only with great difficulty. One might say that it was among the stumbling blocks of classical psychology because it is admittedly incapable of being solved if one confines oneself to the theoretical ideas that were elaborated by academic psychology.

How does such a problem arise for classical psychology? Given the presuppositions with which that psychology works, given the prejudices it adopted from the start without any kind of criticism, the relation with others becomes incomprehensible for it. What, in fact, is the psyche [*psychisme*] - mine or the other's - for classical psychology? All psychologists of the classical period are in tacit agreement on this point: the psyche, or the psychic, is *what is given to only one person*. It seems, in effect, that one might admit without further examination or discussion that what constitutes the psyche in me or in others is something incommunicable. I alone am able to grasp my psyche - for example, my sensations of green or of red. You will never know them as I know them; you will never experience them in my place. A consequence of this idea is that the psyche of another appears to me as radically inaccessible, at least in its own existence. I cannot reach other lives, other thought processes, since by hypothesis they are open only to inspection by a single individual: the one who owns them.

Since I cannot have direct access to the psyche of another, for the reasons just given, I must grant that I seize the other's psyche only indirectly, mediated by its bodily appearances. I see you in flesh and bone; you are there. I cannot know what you are thinking, but I can suppose it, guess at it from your facial expressions, your gestures, and your words - in short from a series of bodily appearances of which I am only the witness.

The question thus becomes this: How does it happen that, in the presence of this mannequin that resembles a man, in the presence of this body that gesticulates in a characteristic way, I come to believe that it is inhabited by a psyche? How am I led to consider that this body before me encloses a psyche? How can I perceive across this body, so to speak, another's psyche? Classical psychology's conception of the body and the consciousness we have of it is here a second obstacle in the way of a solution of the problem. Here one wants to speak of the notion of *cenesthesia*, meaning a mass of sensations that would express to the subject the state of his different organs and different bodily functions. Thus my body for me, and your body for you, could be reached, and be knowable, by means of a cenesthesic sense.

A mass of sensations, by hypothesis, is as *individual* as the psyche itself. That is to say, if in fact my body is knowable by me only through the mass of sensations it gives me (a mass of sensations to which you obviously have no access and of which we have no concrete experience), then the consciousness I have of my body is impenetrable by you. You cannot represent yourself in the same way in which I feel my own body; it is likewise impossible for me to represent to myself the way in which you feel your body. How, then, can I suppose that, in back of this appearance before me, there is someone who experiences his body as I experience mine?

Only one recourse is left for classical psychology – that of supposing that, as a spectator of the gestures and utterances of the other's body before me, I consider the totality of signs thus given, the totality of facial expressions this body presents to me, as the occasion for a kind of decoding. Behind the body whose gestures and characteristic utterances I witness, I project, so to speak, what I myself feel of my own body. No matter whether it is a question of an actual association of ideas or, instead, a judgment whereby I interpret the appearances, I transfer to the other the intimate experience I have of my own body.

The problem of the experience of others poses itself, as it were, in a system of four terms: (1) myself, my 'psyche'; (2) the image I have of my body by means of the sense of touch or of cenesthesia, which, to be brief, we shall call the 'introceptive image' of my own body; (3) the body of the other as seen by me, which we shall call the 'visual body'; and (4) a fourth (hypothetical) term which I must reconstitute and guess at – the 'psyche' of the other, the other's feeling of his own existence – to the extent that I can imagine or suppose it across the appearances of the other through his visual body.

Posed thus, the problem raises all kinds of difficulties. First, there is the difficulty of relating my knowledge or experience of the other to an association, to a judgment by which I would project into him the data of my intimate experience. The perception of others comes relatively early in life. Naturally we do not at an early age come to know the exact *meaning* of each of the emotional expressions presented to us by others. This exact knowledge is, if you like, late in coming; what is much earlier is the very fact that I perceive an expression, even if I may be wrong about what it means exactly. At a very early age children are sensitive to facial expressions, e.g., the smile. How could that be possible if, in order to arrive at an understanding of the global meaning of the smile and to learn that the smile is a fair indication of a benevolent feeling, the child had to perform the complicated task I have just mentioned? How could it be possible if, beginning with the visual perception of another's smile, he had to compare that visual perception of the smile with the movement that he himself makes when he is happy or when he feels benevolent – projecting to the other a benevolence of which he would have had intimate experience but which could not be grasped directly in the other? This complicated process would seem to be incompatible with the relative precociousness of the perception of others.

Again, in order for projection to be possible and to take place, it would be necessary for me to begin from the analogy between the facial expressions offered me by others and the different facial gestures I execute myself. In the case of the smile, for me to interpret the visible smile of the other requires that there be a way of comparing the visible smile of the other with what we may call the 'motor smile' – the smile as felt, in the case of the child, by the child himself. But in fact do we have the means of making this comparison between the body of the other, as it appears in visual perception, and our own body, as we feel it by means of introception and of cenesthesia? Have we the means of systematically comparing the body of the other as seen by me with my body as sensed by me? In order for this to be possible there would have to be a fairly regular correspondence between the two experiences. The child's visual experience of his own body is altogether insignificant in relation to the kinesthetic, cenesthesic, or tactile feeling he can have of it. There are numerous regions of his body that he does not see and some that he will never see or know except by means of the mirror (of which we will speak shortly). There is no point-for-point correspondence between the two images of the body. To understand how the child arrives at assimilating the one to the other, we must, rather, suppose that he has other reasons for doing it than reasons of simple detail. If he comes to identify as bodies, and as animated ones, the bodies of himself and the other, this can only be because he globally identifies

them and not because he constructs a point-for-point correspondence between the visual image of the other and the introceptive
image of his own body.

These two difficulties are particularly apparent when it comes to
accounting for the phenomenon of imitation. To imitate is to
perform a gesture in the image of another's gesture – like the child,
for example, who smiles because someone smiles at him. According
to the principles we have been entertaining, it would be necessary for
me to translate my visual image of the other's smile into a motor
language. The child would have to set his facial muscles in motion in
such a way as to reproduce the visible expression that is called 'the
smile' in another. But how could he do it? Naturally he does not have
the other's internal motor feeling of his face; as far as he is
concerned, he does not even have an image of himself smiling. The
result is that if we want to solve the problem of the transfer of the
other's conduct to me, we can in no way rest on the supposed analogy
between the other's face and that of the child.

On the contrary, the problem comes close to being solved only on
condition that certain classical prejudices are renounced. We must
abandon the fundamental prejudice according to which the psyche is
that which is accessible only to myself and cannot be seen from
outside. My 'psyche' is not a series of 'states of consciousness' that are
rigorously closed in on themselves and inaccessible to anyone but me.
My consciousness is turned primarily toward the world, turned
toward things; it is above all a relation to the world. The other's
consciousness as well is chiefly a certain way of comporting himself
toward the world. Thus it is in his conduct, in the manner in which
the other deals with the world, that I will be able to discover his
consciousness.

If I am a consciousness turned toward things, I can meet in things
the actions of another and find in them a meaning, because they are
themes of possible activity for my own body. Guillaume, in his book
l'Imitation chez l'enfant (1925), says that we do not at first imitate
others but rather the actions of others, and that we find others at the
point of origin of these actions. At first the child imitates not persons
but conducts. And the problem of knowing how conduct can be
transferred from another to me is infinitely less difficult to solve than
the problem of knowing how I can represent to myself a psyche that is
radically foreign to me. If, for example, I see another draw a figure,
I can understand the drawing as an action because it speaks directly
to my own unique motility. Of course, the other *qua* author of a
drawing is not yet a whole person, and there are more revealing
actions than drawing – for example, using language. What is
essential, however, is to see that a perspective on the other is opened

to me from the moment I define him and myself as 'conducts' at work in the world, as ways of 'grasping' the natural and cultural world surrounding us.

But this presupposes a reform not only of the notion of the 'psyche' (which we will replace henceforth by that of 'conduct') but also of the idea we have of our own body. If my body is to appropriate the conducts given to me visually and make them its own, it must itself be given to me not as a mass of utterly private sensations but instead by what has been called a 'postural,' or 'corporeal, schema.' This notion, introduced long ago by Henry Head, has been taken over and enriched by Wallon, by certain German psychologists, and has finally been the subject of a study in its own right by Professor Lhermitte in *l'Image de notre corps* (1939).

For these authors, my body is no agglomeration of sensations (visual, tactile, 'tenesthesic,' or 'cenesthesic'). It is first and foremost a *system* whose different introceptive and extroceptive aspects express each other reciprocally, including even the roughest of relations with surrounding space and its principal directions. The consciousness I have of my body is not the consciousness of an isolated mass; it is a *postural schema*. It is the perception of my body's position in relation to the vertical, the horizontal, and certain other axes of important co-ordinates of its environment.

In addition, the different sensory domains (sight, touch, and the sense of movement in the joints) which are involved in the perception of my body do not present themselves to me as so many absolutely distinct regions. Even if, in the child's first and second years, the translation of one into the language of others is imprecise and incomplete, they all have in common a *certain style* of action, a certain *gestural* meaning that makes of the collection an already organized totality. Understood in this way, the experience I have of my own body could be transferred to another much more easily than the cenesthesia of classical psychology, giving rise to what Wallon calls a 'postural impregnation' of my own body by the conducts I witness.

I can perceive, across the visual image of the other, that the other is an organism, that that organism is inhabited by a 'psyche,' because the visual image of the other is interpreted by the notion I myself have of my own body and thus appears as the visible envelopment of another 'corporeal schema.' My perception of my body would, so to speak, be swallowed up in a cenesthesia if that cenesthesia were strictly individual. On the contrary, however, if we are dealing with a schema, or a system, such a system would be relatively transferrable from one sensory domain to the other in the case of my own body, just as it could be transferred to the domain of the other.

Thus in today's psychology we have one system with two terms (my behavior and the other's behavior) which functions as a whole. To the extent that I can elaborate and extend my corporeal schema, to the extent that I acquire a better organized experience of my own body, to that very extent will my consciousness of my own body cease being a chaos in which I am submerged and lend itself to a transfer to others. And since at the same time the other who is to be perceived is himself not a 'psyche' closed in on himself but rather a conduct, a system of behavior that aims at the world, he offers himself to my motor intentions and to that 'intentional transgression' (Husserl) by which I animate and pervade him. Husserl said that the perception of others is like a 'phenomenon of coupling' [*accouplement*]. The term is anything but a metaphor. In perceiving the other, my body and his are coupled, resulting in a sort of action which pairs them [*action à deux*]. This conduct which I am able only to see, I live somehow from a distance. I make it mine; I recover [*reprendre*] it or comprehend it. Reciprocally I know that the gestures I make myself can be the objects of another's intention. It is this transfer of my intentions to the other's body and of his intentions to my own, my alienation of the other and his alienation of me, that makes possible the perception of others.

All these analyses presuppose that the perception of others cannot be accounted for if one begins by supposing an ego and another that are *absolutely* conscious of themselves, each of which lays claim, as a result, to an absolute originality in relation to the other that confronts it. On the contrary, the perception of others is made comprehensible if one supposes that psychogenesis begins in a state where the child is unaware of himself and the other as different beings. We cannot say that in such a state the child has a genuine communication with others. In order that there be communication, there must be a sharp distinction between the one who communicates and the one with whom he communicates. But there is initially a state of pre-communication (Max Scheler), wherein the other's intentions somehow play *across* my body while my intentions play across his.

How is this distinction made? I gradually become aware of my body, of what radically distinguishes it from the other's body, at the same time that I begin to live my intentions in the facial expressions of the other and likewise begin to live the other's volitions in my own gestures. The progress of the child's experience results in his seeing that his body is, after all, closed in on itself. In particular, the visual image he acquires of his own body (especially from the mirror) reveals to him a hitherto unsuspected isolation of two subjects who are facing each other. The objectification of his own body discloses to the child his difference, his 'insularity,' and, correlatively, that of others.

Thus the development has somewhat the following character: There is a first phase, which we call pre-communication, in which there is not one individual over against another but rather an anonymous collectivity, an undifferentiated group life [*vie à plusieurs*]. Next, on the basis of this initial community, both by the objectification of one's own body and the constitution of the other in his difference, there occurs a segregation, a distinction of individuals – a process which, moreover, as we shall see, is never completely finished.

This kind of conception is common to many trends in contemporary psychology. One finds it in Guillaume and Wallon; it occurs in Gestalt theorists, phenomenologists, and psychoanalysts alike.

Guillaume shows that we must neither treat the origin of consciousness as though it were conscious, in an explicit way, of itself nor treat it as though it were compeltely closed in on itself. The first *me* is, as he says, virtual or latent, i.e., unaware of itself in its absolute difference. Consciousness of oneself as a unique individual, whose place can be taken by no one else, comes later and is not primitive. Since the primordial *me* is virtual or latent, egocentrism is not at all the attitude of a *me* that expressly grasps itself (as the term 'egocentrism' might lead us to believe). Rather, it is the attitude of a *me* which is unaware of itself and lives as easily in others as it does in itself – but which, being unaware of others in their own separateness as well, in truth is no more conscious of them than of itself.

Wallon introduces an analogous notion with what he calls 'syncretic sociability.' Syncretism here is the indistinction between me and the other, a confusion at the core of a situation that is common to us both. After that the objectification of the body intervenes to establish a sort of wall between me and the other: a partition. Henceforth it will prevent me from confusing myself with what the other thinks, and especially with what he thinks of me; just as I will no longer confuse him with my thoughts, and especially my thoughts about him. There is thus a correlative constitution of me and the other as two human beings among all others.

Thus at first the *me* is both entirely unaware of itself and at the same time all the more demanding for being unaware of its own limits. The adult *me*, on the contrary, is a *me* that knows its own limits yet possesses the power to cross them by a genuine sympathy that is at least *relatively* distinct from the initial form of sympathy. The initial sympathy rests on the ignorance of oneself rather than on the perception of others, while adult sympathy occurs between 'other' and 'other'; it does not abolish the differences between myself and the other.

Note
1 In *Revue Française de Psychoanalyse*, vol. 14 (April-June, 1950), pp. 299-310.

6 Embodiment and child development: a phenomenological approach

John O'Neill

Any theory of child socialization is implicitly a theory of the construction of social reality, if not of a particular historical social order. In this essay I propose to give an account of the phenomenological approach to the basic pre-suppositions of child socialization. I shall restrict my account to the writings of Maurice Merleau-Ponty, who, although widely known as a philosopher and political theorist, remains to be known for the lectures on child psychology which he gave for many years at the Sorbonne.[1] For reasons of economy it is not possible to follow the whole of Merleau-Ponty's interpretation and critical evaluation of the literature with which he familiarized himself concerning the physiological, intellectual, moral, and cultural development of the child, not to mention his close reading of psychoanalytical and American anthropological research. Much of the literature is in any case now all too familiar to workers in child psychology, although Merleau-Ponty's close reading and phenomenological critique of Piaget's work might be given special mention because of its continuing interest.

Merleau-Ponty's analysis of the child's relation to others, his family, and the world around him may serve as introduction to the whole of Merleau-Ponty's phenomenology of perception, expression, and the sociohistorical world of human institutions. At all events, the topic and its phenomenological horizons are inseparable and can only be managed in a short space by focusing upon the very fundamental presuppositions of the phenomenon of the child's orientation to the world and others around him through the mediations of the body, language, perception, and reflection. The phenomenological concern with these basic structures of child development involves an implicit concern with the way in which they may be prejudged by the assumptions of unreflexive research.

The starting point in any study of child psychology and

Source: *Recent Sociology* No. 5, ed. H.P. Dreitzel, New York, Collier Books (1973).

socialization must be the child's relation to the adult worl
relations, linguistic, perceptual, and logical categories. B)
on this point, Merleau-Ponty dismisses any notion of a psych
the child, the sick person, man, woman, or the primitive
enclosed nature. Indeed, there is a *complementary feature* ᴏ ᴜᴇ
child-adult relationship, namely, the reverse adult-child relationship.
This obliges us in the methodology of child studies to design research
procedures which are sensitive to the two-way and even asymmetric
relation between the child's orientation to the adult world and the
adult world's interests in fostering, enforcing and moralizing upon its
own interests and hopes in the child world. We cannot here look down
the path toward the 'politics of experience' which this first methodological observation opens up. It must suffice to remark that it points
to a cultural dilemma that is generic to human relations and thus
makes it impossible to conceive of child psychology and psychoanalysis outside of specific cultural frameworks.

Another general conclusion which we may elicit from the
interactional nature of the object of child studies refers to a
phenomenon that is common to the object of all social studies. The
natural scientist for most purposes is concerned only with the
observer's experience, however mediated by his instruments, of the
object under study. Even if we take into account the problems of
interference referred to by the Heisenberg uncertainty principle, the
problem here is merely that the scientist must allow for changes in
the behaviour of experimental objects due to the interference effects
of his own methods of study. But although this problem produces a
greater similarity between the natural and social sciences than was
imagined earlier, it leaves unchanged an essential difference between
them. Namely, where the object of science is a human relationship or
set of human relationships, a custom or institution, the 'ordering' of
the relationship it is not merely a scientific construct. It is first of all a
pre-theoretical construct which is the unarticulated 'commonsense'
knowledge of others as 'relatives' who experience dependable needs
and wants expressed through the 'relevances' of the human body,
time, and place.

The burden of Merleau-Ponty's methodological critique of
research methods in studies of child perception, language, and
morals is that they proceed without the benefit of any reflection upon
the way their methods already prejudge the nature of the phenomena
they are intended to elicit. In the first place we must rid ourselves of a
'dogmatic rationalism' which consists in studying the child's world
from above and thereby construing the child's efforts as pre-logical
or magical behaviour which must be sloughed off as a condition of
entry into the objective, realist world of adults. Such a prejudice

overlooks the way in which child and adult behaviour are solidary, with anticipations from the side of the child and regressions on the side of the adult which makes their conduct no more separable than health and sickness. Indeed, the real task of a genuine psychology must be to discover the basis of *communication* between children and adults, between the unconscious and consciousness, between the sick and the sane.

'We must conceive the child neither as an absolute "other" nor just "the same" as ourselves, but as polymorphous.' This remark may serve as a guiding principle in following Merleau-Ponty's subtle interweaving of the processes of structure and development in the child's relation to others. The notion of *development* is, of course, central to the psychology of the child; it is, however, a complex notion since it implies neither an absolute continuity between childhood and adulthood nor any complete discontinuity without phases or transitions. It is here that we need to avoid the twin reductions of the phenomena of development which Merleau-Ponty labels 'mechanist' and 'idealist' exemplified respectively by the learning theory approach originated by Pavlov and the cognitive approach of Piaget. Here we are on explicitly philosophical ground because the continuity between childhood and adult life raises the question of how it is in principle that individual and inter-subjective life are possible.

Mechanist, reflex or learning theory accounts of child development involve us in the difficulty that their causal explanations fail to cover the phenomena of adult initiative, creativity and responsibility. Reflex theory reduces conduct to a structure of conditioned reflexes built into increasingly complex patterns whose principle of organization is always conceived as an environmental stimulus to which the responses of adaptation occur without internal elaboration. Reflex theory attempts to explain conduct in terms of physiological process without norms or intentionality. But even at its own level reflex theory is not sure of its foundations. Once one attempts to make the notions of stimulus, receptor and reflex more precise, reflex theory becomes riddled with question-begging hypotheses about mechanisms of inhibition and control, acquired drives and the like. The case of 'experimental neurosis' in one of Pavlov's dogs involved in repeated experiments reveals that the consequences of the restriction of a biologically meaningful environment in order to induce conditioned reflexes results in pathological behaviour. By the same token, the acquisition of human habits is not a strictly determined reflex but the acquisition of a capability for inventing solutions to situations which are only *abstractly* similar and never identical with the original 'learning situation.' What is involved in the formation of human habits is the aquisition of a 'categorical attitude' or a power of 'symbolic expression,' and it is only in pathological conduct that atomistic and associationist explanations appear plausible.

While rejecting naturalistic reductions of child development, Merleau-Ponty is equally critical of idealist or cognitive accounts of the phenomena of perception, intelligence and sensory-motor behaviour. The basic fault in cognitive approaches to the child's relation to the world and others is that they sacrifice the immediate, *visceral knowledge* of self, others and the world which we possess without ever having apprenticed ourselves to the 'rules' of perception language, and movement. This preconceptual knowledge is neither subjective nor objective and requires a conception of *symbolic form* which rests neither upon a realist nor an idealist epistemology but instead seeks what is complementary in them. Because the philosophical presuppositions of psychology are implicitly dualistic, consciousness is usually described as the transparent possession of an object of thought in distinction from perceptual and motor acts which are described as a series of events external to each other. Thought and behaviour are juxtaposed or else set in a speculative hierarchy. Against these alternatives, Merleau-Ponty proposes to classify behaviour according to a continuum whose upper and lower limits are defined by the submergence of the structure of behaviour in content, at the lowest level, i.e. 'synenetic forms,' and, at the highest level, the emergence of structure as the proper theme of activity, i.e., 'symbolic forms.'

The conceptualization of behaviour requires the category of Form in order to differentiate the structures of quantity, order and value or signification as the dominant characteristics respectively of matter, life and mind and at the same time to relativize the participation of these structures in a hierarchy of forms of behaviour. Form is itself not an element in the world but a limit toward which biophysical and psychobiological structures tend. In a given environment each organism exhibits a preferred mode of behaviour which is not the simple aim or function of its milieu and its internal organization but is structured by its general attitude to the world. In other words, the analysis of form is not a matter of the composition of real structures but the perception of wholes. Human behaviour, which is essentially symbolic behaviour, unfolds through structures or gestures which are not in objective space and time, like physical objects, nor in a purely internal dimension of consciousness unsituated with respect to historical time and place.

Merleau-Ponty calls the objects of perception 'phenomena' in order to characterize their openness to perceptual consciousness to which they are not given *a priori* but as 'open, inexhaustible systems which we recognize through a certain style of development.' The matrix of all human activity is the *phenomenal body* which is the schema of our world, or the source of a vertical or human space in which we project our feelings, moods and values. Because the human body is a 'community of senses' and not a bundle of contingently related impression, it functions as the universal setting or schema for all possible styles or typical structures of the world. These, however, are not given to us with the invariable formula of a *facius totius universi* but through the temporal synthesis of horizons implicit in intentionality. 'For us the perceptual synthesis is a temporal synthesis, and subjectivity, at the level of perception, is nothing but temporality, and that is what enables us to leave to the subject of perception his opacity and historicity.' The cognitive approaches to child development overlook the *tacit* subjectivity which does not constitute its world *a priori* nor entirely *a posteriori* but develops through a 'living cohesion' in which the embodied self experiences itself while belonging to this world and others, clinging to them for its content.

Thus in his analysis of the child's perception of causal relations Merleau-Ponty argues that it is not a matter of a simple ordering of external data but of an 'informing' [*Gestaltung*] of the child's experience of external events through an operation that is properly neither a logical nor a predicative activity. Similarly, in the case of the child's imagination, it proves impossible to give any objective sense of the notion of *image* even as photograph, mimicry, or picture, apart from an 'affective projection.' Imagination is therefore not a purely intellectual operation but is better understood as an operation beneath the cognitive relation of subject and object. The 'imaginary' and the 'real' are two *forms of conduct* which are not antithetical but rest upon a common ambiguity which occasionally allows the imaginary to substitute for the real. The child lives in the hybrid world of the real and the imaginary which the adult keeps apart for most purposes or is otherwise careful of any transgression wherein he catches his own conscience. Again, in the analysis of the child's drawing, it is also improper to treat the child's efforts as abortive attempts to develop 'adult,' or rather perspectual, drawing, which is itself an historical development in art dominated by the laws of classical geometric perspective. The child's drawing is not a simple imitation of what he sees any more than of what he does not see through lack of detailed 'attention.' The child's drawings are expressive of his relations to the things and people in this world. They develop and change along with his experience with the objects, animals, puppets, and persons around him, including his own experience of his body, its inside and outside. 'The child's drawing is *contact* with the visible world and with others. This tactile relation with the world and with man appears long before the looking attitude, the posture of indifferent contemplation between the spectator and the spectacle which is realized in adult drawing.'

It is above all in the child's acquisition of language that we observe the complex interrelation of cognition and affectivity which can only be made thematic in later phases of development by presupposing the massive inarticulatable background of the world into which we import our categories, distinctions and relations. Language and intelligence presuppose one another without priority and their development rests rather upon the ability of the child to assimilate his linguistic environment as an open system of expression and conduct, comparable to his acquisition of all his other habits. Again, for reasons of economy we cannot deal with the broad range of the phenomenology of language. Instead, we must focus attention upon Merleau-Ponty's interpretation of the social contexts of the acquisition of language.

It is a commonplace that the child's acquisition of language is also correlated with his relation to his mother. Children who have been suddenly and forcibly separated from their mothers always show signs of a linguistic regression. At bottom, it is not only the word "mama" that is the child's first; it is the entire language which is, so to speak, maternal.

The acquisition of language might be a phenomenon of the same kind as the relation to the mother. Just as the maternal relation is (as the psychoanalysts say) a relation of *identification*, in which the subject projects on his mother what he himself experiences and assimilates the attitudes of his mother, so one could say that the acquisition of language is itself a phenomenon of identification. To learn to speak is to learn to play a series of *roles*, to assume a series of conducts or linguistic gestures. ('The Child's Relations with Others')

This hypothesis on the development of language in relation to the child's familial roles is illustrated in terms of analysis of the expression of child jealousy. Upon the birth of a new baby the younger of two children displays jealousy, behavioural regression (carrying himself as though he were the baby), and language regression. There, phenomena represent an initial response to the threatened structure of the child's temporal and social world of the 'latest born' child. The emotional response of jealousy expresses the child's attachment to a hitherto eternal present. A little later the child begins to identify with his older brother, adopting the latter's earlier attitudes towards himself as the 'youngest.' The chance circumstance of the visit of another child bigger than his older brother relativizes once and for all the 'absolute eldest' and the child's jealousy recedes. At the same time as these 'sociometric' experiences are acquired the child's linguistic experience of temporal structure also expands. 'He considered the present to be absolute.

Now, on the contrary, one can say that from the moment when he consents to be no longer the latest born, to become in relation to the new baby what his elder brother had until then been in relation to him, he replaces the attitude of "my place has been taken" with another whose schema might be somewhat like this: "I *have been* the youngest, but I *am* the youngest no longer, and I *will become* the biggest." One sees that there is a solidarity between the acquisition of this temporal structure, which gives a meaning to the corresponding linguistic instruments, and the situation of jealousy that is overcome.'

The child's resolution of his jealousy permits us to make some general remarks upon the relation of the cognitive and affective elements in the child's conception of the world and others around him which will then permit us to deal finally with the fundamental problem of the possibility of social relations of any kind. In overcoming his jealousy we might, as Piaget would say, speak of the child having solved the egocentric problem by learning to decenter himself and to relativize his notions by thinking in terms of reciprocity. But these are clearly not purely intellectual operation; rather, what is called *intelligence* here really designates the mode of intersubjectivity achieved by the child. The intellectual and linguistic elaboration of our experience of the world always rests upon the 'deep structures' of our affective experiencce of the interpersonal world against which we elaborate only later our modes of inductive and deductive thinking.

The perception of other people and the intersubjective world are problematical only for adults. The child lives in a world which he unhesitatingly believes accessible to all around him. He has no awareness of himself or of others as private subjectivities, nor does he suspect that all of us, himself included, are limited to one certain point of view of the world. That is why he subjects neither his thoughts, in which he believes as they present themselves, without attempting to link them to each other, nor our words, to any sort of criticism. He has no knowledge of points of view. For him men are empty heads turned towards one single, self-evident world where everything takes place, even dreams, which are, he thinks, in his room, and even thinking, since it is not distinct from words. Others are for him so many gazes which inspect things, and have an almost material existence, so much so that the child wonders how these gazes avoid being broken as they meet. At about twelve years old, says Piaget, the child achieves the *cogito* and reaches the truths of rationalism. At this stage, it is held, he discovers himself both as a point of view on the world and also as called upon to transcend that point of view, and to construct an objectivity at the level of judgement. Piaget brings the child to a mature outlook as if the thoughts of the adult were self-sufficient and disposed of all contradicitons. But, in reality, it must be the case that the child's outlook is in some way vindicated against the adult's and against Piaget, and that the unsophisticated thinking of our earliest years remains as an indispensible acquisition underlying that of maturity, if there is to be for the adult one single intersubjective world. My awareness of constructing an objective truth would never provide me with anything more than an objective truth for me, and my greatest attempt at impartiality would never enable me to prevail over my subjectivity (as Descartes so well expresses it by the hypothesis of the malignant demon), if I had not, underlying my judgments, the primordial certainty of being in contact with being itself, if, before any voluntary *adoption of a position* I were not already *situated* in an intersubjective world, and if science too were not upheld by this basic δοξα. With the *cogito* begins that struggle between consciousnesses, each of which, as Hegel says, seeks the death of the other. For the struggle ever to begin, and for each consciousness to be capable of suspecting the alien presences which it negates, all must necessarily have some common ground and be mindful of their peaceful co-existence in the world of childhood. (*Phenomenology of Perception*)

Classical psychology, however, renders the intersubjective world which is the presupposition of all socialization entirely problematic. This arises from the assumption that the psyche is *what is given to only one person*, intrinsically mine and radically inaccessible to others who are similarly possessed of their own experiences. The same assumption is also made with regard to the body, namely, that it is as *individual* as the psyche and knowable by me only through the mass of sensations it gives me. So conceived, the problem of the experience of others presents itself as a system with four terms: (1) myself, my 'psyche'; (2) the image I have of my body by means of the sense of touch or cenesthesia, i.e., the 'introceptive image' of my own body; (3) the body of the other as seen by me, i.e., that 'visual body'; (4) the hypothetical 'psyche' of the other, his feeling of his own existence which I must reconstitute by means of (3) the 'visual body.'

The difficulties intrinsic to the operation of this schema are apparent from what it assumes in the analysis of the child's response to the other's smile. The child responds very early to facial expressions and, of course, verbal expressions of 'do's' and 'don'ts' without being able either to compare his 'motor smile' with the 'visible smile' of the other or to correlate just what it is that he is doing that meets with approval or disapproval. Rather than engage in point for point comparisons the child can only respond to global situations and attitudes, in other words to his surroundings as motivation or conduct. This means that we must reject the individualist and solipsistic conceptions intrinsic to the dual worlds of the mind and body as conceived in classical psychology and its philosophical tradition. We can no longer conceive of the psyche as a series of enclosed 'states of consciousness' inaccessible to anyone but myself. Consciousness is turned towards the world; it is a mode of conduct toward things and persons which in turn reveal themselves to me through their style and manner of dealing with the world. By the same token we must revise our conception of the body as an agglomeration of senses that are mine and which are only to be guessed at in the case of others. My awareness of body is the activity of a postural or corporeal schema which is the lived experience of a cenestesia or play between my various senses and the senses of others visible in their comportment.

Thus in today's psychology we have one system with two terms (my behaviour and the other's behaviour) which functions as a whole. To the extent that I can elaborate and extend my *corporeal schema*, to the extent that I acquire a better organized experience of my own body, to that very extent will my consciousness of my own body cease being a chaos in which I am submerged and lend itself to a transfer to others. And since at the same time the other who is to be perceived is himself not a 'psyche' closed in on himself but rather a *conduct*, a system of behaviour that aims at the world, he offers himself to my motor intentions and to that 'intentional transgression' (Husserl) by which I animate and pervade him. Husserl said that the perception of others is like a 'phenomenon of coupling' [*accouplement*]. The term is anything but a metaphor. In perceiving the other, my body and his are coupled, resulting in a sort of action which pairs them [*action à deux*]. This conduct which I am able only to see, I live somehow from a distance. I make it mine; I recover [*reprendre*] it or comprehend it. Reciprocally I know that the gestures I make myself can be the objects of another's intention. It is this transfer of intentions to my own, my alienation of the other and his alienation of me, that makes possible the perception of others. ('The Child's Relations with Others')

Here we can only point to the complementarity between the role of the corporeal schema and the work of social actors in elaborating the field of impressions and visual data inadvertently and deliberately presented to him as the motives and expectations of social interaction or the typification of personal and institutional conduct. Likewise, without any further comment upon the relation between transcendental phenomenology and mundane intersubjectivity, we must now conclude with an analysis of the formation of the child's corporeal schema in the early stages of socialization.

The problem is to account for how it is that we become aware of the distinction between our own body and the other's body while simultaneously acquiring the ability to transfer our intentions to the facial and linguistic expressions of the other as the *prima facie* basis of their further elaboration and making our own gestures similarly available to the other's intentions and expectations. We may distinguish three principal stages in this process, at each point commenting upon the conceptual revisions which are implicit in their structure and development during the first three years of the child's life.

The first phase is that of *pre-communication* in which the child does not experience himself as a single individual set over against all others. The first *me* is still a latent or vertical possibilty within our experience of an anonymous or collective existence. What is sometimes called egocentrism at this stage refers not to an experience of self-other contrast but precisely to the experience of a *me* which dwells as easily in others as in itself and is in fact no more aware of itself than it is of others. For this reason, however, the child's *me* can be extremely demanding and volatile. But the phenomena of the child appearing to be wilfully different from situation to situation, playing several roles with himself and even attributing his experiences to others ('transitivism') mislead us into attributing them to the child's egocentrism. But these phenomena are actually symptomatic of the as yet unacquired structure of his own perspective as an *I* and that of others in which every *you* is also an *I* and neither he nor they an undifferentiated *me* without limits of time and space. The full development of this structure of experience has as its 'correlate' the development of lingustic competence with the system of pronouns which in turn elaborates an interpersonal order through this very perspective.

The second phase which we distinguish intervenes, in the development of the first phase from pre-communication to the acquisition of personal perspective and its implicit competence with orderly social life gained by the child's second year or so. This is the stage of the child's awareness of his *own body (corps propre)* and the *specular image (l'image speculaire)*. At this stage the development of consciousness towards what is called intelligence proceeds by means of an expanded awareness of the child's own body through the acquisition of its specular image which in turn involves a general mode of conduct beyond the episodic event of seeing his body image in a mirror. Moreover, the mastery of this specular image is more difficult for the child to achieve than the distinction between his father, say, and his father's image in the mirror – even though he still allows the image a quasi-reality similar to that we feel in the presence, of portraits, however much we 'know better.' But in the case of his own specular image the child can make no visual comparison to establish the difference between the experience of his body seen in the mirror and his body of which he can only see the hands, feet or other parts but is otherwise a totality of which he has only a lived experience. Yet the child has now to understand that although he is his own body and not its image in the mirror, his own body is nevertheless visible to others like its mirror image.

Since Merleau-Ponty is not concerned to make an absolute distinction between the three phases of early child development, we may mention the overlap between the second and third phase here, i.e., the 'crisis at three years.' This phase is marked by the child's refusal of his body and thoughts falling under any perspective or interpretation than his own. He wants his own way and this he works out by stubbornly requiring the resistance of others to his own negativity. Through everything the child refuses, his parents, their words, and their food, there arises the structure of oedipal relations in which again the child's world and his conception of social reality are reducible neither to cognitive nor solely affective factors.

The interpretation of the development of the specular image again involves taking a position on the reduction of cognitive and affective behaviour. Merleau-Ponty rejects the view that the specular image involves a cognitive process in which the relation between reality and image, the body here and its image or shadow over there, is established once and for all. The specular image involves a new form of conduct, a shift from the lived body to the visible body, the object of social attention, projection and mimesis. The body is now a form of conduct, of an identification with others which is never quite stabilized but is the basis of the child's joys and sorrows, his jealousies and tender loyalties which are the experiences of growing up among others – the possibility of a super ego.

Thus one sees that the phenomenon of the specular image is given by psychoanalysts the importance it really has in the life of the child. It is the acquisition not only of a new content but of a new function as well: the narcissistic function. Narcissus was the mythical being who after looking at his image in the mirror of water, was drawn as if by vertigo to rejoin his own image in the mirror of water. At the same time that the image of oneself makes possible the knowledge of oneself, it makes possible a sort of alienation. I am no longer what I felt myself, immediately, to be; I am that image of myself that is offered by the mirror. To use Dr. Lacan's terms, I am 'captured, caught up' by my spatial image. Thereupon I leave the reality of my lived *me* in order to refer myself constantly to the ideal, fictitious, or imaginary *me*, of which the specular image is the first outline. In this sense I am torn from myself, and the image in the mirror prepares me for another still more serious alienation, which will be alienation by others. For others have only an exterior image of me, which is analogous to the one seen in the mirror. Consequently others will tear me away from my immediate inwardness much more surely than will the mirror. 'The specular image is the "symbolic matrix,"' says Lacan, 'where the I springs up in primordial form before objectifying itself in the dialectic of identification with the other.' ('The Child's Relations with Others')

The acquisition of the specular image introduces the child into the drama of social life, the struggle with the other, ruled by desire and recognition, even to death. It lies outside of the scope of this essay to pursue these themes in terms of the conjuncture between Hegelian phenomenology and Lacanian psychoanalysis. But this is certainly a direction in which we might pursue the dialectic between personal and public life which we repeat in the spectacle of the *body-politic* and the struggle between the 'organization' of authority and the delinquencies of love's body.

Note
1 These lectures are contained in the form of student notes published with Merleau-Ponty's approval in *Bulletin de Psychologie*, No. 236, tome XVIII 3-6, Novembre 1964. Of these lectures 'The Child's Relations with Others' has been translated by William Cobb in Maurice Merleau-Ponty, *The Primacy of Perception*, and other essays, edited by James M. Edie, Evanston, Northwestern University Press 1964, pp. 96-155.

7 The emergence of mind within sociality

Gibson Winter

George Herbert Mead's triadic structure of the emergence of mind can be reconstituted in a more balanced way as the coming to consciousness of the 'We-relation.' Mead's original formulation can be schematized as follows:

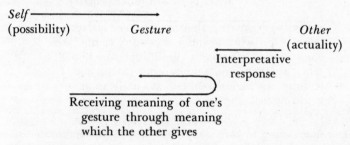

In this schematization, the self is a reflection of society; as the self takes the other's perspective, he apprehends his fumbling gesture as meaningful sign. On more complex levels of language and culture, he assumes the perspective of the generalized other, achieving mind and rationality by calling out in himself the response which he arouses in others by gesture and sign. The problem with this account is that the use of an explanatory hypothesis of social determination leads to the paradox of selves emerging from a social process which itself presupposes selves. The problem is how internally related selves can emerge from externally related entities. The evidence of the 'We-relation' suggests that selves are internally related on a primordial level; thus, the emergence of sign, symbol, and mind reflects the increasing interiority of this sociality as self-consciousness and the cultural enrichment of the sociality as the shared world of cultural meanings.

A new schematization of the triadic structure can be sketched from

Source: Gibson Winter, *Elements for a Social Ethic*, New York, Macmillan (1966).

the pregiven relatedness of self and other in vivid simultaneity in the following way:

underlying relatedness

Self ◄───────────────────────────► *Other*

Subjective   Subjective center
  center of   of relational being
  relational being

> (Dynamic) The gesture expresses the impulse to actualization of pregiven sociality through eliciting response of the other

> > (Form) Interpretative response actualizing pregiven sociality as meaning (arising in intimacy of 'We-relation' of shared inner process)

> (Unification) Empathic sharing in other's interpretative response as meaning of gesture, coming to consciousness of sociality (unification of self and other as 'We'), and simultaneous emergence of identity (self-consciousness as unification of gesturing self and expressed meaning in intentionality)

The basic innovations in this model are: (1) the presupposition of sociality coming to consciousness as mind through gesture, sign, and symbol; (2) the balance of the gesturing self (dynamic) with the meaning-receiving and meaning-giving interpretative response of the other.

In this schematization, three basic elements can be identified: dynamic, form, and unification. These are very general elements with a long history in philosophic discussion and most recently developed in the theological milieu by Paul Tillich. There may well be additional structural components for an exhaustive account of social experience, but these elements serve to clarify the triadic relationship in Mead's analysis.

Unification is the crucial element in this analysis: sociality comes to consciousness in the process of gesture (dynamic); concern for response is expressed through the communicative gesture (form), which becomes the basic structure of sociality. Thus, all three elements appear in each dimension of the emergence of mind, self, and society from sociality.

1 The gesture is dynamic, eliciting attention (a standing over against

the other and reaching toward the other); however, the gesture itself presents an intention, expresses meaning with some form; it also reflects a relatedness and need for response – an anxiety over a lost unity and a concern for response.

2 The interpretative response is a meaning-giving (form-receiving and form-giving) act; this dominance of form in the interpretative response should not obscure the implicit dynamic of the openness to the other and the reflection of relatedness in the attention to the other.

3 The dominance of unification becomes fully manifest in the reciprocity of perspectives, which is presupposed in seeing the gesture from the perspective of the other; however, this empathic seeing from the stance of the other involves the dynamic of distance from oneself, which is mediated by the other's giving of form to the gesture – making possible a sharing in a common world of form. The unity of self and other is actualized as a social world through the sharing of gestures, signs, and language; the unity of the self is actualized simultaneously, as personal identity in the consistency of the intentionality of the self with the responses of the social world and particularly the world of significant others. The structure of dynamic and form in their unity as self-consciousness reveals man's essential tendencies as: (1) care for response; (2) reflective awareness and openness to form; (3) thrust to integrity and unity.

We could summarize the restatement of Mead's schema as a shift from the dominance of form and social determination to the principle of unification, or sociality, in which internal dynamics (the intentional self) and shared forms (the social self) develop in dialogue and enriching counterpoint. This basic structure thus reflects essential tendencies of the self which are disclosed as fundamental conditions of experience itself. The dynamic freedom of distance and openness to being is an essential element of experience, emerging in the actualization of sociality. The shared forms of a public world mediate the self-consciousness of personal identity and reflect the sociality which underlies the communicative process itself. In turn, the relatedness of being is presupposed in this social process – appearing in the form of immediacy as the 'We-relation' and amplified in a social and cultural milieu through the dialogue of gesture, sign, and higher-order symbols. Hence, the 'We-relation' is the immediate givenness of sociality and also the matrix of language and mind. In this respect, self and symbolization are interdependent expressions of creativity (dynamics) and shared meanings (forms) which emerge as the coming to consciousness of sociality in evolution.

A symbol is a vehicle of conception, to use Susanne Langer's rather general definition. In this sense, a symbol is the mode of the self's openness toward the world; it is also the mode of its distance from the world – distance through which it surpasses the immediacy of its environment and transforms what surrounds it from an environment into a situation. The subject-object relationship implies a standing-over-against the other or the situation. Thus, being 'situated' rather than being 'conditioned by an environment' implies a self which can set itself apart from its world while at the same time being open toward that world. Symbolization is precisely this possibility. Reality is given through the symbol – whatever that reality may be – and the reality is both intended by the self in the symbol and set at a distance from the self through the symbol. Being conscious of the other, to return to the 'We-relation,' is not merely a matter of being united in a sense of sympathy or common feeling; being conscious is also aware-ness of this other as that other person who is speaking, gesturing, expressing fear or joy, turning toward us or away from us, etc. Thus, being conscious of the other is grasping the other's meaning. When the other enters into a 'We-relation,' he implies a willingness not only to give his presence but also to disclose his feelings and thoughts; similarly, the sharing of the self in a 'We-relation' is an attempt to enter this symbolic world through interpretative activity. Being conscious of oneself, moreover, is reflective awareness that one is the intentional source of encounter; in brief, self-consciousness, or distance from oneself as acting, thinking, feeling, etc., is dependent upon the symbolization through which the process of consciousness can be given to itself. The self as self-consciousness comes into being not only through the response of the other but also through the process of symbolization.

The 'We-relation' can be understood as the social matrix of symbolization, because the self gains distance through the response of the other to its gestures and disclosures; thus, the self receives from the other the meaning of gesture and symbol through which its own consciousness can become an object of reflective awareness. The self discovers its intentional structure through the fulfillment of its meaning-intention in the response of the other. The other is thus a source of distance from oneself through symbols, as well as a source of confirmation of being by his attention in the vivid simultaneity of mutual presence. This second aspect of the 'We-relation' is the source of symbolization to which George Herbert Mead's analysis was addressed – the emergence of mind through the recognition of the meaning of gesture in the other's response. Thus, the social character of human being is fundamental to the self in its anxiety for being – the impulse to find response in the other and the impulse toward gesture and language – and also to the intentional thrust of the self toward a consciousness of its own meaning as the meaning of being-in-the-world.

The analysis of the 'We-relation' involves two dimensions – 'impulse to confirmation of being' and 'impulse to meaning' – which can be separated only analytically. The very notion of 'anxiety over being,' which was introduced as a root of the 'We-relation,' implies the distance from self and other which arises in symbolization and self-consciousness. The notion of intentional expression implies consciousness of self which is mediated through the distance offered by the other's response. Hence, to speak of the human world is to speak of an intersubjective world which is a world of presence and distance, of impulse to relatedness and thrust to distance. The human world is thus an intersubjective world in which self and other are united in their essential relatedness and yet separate in their actualization of this relationship. In affirming the other, the self expresses its distance and freedom. The self is ultimately, then, a freedom or distance from the self, the other, and the world – a freedom made possible by sociality and yet a freedom through which sociality emerges.

The self as embodied consciousness is thus free in its self-surpassing power to reconstitute any situation. However, this freedom is mediated through the other person and through symbol. Moreover, the content of the self – its structure as a continuing form – is mediated by society and culture. The self is constituted in its biography; the self is simultaneously the intentionality toward the future through which that sedimented past is reconstituted in a grasping at enlarged meaning and fuller integrity. Here again the dominance of unification suggests the essential character of the dialectic of dynamics and form with which the self experiences its identity as given and yet reconstitutes that given selfhood. Unification discloses itself as the internal thrust of embodied consciousness to achieve a richer world and thus an enlarged scope of internal meaning; this thrust to self-surpassing involves simultaneously a reaching beyond any unity of the world which is already given toward a more comprehensive meaning. The reach for embracing unity thus includes the self-surpassing dynamic of freedom toward richer experience for the self within a world of more comprehensive meaning.

We have, in this preliminary consideration, focused only upon the 'We-relation' in its positive or creative aspect. However, the dependence of the other upon the self's disclosure in the 'We-relation,' as in all the other relationships which will be considered later, arises from the freedom of the self. The possibility of bad faith also arises in this self-transcendence of the 'I.' The 'We-relation' may be an occasion in which we encounter deceit. Even as the 'I' subject has the power to negate every social and cultural form, up to and including his own existence, so the 'I' subject may engage the other in mutual confidence which he intends to betray or may later betray for other reasons. Hence, the 'We-relation' is not only matrix of being and meaning but also occasion of man's deepest betrayals. The ambiguity of the 'I,' and thus of the 'We-relation,' arises from self-transcendence and belies any social determinism.

When we speak of the 'I,' then, in terms of its creativity and power, we confront the question of the content of the 'I.' What can be said about the 'I' subject in reference to ultimate fulfillment or meaning? This problem was already suggested in the notion of an anxiety of being and meaning. The self, so far as can be discovered in pheno-menological reflection on its intentionality toward the world, reflects a thrust toward wholeness both in its self and in the harmony of the world in relation to which it is constituted. We can speak here, then, of a passion for unity which presses the self beyond any level of integration of self or world which is already achieved; any coherence of the world already grasped is subject to reconsideration and new levels of formulation. These general notions, then, point to the form of the 'I' subject as intentionality stretched upon the world with care for response (anxiety of being), concern for meaning (enrichment as self-consciousness), and infinite passion for unity (lured to harmony) in its own being and in relation to an ultimate horizon of meaning. However, the content of this 'I' subject is mediated through the physical, social, and cultural world; the enrichment of the 'I' is inseparable from the enrichment of its world. George Herbert Mead's insight into the social mediation of the self points to the content of the self which is the objective correlate of intentional being-in-the-world. Much more can be said about the content which is mediated by a particular structure of social and cultural possibilities; in the present context, we need to recognize that the world is always the limited, finite possibility available to this infinite passion for unity. Hence, the social self is the vehicle of actualization of the 'I' but is also its limitation and the focus of transcending projection to new possibilities. The key term, however, is 'unity,' and the integrity of self, social world, and cultural actualization is subject to this principle.

The infinite concern of the 'I' for integrity also implies that the objective reality of its ultimate commitment becomes creative or destructive for the content of its fulfillment or defeat. The internal unity of the 'I' is inseparable from the richness of its ultimate horizon. The 'I' constitutes itself in its intentionality toward the social and cultural world, but it is in turn constituted by the meaning of the world toward which it moves. Bad faith, for example, which arises in the anxiety of being, ultimately reflects the choice of the 'I' in its reach toward fulfillment; in bad faith, the harmony of self and other to which the 'I' belongs is sacrificed for a lesser reality of the 'I's choice, and the basic relatedness of self and other is denied. This possibility, as indicated, arises in the freedom and distance through which the 'I' comes into being in self-consciousness, but its content as bad faith arises in a violation of the essential unity of self and other, in the 'false' commitment of the self to its own fulfillment. Hence, the content of the 'I' can be discussed normatively; for the moment, it is essential only to recognize that the reality of ultimate commitment – the ultimate horizon of meaning in which choosing and valuing occur – reflects an adequate or inadequate expression of the project of the 'I,' *i.e.*, its apprehension of fulfillment as particular being in the context of universal being.

Origins of the child in myth and dream

Children are much closer to the unconscious than are adults; fantasy and reality are less clearly separated for them. However, while adults strive for a clarity of vision, an undistorted view of the 'real', they do so symbolically. This capacity to symbolize we quite simply take for granted in man, it equates with the origins of his sociality. Nevertheless we attempt to gain access to the individual unconscious through dreams and to the collective unconscious through mythology. Both avenues lead us to the necessary character of the child in social life; our reveries and our legends depend upon the child within us for their sensibility. They take us inevitably to the origins of our living together.

8 Abandoning the child

James Hillman

What is this 'child' - that is surely the first question. Whatever we say about children and childhood is not altogether really about children and childhood. We need but consult the history of painting to see how peculiar are the images of children, particularly when comparing them in their distortions with contemporary exactitude in depicting landscapes and still lives or the portraits of adults. We need but consult the history of family life, education and economics to realize that children and childhood as we use the terms today are a late invention. (Ariès, Part I.) What is this peculiar realm we call 'childhood', and what are we doing by establishing a special world with children's rooms and children's toys, children's clothes, and children's books, music, language, caretakers, doctors, of playing children so segregated from the actual lives of working men and women. Clearly, some realm of the psyche called 'childhood' is being personified by the child and carried by the child for the adult. How curiously similar this *daseinsbereich* is to the realm of the madhouse some centuries ago and even today, when the madman was considered a child, the ward of the state or under the parental eye of the doctor who cared for his 'children', the insane, like for his family. Again, how extraordinary this confusion of the child with the insane, of childhood with insanity ('Madness is childhood'. - Foucault, 1965).

The confusion between real child and his childhood and the fantasy child that obfuscates perception of child and childhood is classical to the history of depth psychology. You may remember that Freud at first believed that repressed memories causing neuroses were forgotten emotions and distorted scenes from actual childhood. Later he abandoned this child, realizing that a fantasy factor had placed in childhood events that had never actually happened; a fantasy child was at work and not an actual occurrence in the life of the person. He

Source: James Hillman, *Loose Ends*, Irving (Texas), Spring Publications (1975).

was obliged then to separate child of fact from that of fantasy, outer child events from inner childhood. Nevertheless, he stuck to his belief that the job of therapy was the analysis of childhood. A statement of 1919 is typical:

Strictly considered ... analytic work deserves to be recognized as genuine psycho-analysis only when it has succeeded in removing the amnesia which conceals from the adult his knowledge of his childhood from its beginning (that is, from about the second to the fifth year) ... The emphasis which is laid here upon the importance of the earliest experience does not imply any underestimation of the influences of later ones. But the later impressions of life speak loudly enough through the mouth of the patient, while it is the physician who has to raise his voice on behalf of the claims of childhood. ('A child is being beaten', CP II, p. 177.)

What childhood did Freud mean? Actual children were never analyzed by Freud. He did not analyze children. Was the 'childhood' which the analyst had to recapture actual childhood? Here, Freud himself remains ambiguous, for the actual small young human we call 'child' merges in Freud with a Rousseauian, even Orphic-Neoplatonic child who is 'psychologically a different thing than an adult...'. (NIL, p. 190.) ('Childhood has its own ways of seeing, thinking and feeling; nothing is more foolish than to try to substitute our ways'. Rousseau, *Emile*, II.) The difference lies in the child's special way of reminiscing: '... a child catches hold on ... phylo-genetic experience where his own experience fails him. He fills in the gaps in individual truth with prehistorical truth; he replaces occurrences in his own life by occurrences in the life of his ancestors. I fully agree with Jung in recognizing the existence of this phylogene-tic inheritance...'. ('From the history of an infantile neurosis' (1918), CP III, pp. 577-78).

The actual child itself was not altogether actual because its experiences consisted in the confabulations of 'pre-historic' occurrences, i.e., non-temporal, mythical, archetypal. And childhood thus refers in Freud partly to *a state of reminiscence*, like the Platonic or Augustinian *memoria*, an imaginal realm which provides the actual child with 'its own ways of seeing, thinking, and feeling' (Rousseau). This realm, this mode of imaginal existence, is to be found, according to popular and depth psychology, in primitive, savage, madman, artist, genius, and the archeological past; the childhood of persons becomes merged with the childhood of peoples. (Cf. CP III, p. 470: the last paragraph of Freud's discussion of the Schreber case.)

But the child and the childhood are *not* actual. These are terms for a mode of existence and perception and emotion which we still today insist belongs to actual children, so that we construct a world for them following our need to place this fantasy somewhere in actuality. We do not know what children are in themselves, 'unadulterated' by our need for carriers of the imaginal realm, of 'beginnings', (i.e., 'primitivity', 'creation'), and of the archetype of the child. We cannot know what children are until we have understood more of the working of the fantasy child, the archetypal child in the subjective psyche.

Freud gave to the child image and to the fantasy of childhood a group of startling attributes which you may remember: child had no super-ego (conscience) like the adult; no free associations like the adult but confabulated reminiscences. The child's parents and problems were external, rather than internal as with the adult, so that the child had no symbolically transferred psychic life (NIL, p. 190). How close to the mental life of 'madness', of artist, and how close to what we call 'primitive' – this absence of personal conscience, this mixture of behaviour and ritual, of memory and myth.

But more startling than the attributes Freud enunciated are those which we may draw from his ideas. First, Freud gave the child *primacy*: nothing was more important in our lives than those early years and that style of thought and emotion of imaginal existence called 'childhood'. Second, Freud gave the child *body*: it had passions, sexual desires, lusts to kill; it feared, sacrificed, rejected; it hated and longed and it was composed of erogenous zones, pre-occupied with feces, genitals, and deserved the name polymorphous perverse. Third, Freud gave the child *pathology*: it lived in our repressions and fixations; it was at the bottom of our psychic disorders (CP II, p. 188); it was our suffering.

These are startling attributes indeed if they be compared with the child of Dickens, for Dorrit and Nell, Oliver and David had little passion and little body, and no sexuality at all, especially in view of little Hans and little Anna and other children of psychoanalytic literature. Perversity, when it entered in Dickens at all, came from adults, from industry, education and society; pathology was in deathbed scenes that claimed children back to paradise. Against Dickens we can see Freud's vision most sharply, even if in both the child as fact and the child as image were still not disentangled.

Jung's essay 'The Psychology of the Child Archetype' in 1940 moved the matter much further; actual child is abandoned and with it the fantasy of empiricism, the notion that our apperception of the factor in our subjectivity results from empirical observation of actual childhood. Jung writes:

It may not be superfluous to point out that lay prejudice is always inclined to identify the child motif with the concrete experience 'child', as though the real child were the cause and pre-condition of the existence of the child motif. In psychological reality, however, the empirical idea 'child' is only the means . . . by which to express a psychic fact that cannot be formulated more exactly. Hence by the same token the mythological idea of the child is emphatically not a copy of the empirical child . . . not – and this is the point – a human child (CW 9, 1, p. 161 fn.).

What accuracy can our studies of the human child have so long as we have not recognized enough the archetypal child in our subjectivity affecting our vision? So let us leave the child and childhood to one side and pursue, what Jung calls, the 'child motif' and the 'childhood aspect of the collective psyche'.

Our question now becomes what is the child *motif* which projects so vividly and draws such fantasies onto itself? Jung answers:

The 'child' is all that is abandoned and exposed and at the same time divinely powerful; the insignificant, dubious beginning and the triumphal end. The 'eternal child' in man is an indescribable experience, an incongruity, a handicap, and a divine prerogative; an imponderable that determines the ultimate worth or worthlessness of a personality (CW 9, 1, §300).

Jung elaborates these general and special features: futurity, divine heroic invincibility, hermaphroditism, beginning and end, and the motif of abandonment from which my theme is drawn. Jung's elaborations of 1940 should be taken as an addition to those in his previous works where the child motif is related to archaic mythical thinking and the mother archetype (CW 5, *passim*) and to paradisiacal blissfulness (CW 6, §§422f, 442). Some of the aspects which Jung discusses Freud had already described in his language-style. The idea of the creative child occurs in Freud's equation child = penis, and the rejected child in his equation child = feces. '"Feces", "child", and "penis" thus form a unity, an unconscious concept (*sit venia verbo*) – the concept, namely, of a little thing that can become separated from one's body'. ('From the history of an infantile neurosis', (1918) CP III, p. 562f.)

To these features I would add two others from our Western tradition, the first specifically Christian, the second specifically Classical. In the Christian tradition 'child' refers also to the simple, the naive, the poor and the common – the orphan – of society and of the psyche, as it did in the language of the Gospels, where child meant outcast, the pre-condition for salvation, and was later placed in association with the feelings of the heart opposed to the learning of the mind. In the Classical tradition the child appears in those con-figurations of masculine psychology represented specifically by Zeus, Hermes and Dionysos, their imagery, mythemes and cults. The child motif there may be kept distinct from the child-and-mother motifs and also the child-hero motifs which have a distinctly different psychological import.

Our theme follows Jung literally when he says: 'The child motif represents something not only that existed in the distant past but something that exists *now* ... not just a vestige but a system functioning in the present whose purpose is to compensate or correct, in a meaningful manner, the inevitable onesidedness and extravagances of the conscious mind' (CW 9, 1, §276). If, according to Freud, the essence of the psychoanalytic method is to alter something, and if the child, according to Jung, is that which acts as psychological corrector, our reflections require that we bring the child back from his abandonment even while we speak of him. Then the general theme may become specifically focussed in the private subjectivity of each and may act to alter the onesidedness of consciousness in regard to the child.

We find the abandoned child first of all in dreams, where we ourselves or a child of ours or one unknown, is neglected, forgotten, crying, in danger or need, and the like. The child makes its presence known through dreams; although abandoned, we can still hear it, feel its call.

In modern dreams we find the child endangered by: drowning, animals, road traffic, being left behind in a car trunk (the 'chest' motif), or a pram or supermarket cart (the 'basket' motif); kidnappers, robbers, members of the family, incompetent; illness, crippling, secret infections, mental retardation and brain damage (the idiot child); or a wider less specific catastrophe such as war, flood or fire. Sometimes, one wakens in the night with the sensation of having heard a child crying.

Usually the dreamer's response to the motif of abandonment is acute worry, a guilty responsibility: 'I should not have let it happen; I must do something to protect the child; I am a bad parent'. If it is an infant in the dream, we believe we must keep the sense of this 'child' with us all the time, feed it every three hours with thoughtful attention, carry it on our backs like a papoose. We tend to take the child as a moral lesson.

But guilt puts the burden of altering something (Freud) and correcting something (Jung) altogether upon the ego as doer. After all, the dreamer is not only in charge of the child; he also *is* the child. Consequently the emotions of worry, guilt and responsibility, morally virtuous as they may be and even partly corrective of neglect, may also prevent other emotions of fright, loss and helplessness. Sometimes the more we worry over the child the less the child really reaches us. So, as long as we take up any dream mainly from the position of the responsible ego, by reacting to it with guilt and the energetics of seeing matters straight, improving by doing, by changing attitudes, extracting from dreams moral lessons for the ethically responsible ego, we reinforce that ego. We thereby emphasize the parent-child cleavage: the ego becomes the responsible parent, which only further removes us from the emotions of the child.

Crucial in all dream integration – integration, not interpretation, for we are speaking now of integrity with the dream, standing with it and in it, befriending it in all its parts, participating in its whole story – is the emotional experience of *all* its parts. Gestalt therapy attempts to drive this home by demanding that the dreamer feel himself into all the parts: the distraught parent, but also the wild dogs, the flooding river, the secret infection, and the exposed child. It is as important to collapse with the child's crying, and to hate savagely the childish, as it is to go home from the analytical hour resolved to take better care of the new and tender parts that need help to grow.

As interpretation and ego responsibility may strengthen the parent at the expense of the child, so too may amplification not reach the child who is abandoned. An amplification of the child in the river, wandering lost in the forest or attempting a task beyond his strength, in terms of fairytales and myths and initiation rites may stain the motif accurately so that we see certain aspects clearly – mainly heroic new consciousness emerging – but the staining technique of amplification to bring out the objective meaning may also obliterate the subjective reality of dereliction. Amplification often takes us away from the misery by placing it on a general level. For many psychic events this extension of awareness through amplification is just what is needed, but for precisely this motif it would seem contraindicated because the forsaken child can best be refound by moving closer to subjective misery and noting its precise locus.

Both responsibility and amplification are insufficient methods for this motif. As activities of the reasoned, mature person they distance us yet further from the child.

Evoking the child

We are familiar with situations that call the child back from where we have left it. Going backwards into familiar places, sounds, smells; each *abaissement du niveau mental*, new conditions that constellate thrill and the fantasy of complete newness, that one can make of something whatever one wishes; also sudden falls into love, into illness, into depression. The child is also evoked by unfamiliarity where imagination is asked for and we respond instead with stubborn petulance, inadequacy, tears.

But the regressed condition that no one wants can also be directly prompted in psychotherapy. For here is a haven, to creep out of hiding; here one may show one's unwanted, unlovable, ugly concealments, and one's huge hopes. These feelings have all been given appropriate psychological names: infantile desires, self-destructive fantasies, omnipotence cravings, archaic impulses. But in deriding these names we ought not to forget – and we are each therapists of the psyche since it is a devotion that cannot belong to a profession only – that always these childish *pathological conditions contain futurity*. The very way forward through the condition so unwanted, ugly and preposterously expectant lies just in the conditions themselves. The pathology is also the futurity. In it the insights lie; from it the movement comes.

By recognizing a basic cry we may evoke this child in the pathology; it is as if there were a basic cry in persons that gives direct voice to the abandoned content. For some persons it is: 'Help, please help me'; others say, 'take me, just as I am, take me, all of me without choice among my traits, no judgement, no questions asked'; or 'take me, without my having to do something, to be someone'. Another cry may be 'hold me', or 'don't go away; never leave me alone'. We may also hear the content saying simply, 'Love me'. Or we can hear, 'teach me, show me what to do, tell me how'. Or, 'carry me, keep me'. Or the cry from the bottom may say, 'let me alone, all alone; just let me be'.

Generally the basic cry speaks in the receptive voice of the infant, where the subject is an object, a 'me' in the hands of others, incapable of action yet poignantly enunciating its knowledge of its subjectivity, knowing how it wishes to be handled. Its subjectivity is in the crying by means of which it organizes its existence. So, as well, we hear it in the basic cry a person addresses to his environment, turning his entourage into helpers, or lovers, or constant companions (a *thiasos*) who will nurse, dance attendance, or teach, or accept all blindly, who will never let him alone, or the reverse, from whom he flees in continual rejection. And the cry says how a person is unable to meet his needs himself, unable to help himself, or let himself alone.

It is worth insisting here that the cry is never cured. By giving voice to the abandoned child it is always there, and must be there as an archetypal necessity. We know well enough that some things we never learn, cannot help, fall back to and cry from again and again. These inaccessible places where we are always exposed and afraid, where we cannot learn, cannot love, and cannot help by transforming, repressing or accepting are the wildernesses, the caves where the abandoned child lies hidden. That we go on regressing to these places states something fundamental about human nature: we come back to an incurable psychopathology again and again through the course of life yet which apparently does go through many changes before and after contact with the unchanging child.

Here we strike upon the psychological relationship between what philosophy calls becoming and being, or the changing and the changeless, the different and the same, and what psychology calls growth on the one hand and on the other psychopathy: that which cannot by definition reverse or alter but remains as a more or less constant lacuna of character throughout life. In the language of our theme we have the eternal vulnerability of the abandoned child, and this same child's evolving futurity.

In this conundrum we usually pick up one side or the other, feeling ourselves different, changing, evolving, only to be smashed back by the shattering recurrence of a basic cry which in turn leads to the belief of being hopelessly stuck, nothing moving, just the same as always. The history of psychotherapy has also been driven back and forth by this apparent dilemma. At times degeneration theory (inheritance and constitution, or an idea of predestination) declare character is fate and that we can but move within pre-determined patterns. At other times, such as today in American humanistic developmental psychology, the category of growth through trans-formation covers all psychic events.

Neither position is adequate. Like the metaphorical child of Plato's *Sophist* who, when asked to choose, opts for 'both', the abandoned child is both that which *never grows*, remaining as permanent as psychopathy, and also that futurity springing from vulnerability itself. The complex remains, and the lacunae; that which becomes different are our connections with these places and our reflections through them. It is as if to change we must keep in touch with the changeless, which also implies taking change for what it is, rather than in terms of development. Evolution tends to become a 'means of disowning the past' (T. S. Eliot); what we want to change we wish to be rid of. A subtle psychological perception is required to distinguish in our natures the changeable from the changeless, and to see the two as intimately connected so as not to search in the wrong place for growth and the wrong place for stability, or to presume that change leaves stability behind and that stability is never vulnerable.

The return of the child

It the child is repressed in the amnesia of 'the second to the fifth year', as Freud wrote, then it is the little child who shall return. Abandonment does not succeed; the murderer's hand fails; fishermen, shepherds, maids appear; the child becomes a foundling to come back and carry the day.

It is not merely that the childish returns in the left-overs of childhood, but *everything that emerges from unconsciousness comes back too young*. Everything begins in youthful folly because the doors to the cellars and gardens of the mind are barred not only by a censor, a flaming sword, or a Cerberus, but by a little boy or girl who magically transforms everything passing over the threshold into its own condition.

Thus, as Freud saw, the world of the unconscious is the world of childhood, not actual childhood or the childhood of the human race, but a condition governed by the archetype of the child; thus, as Jung saw, this archetype is herald, the pre-figuration of every change that we go through in depth. Everything comes back too young, implying that the adequate connection with the unconscious will have to show inadequacy. We are not able, still dependent on that child, its whims, its atmosphere of specialness, still needing our hurts, the way it touches our eros, making us each at moments into paedophiles, child-lovers.

Moreover, all the other faces of the repressed, the personally forgotten and the primordially unknown, will return in a child-like style. Besides the revolution, all those other things ostracized from the agora of daily life - art, insanity, passion, despair, vision - will come in with this peculiar childishness which at times we ennoble as the childlikeness of the creative.

The childishness that returns as the personal shadow deserves better treatment than merely the Freudian one. Jung indicated that the treatment of childishness, of psychopathology, at the archetypal level is to '*dream the myth onwards*' (CW 9, 1, §271), to let its prospective nature speak. By allowing the child to be the corrector. it performs one of its archetypal functions: futurity. What comes back points forward; it returns as the repressed and at the same time comes back in order to fulfill a biblical cure for psychopathology: 'and a little child shall lead them' (Isaiah 11:6).

Consequently, the cue to the future is given by the repressed, the child and what he brings with him, and the way forward is indeed the way back. But it is immensely difficult to discriminate among the emotions that come with the child, mainly because he does not re-turn alone.

It is as if the little girl abandoned returns with a protector, a new found father, a strong male figure of muscular will, of arguments and cunning, and his outrage, his blind striking out mingles with her pained tantrums, his sullen melancholy becomes indistinguishable from her withdrawn pouting. Though they coalesce, child and guardian also struggle for separation. In face and gesture there are alternating movements, an alternating look in the eye, appeal for help, resistance to it, bitterness of tears coming grudgingly, fought off, clenched, and then abandoned cataclysmic sobbing. Sometimes the little girl returns as a gamin of the streets, dirty, or a tomboy of the fields, earthy, half-male, hardened from the long neglect and the tutorials of the animus, a girl-child almost wolf-child, all thumbs and elbows, returning yet saying 'let me alone'.

In the little boy a similar pattern occurs for it is equally difficult to distinguish him from the milkmaids and nymphs and sisters who have succoured him during the repression. The softness and vanity and demands which he brings with him, passivity and vulnerability, the reclusive nursing of himself, hardly differ from what psychology has called anima states.

With the child's return comes childhood, both kinds: actual with its memories and imaginal with its reminiscences. We have come to call this memorial factor with its two kinds of remembrances 'the unconscious', personal and collective. But this term, 'the unconscious', only adds to the burden of differentiating the complexity of psychic life. It might be more beneficial to separate the child (as the reminiscent factor which returns a person to the primordially repressed of non-actual sub-structures) from a category so indefinite as the unconscious. Then we would be in a better position to free 'childhood' as an imaginal mode of perceiving and feeling from its identification with actual childhood which usually had less freedom and joy, less fantasy and magic and amorality than we sentimentally attribute to it. *Our cult of childhood is a sentimental disguise for true homage to the imaginal.* Could childhood be called by its true name – the realm of archetypal reminiscence – then we would not have to become unconscious to find the mythical. We have psychologically confused the 'coming up' of events from 'the unconscious' with the 'coming back' of reminiscence.

Psychology has taken the repressed child to be an axiomatic metaphor of psychic structure. Psychology assumes the repressed is less developed than the repressor, that consciousness is topographically, historically and morally superior to the unconscious, characterized by primitive, amoral and infantile impulses. *Our notion of consciousness inherently necessitates repression of the child.* This constellates our main fear: the return of the inferiority, the child, who also means the return of the realm of archetypal reminiscence. Archetypal fantasy is the most threatening activity of the human soul as we now conceive it, for our Western rational tradition has placed this activity in the ontologically inferior, the primitive amoral realm of actual childhood.

Thus a restoration of the mythical, the imaginal and the

archetypal implies a collapse into the infantile realm of the child. Our strong ego-centered consciousness fears nothing more than just such collapse. The worst insult is to be called 'childish', 'infantile', 'immature'. So we have devised every sort of measure for defending ourselves against the child – and against archetypal fantasy. These defenses we call the consciousness of the strong, mature and developed ego.

Though ego-consciousness has its defenses, or *is* defenses, the child is defenselessness itself. Exposure, vulnerability, abandonment are its very nature. Its defense is mainly that of innocence. Without structured walls, lost in the woods or afloat on the waters in a frail basket, its predilection is to remain protected by its own helplessness. Its style of defense, of paranoia, is innocence: 'I don't know', 'I didn't realize', 'I didn't mean anything', 'It just happened'. The world is *systematically* haphazard, afloat; all things held together by spontaneous amazing synchronicities; all things intending the child, pointing to him, keeping him alive in the center of importance, even while he does nothing, wills nothing, knows nothing.

The shadow that we fear most and repress primordially, i.e., the kind of fantasy reminiscence that we name madness, is brought with the child. The fear of yielding control to him governs our profound amnesia. And so we have forgotten an evident psychological truth: anxiety reveals the deepest shadow. Rather than see the child in the shadow, recent psychology has been concentrating upon the shadows of aggression and of moral evil. But aggression can be enjoyable, and moral evil, attractive. They are not fearful, shameful to the same degree as the child. Jungian focus upon the devil and the dark side of the God image has covered over our anxiousness, so that we have neglected the dark side of the Bambino, the other *infans noster* who was the first shadow found in the anxieties of classical analysis. The ruling power contaminating the imaginal with the impulsive is a monster child whom we have been abandoning for centuries.

So, when the cry goes up *'l'imagination au pouvoir'* (Sorbonne rebellion in 1968) we should not feel deceived that a monster has been released, that the revolution becomes puerile nonsense, obscene, scatological, polymorphously perverse. The imagination to power is the child to power, because Western consciousness with its onesided extravagances of will and reason at the expense of memoria, has abandoned the *mundus imaginalis* to children.

Childishness – childlikeness

The deepest dilemma concerning the return of the child is that conundrum inherent to any archetype, its supposedly good and bad sides, the digestible and indigestible portions, according to whatever model of integration we are serving. In the case of the child these poles become childishness and childlikeness. On the one hand, one works to become mature, to put all childish things away, to develop out of infantilisms and *avidya* of ignorance. On the other hand, one is to become a child, for only into the child enters the kingdom of heaven, and the child should lead the psyche and be its 'end'. How does one then reconcile the two contradictory instructions: to overcome the child and to become the child?

The poles appear already in Plato for the child of the *Meno* is not the same as the child of the *Lysis*, the *Republic* and the *Laws*. And the poles appear in Paul (I Cor. 14:20) who appeals for childlikeness of heart but will not have childishness of mind. Or, as Augustine put the dilemma: 'Childhood is proposed to us as a model of humility which we should imitate, but it is equally proposed as a type of folly to be avoided' (*Enar. in Ps.* XLVI, 2). The division in the archetype also appears in what Philippe Ariès calls 'the two concepts of childhood', on the one hand the indulgent coddling provided by the family, on the other, the rational disciplining provided by society, church, and education. The division finally appears in education theory today, between the tender-minded who take their lead from Rousseau, Froebel and the Romantics and their vision from 'childlikeness', and the tough-minded who follow a pattern more classical, more medieval, seeing in the child a miniature adult whose waxlike impressionable 'childishness' requires moulding by disciplined *Bildung*.

Jung suggests a choice between the opposites and an end to the ambivalence inherent in any archetypal pattern. He offers childhood recaptured without its childishness. The solution he suggests is that by sacrificing childishness, one creates a new childlikeness. Innocence, play and spontaneity are regained by giving up ignorance, games and unruliness. We move from false liberty to true freedom; only a childishness abandoned can be refound as childlikeness; clinging to silliness and innocence never makes the wise and holy fool. Surely this suggestion I have elaborated from Jung (CW 11, §742) seems right, for what place is there in the reborn man of individuation for childish petulance and incapacity, foibles and single-minded desires, and for the magical wishful hopes so subjective and so unconditioned by past experience. What else is consciousness but putting away all childish things?

Nevertheless, the distinction between the child and his childishness is difficult to maintain. In actuality is separation possible; can we choose one pole? Is not the child this very complex of opposites whose psychic impact derives precisely from the tension of its 'good' and 'bad', its static and changing, sides. Extract the childishness from the child and we are left not with an angel (which are anyway demons of might and terror), but with an idealized image of how one thinks one ought to be, the innocence of repression, again constellating an abandoned child who willynilly must return. We cannot advance psychology, or the psyche in the throes of its complexes, one jot by attempting to separate out even through sacrifice or for the sake of eschatology the pathological elements.

Perhaps this is what to become as a child now means psychologically. It means what it says: the state as a whole with its pathological childishness, to think as a child and to speak as a child, still babes in wisdom of perfected praise (Ps. 8:2; Matt. 21:16) whose reminiscences do indeed transcend experience.

Without the shadow of childishness how do we enter truly the consciousness of the child? Is there another way to innocence and humility than through ignorance and humiliation, by being made simple, small, fearing? To be led by the little child then psychologically implies to be led not only by one's spontaneous surprise and frank wonder where something is new and we are innocent, but also by one's childishness: by the sense of loneliness and abandonment and vulnerability, by the idealizations of Greatness upon outer authorities and the inner powers of our complexes who give us parentage, by the intoxications of magical invincibility, by the peculiar sexuality which is both hermaphroditic and incapable of being actualized, and by the unadapted pitiless feelings, the child's cruelty, the short memory, stupidity, which too form the stuff of innocence.

Especially Freud's discoveries concerning the child need to be recollected in relation with the idea of rebirth that is so representative of the child archetype. Because the resurrection of the whole man includes the body, its sinful, weak, lustful members (Rom. 6:12-13), we cannot neglect the child in the body which Freud reaffirmed. If we are anywhere most the victim of childishness, or more at war with it, it is in the body, treated as an enemy, as an inferior to be disciplined or indulgently coddled. Yet if the child – even Freud's – is at least partly a reminiscing imaginal factor, then the body impulses which we associate with the child also must at least partly refer to an imaginal body. Then even our polymorphous perversions and our longings of childishness would provide entry to the childlikeness of resurrection, where the work of rebirth would proceed through infantile sexuality, a discipline of perversion. We could no longer insist upon distinction between childlike and childish.

But must so much be given over to this one archetype so that it personifies not only body and the concrete mode of direct experience but almost all of our subjectivity as well? Must the child carry our bodily delights and our imaginal reminiscing, our wholeness and our creative liberation, our play and our eros, our past and our future? If we give all these aspects of existence to the child, then of course these areas of experience become childish. Then eros is loaded with childish longings, the body a childish complaint, the revolution a childish enactment, imagination a childish fantasy and concrete play an inferior activity. Then too we can never be satisfied with any of these areas as they are; they must be 'developed' – our fantasy by means of active imagination or art therapy, and our bodies, our eros, our fun, and the revolution too, must go through a process of becoming more conscious, more 'mature', to lose 'primitivity'.

Even childhood does not have to remain a province of the child. For childhood is mainly a word we use to cover modes of experience and perception, imaginal modes which we abandon every moment for the sake of more adult behaviour, that is, more conceptual and more willed. If we abandon 'childhood' as a cover for what is most valuable to human life, then the dilemma of childish and childlike may be resolved. Because we do not need to be fresh, naive and simple 'to become as a child', we could abandon the idealization of play as the path to the imaginal. We would no longer believe that we must be innocent to be new, simple to be whole. The restoration of the childish shadow to the ideal of childlikeness would return to wholeness its affliction and weakness, and to the imaginal both its psychopathological distortions and the hard work of actualization.

Bearing the child

Because abandoning the child is a mythological motif, it stands as a permanent psychological reality, not to be cured but to be enacted. But how? Mythology may give theme and pattern, but depth psychology with its practical aim 'to alter something' (Freud) leaves to the subject the manner of enactment. We have no simple answer, and what has gone before has deliberately complicated a rather uncomplicated motif. Thomas Mann wrote that only the exhaustive is truly interesting; in psychology, only the complicated is truly representative.

The pattern we have been exposing shows a vicious circle. Abandoning *of* the child in order to become mature and then abandonment *to* the child when it returns. Either we repress or we coddle this face of our subjectivity. In both cases the child is unbearable: first we cannot support it at all, then we give way to it altogether. We follow a pattern contained in the word 'abandon' itself, alternating between the opposite meanings of 'losing' and of 'releasing'. On the one hand we free ourselves of a condition by letting it go from us, and on the other hand, we free ourselves by letting go to it.

One of the ways we abandon ourselves to the child has been in the form of fantasies, called ideas, by means of which the child in sublimated form captures our consciousness. It is a psychological axiom that the more we move away from the repressed child the more vulnerable we are to possession of this abandoned part (CW 9, 1, §277). The more unbearable we find the childish emotionalisms in our subjectivity, the more are we prey to childlike simplifications in our ideas that attempt to reflect objectivity, maturity and responsible unemotionality. Then the child dominates our theory-forming with naive concepts of psyche and therapy, of growth and wholeness, of revolution and freedom, of love and genius. Then we choose, or are chosen by, sentimental philosophies of feeling that deny value to intellect – only connect, relate, believe, encounter – for the child represents the good, innocent heart. And this child is the primary anti-intellectual, who knows without learning things which are hidden from the learned but revealed unto babes (Luke 10:21-22).

Indirectly we have also been examining the way in which we con-stellate this mythical motif in our individual subjectivities. The rela-tion between psyche and myth goes in two directions; the mythemes govern the soul, but at the same time as it lives they are drawn into enactment. Of these enactments, the heroic model of consciousness always refers back to the child for its origins. We can never perform the ego's tasks, coping, struggling, advancing into light and knowl-edge, without also regressing to the child. The concept of ego so permeated by hero mythemes is based also upon the abandoned child as its pre-condition. (CW 9, 1, §281-84) The child returns hidden in the hero's boots, to swagger and control his naively literal notion of reality.

But the child does not have to return only as hero. In fact he does not have to 'return' at all, if he is never repressed, never abandoned. Dionysian consciousness keeps the child with it as a permanent aspect of its archetypal structure: at the oldest Dionysian Spring festival in honour of the God in the new wine, the second day belonged to the child; small children took part in the ritual and the children's drinking jugs show them with toys and crowns.

Because myths are always true, they are always happening; we abandon the child daily in our attitudes and acts. Whatever we do not acknowledge as having begotten, whatever we disown, to whatever we refuse historical lineage becomes one more orphan. The orphan has no history, everything lies ahead, complete futurity. History provides parentage to psychic events, giving them background in race, culture, tradition. When we refuse the historical aspect in our complexes, how history reaches us through our complexes – for it is in them that my race, my ancestors and my historical culture affect me most closely – then we create orphans: we abandon our complexes to the power of the child archetype. They go to the orphanage, the breeding ground of renegade psychopathy.

Thus, as a psychologist I must refuse the attack upon history now coming from two sides: from the mystics of religion who would make way for spiritual rebirth by breaking through the historical, and from the heralds of political change who would start anew, the past 'a bucket of ashes' (Carl Sandburg). The cults of immediacy, of relevance, of transcendence, of revolution, whether in mind expansion or in social liberation are the cult of childhood in a new form (but read Marcuse!), negating the historical roots of the complexes turning them into orphans with nothing behind them. Then history, as to Oedipus, comes out of a void. Oedipus' delusion about his history was material to his tragedy.

It may seem odd for an American psychologist speaking to European intellectuals to stress history, since for Europe, as Joyce – I believe – said, 'History is a nightmare from which I am trying to awaken'. Yet, psychological reality is only partly separable from historical reality. Our subjectivity is complicated throughout with our Western history, and we can never awaken from it unless we recognize it in our complexes. If psychotherapy conceives its task in altering and in correcting 'the one-sided extravagances of consciousness' (Jung), then psychotherapy is an attempt also to re-vision history and its work in the complexes. Change in psyche is change in history, and that is why psychic change is so difficult, for it means moving history. Yet, nothing moves in ourselves or in the world if history be not borne. A revolution that neglects taking history with it will change nothing; it will leave the psyche untouched, and thus become a new repression.

The child archetype, because of its a-historical and pre-historical tendencies, by moulding consciousness after itself would have us lose history producing a generation of abandoned children who see all things in their beginnings and ends, an existence of omnipotent hope and catastrophic dread. The obsession with this archetype also has its other side, the parental other pole to the child, which gives us a burdening sense of parentage, of worldwide responsibility, the parental inflation compensatory to the child. Then we become all *Sorge* amidst the existential *Geworfenheit*.

History gives a sense for what is authentic; it limits the possible. Without this historical sense everything is new and anything can happen. Any delusional course of salvation lies open – and the confusion in subjectivity about 'how to be' and what the soul wants is matched with a myriad of liberation programs, including the turn Eastwards as a way out of Western History. Psychology itself tends to be just one more 'trip', owing to the child's influence.

But Jung's psychology is altogether a reflection of the historical psyche and is not a program for its transcendence. Jung's vision of a complex polyvalent wholeness, pregnant with innumerable possibilities and individually different, is too precious, too fertile to become but another delusional omnipotence fantasy with goals of stalwart independence achieved through naive growth to oneness, where becoming self and becoming God conflate.

Surely psychology can be more critical and less childlike in its use of 'wholeness' and 'self'; surely psychology can abandon in its theory its fantasies of growth, creativity, independence and futurity, so that change might be left as change and its kinds more accurately noted – not always newness and development – and the unchanging may be viewed less sadly. Then individuation may be separated from development so as to reflect more precisely the actualities of experience. For is not psychology's task to reflect the psyche *as it is* rather than to structure it with a hermeneutic system or inculcate through therapy a psychological dogma?

Reflecting the psyche as it is has been the concern of this essay. And I do mean 'essay' – an attempt to articulate and thereby constellate that level of archetypal subjectivity which is the child. But our attempt must inevitably fail in order to correspond with the subject itself. Our inadequacy reflects its helplessness. So, we may not expect that what the psyche says through the word 'childhood' can be translated into the mature and intellectual speech of science or scholarship. Psychology, it seems to me, has too long laboured in this mistake. Our essay rather follows some lines from T. S. Eliot (*East Coker*, V): 'every attempt/Is a wholly new start, and a different kind of failure . . . And so each venture/Is a new beginning, a raid on the inarticulate . . .'. In this way the failure and the venture belong together. They are each part of instigating the new start in regard to the child by stimulating our imagination about archetypal childhood.

The dominance of the child archetype in our psychological thinking, besides softening our intellect, has deprived the adult of his imagination. This 'inferior' activity has been relegated to childhood, like so much else unreal, autoerotic and primitive. The adult must go back to childhood to re-find imagination – feeling it unreal, autoerotic, primitive – for lost childhood has meant lost imaginal power, amnesia as lost *memoria*, an abandoned capacity for reminiscence in the Neoplatonic sense. Thus 'adult' and 'mature' have come to signify demythologized existence whose underlying mythemes return to possess the adult and his psychology in the sentimental and simplified ways we have suggested. We might condense this psychological process into a formula: *the less the child is borne as an emotional vulnerability and imaginal reality, the more we shall be abandoned to it in our rationalized fantasies.*

Preferable to the division into child and adult and the consequent patterns of abandonment which we have been sketching, would be a psychology less given over to the child, its woes and romanticism. We might then have a psychology descriptive of man, an aspect of whom is perennially child, carrying his incurable weakness and nurse to it, enacting the child neither by development nor by abandonment, but bearing the child, the child contained. Our subjective experience might then be mirrored by a psychology both more exact in its description and more sophisticatedly classical, where the child is contained within the man who carries in his face and mien the shame of the childish, its unchanging psychopathology – untranscended, untransformed – and the invincible high hopes together with the vulnerability of these hopes, who bears his abandonment in dignity, and whose freedom comes from the imaginal redeemed from the amnesia of childhood.

References

ARIÉS, P. *Centuries of Childhood* tr. Robert Baldick, Cape, 1962.

FREUD, S. *Collected Papers* vols. II and III, Hogarth, 1924, 1925, (CP).

FREUD, S. *New Introductory Lectures on Psycho-Analysis* tr. Sprott, Hogarth, 1933, (NIL).

JUNG, C.G. *Collected Works* vols: 9, 10 (2nd ed. 1968), 12 (2nd ed. 1968), 13 (1967), Routledge, (CW).

9 Reveries toward childhood
Gaston Bachelard

I

When, all alone and dreaming on rather at length, we go far from
the present to relive the times of the first life, several child faces come
to meet us. We were several in the trial life (*la vie essayée*), in our
primitive life. Only through the accounts of others have we come to
know of our unity. On the thread of our history as told by the others,
year by year, we end up resembling ourselves. We gather all our
beings around the unity of our name.

But reverie does not recount. Or at least there are reveries so deep,
reveries which help us descend so deeply within ourselves that they
rid us of our history. They liberate us from our name. These solitudes
of today return us to the original solitudes. Those original solitudes,
the childhood solitudes leave indelible marks on certain souls. Their
entire life is sensitized for poetic reverie, for a reverie which knows
the price of solitude. Childhood knows unhappiness through men. In
solitude, it can relax its aches. When the human world leaves him in
peace, the child feels like the son of the cosmos. And thus, in his
solitudes, from the moment he is master of his reveries, the child
knows the happiness of dreaming which will later be the happiness of
the poets. How is it possible not to feel that there is communication
between our solitude as a dreamer and the solitudes of childhood?
And it is no accident that, in a tranquil reverie, we often follow the
slope which returns us to our childhood solitudes.

Let us leave to psychoanalysis then the task of curing badly spent
childhoods, of curing the puerile sufferings of an *indurate childhood*
which oppresses the psyche of so many adults. There is a task open to
a poetico-analysis which would help us reconstitute within ourselves
the being of liberating solitudes. Poetico-analysis ought to return all
the privileges of the imagination to us. Memory is a field full of

Source: Gaston Bachelard, *The Poetics of Reverie*, tr. Daniel Russell, New York,
Grossman (1969).

psychological ruins, a whatnot full of memories. Our whole child-hood remains to be reimagined. In reimagining it, we have the possibility of recovering it in the very life of our reveries as a solitary child.

From then on, the theses which we wish to defend in this chapter all return to make us recognize within the human soul the perman-ence of a nucleus of childhood, an immobile but ever living childhood, outside history, hidden from the others, disguised in history when it is recounted, but which has real being only in its instants of illumination which is the same as saying in the moments of its poetic existence.

When he would dream in his solitude, the child knew an existence without bounds. His reverie was not simply a reverie of escape. It was a reverie of flight.

There are childhood reveries which surge forth with the brilliance of a fire. The poet finds his childhood again by telling it with a tone (*verbe*) of fire.

Tone on fire. I shall tell what my childhood was.
We unearthed the red moon in the thick of the woods.
Alain Bosquet, *Premier Testament*

An excess of childhood is the germ of a poem. One would laugh at a father who, for love of his child, would go 'unhook the moon.' But the poet does not shy away from this cosmic gesture. In his ardent memory, he knows that that is a childhood gesture. The child knows very well that the moon, that great blond bird, has its nest somewhere in the forest.

Thus, childhood images, images which a child could make, images which a poet tells us that a child has made are, for us, manifestations of the permanent childhood. Those are the images of solitude. They tell of the continuity of the great childhood reveries with the reveries of the poet.

II

So it seems that, with the aid of the poet's images, childhood will be revealed as psychologically beautiful. How can we avoid speaking of psychological beauty when confronted with an attractive event from our inner life. This beauty is within us, at the bottom of memory. It is the beauty of a flight which revives us, which puts the dynamism of one of life's beauties within us. In our childhood, reverie gave us freedom. It is striking that the most favorable field for receiving the consciousness of freedom is none other than reverie. To grasp this liberty when it intervenes in a child's reverie is paradoxical only if one forgets that we still dream of liberty as we dreamed of it when we were children. What other psychological freedom do we have than the freedom to dream? Psychologically speaking, it is in reverie that we are free beings.

A potential childhood is within us. When we go looking for it in our reveries, we relive it even more in its possibilities than in its reality.

We dream of everything that it could have been; we dream at the frontier between history and legend. To reach the memories of our solitudes, we idealize the worlds in which we were solitary children. So it is a problem in practical psychology to take into account the very real idealization of childhood memories and the personal interest we take in all childhood memories. And for that reason there is communication between a poet of childhood and his reader through the intermediary of the childhood which endures within us. Furthermore, this childhood continues to be receptive to any opening upon life and makes it possible for us to understand and love children as if we were their equals in original life.

A poet speaks to us and we are a living water, a new wellspring. Let us listen to Charles Plisnier:

Ah, provided I consent to it
my childhood there you are
as alive, as present
Firmanent of blue glass
tree of leaf and snow
river that runs, where am I going?
Sacre XXI

Reading these lines I see the blue sky above my river in the summers of the other century.

The being of reverie crosses all the ages of man from childhood to old age without growing old. And that is why one feels a sort of redoubling of reverie late in life when he tries to bring the reveries of childhood back to life.

This reinforcement of reverie, this deepening of reverie which we feel when we dream of our childhood explains that, in all reverie, even that which takes us into the contemplation of a great beauty of the world, we soon find ourselves on the slope of memories; imperceptibly, we are being led back to old reveries, suddenly so old that we no longer think of dating them. A glimmer of eternity descends upon the beauty of the world. We are standing before a great lake whose name is familiar to geographers, high in the mountains, and suddenly we are returning to a distant past. We dream while remembering. We remember while dreaming. Our memories bring us back to a simple river which reflects a sky leaning upon hills. But the hill gets bigger and the loop of the river broadens. The little becomes big. The world of childhood reverie is as big, bigger than the world offered tò today's reverie. From poetic reverie, inspired by some great spectacle of the world to childhood reverie, there is a commerce of grandeur. And that is why childhood is at the origin of the greatest landscapes. Our childhood solitudes have given us the primitive immensities.

By dreaming on childhood, we return to the lair of reveries, to the reveries which have opened up the world to us. It is reverie which makes us the first inhabitant of the world of solitude. And we inhabit the world better because we inhabit it as the solitary child inhabits images. In the child's reverie, the image takes precedent over every-thing else. Experiences come only later. They go against the wind of every reverie of flight. The child sees everything big and beautiful. The reverie toward childhood returns us to the beauty of the first images.

Can the world be as beautiful now? Our adherence to the original beauty was so strong that if our reverie carries us back to our dearest memories, the present world is completely colorless. A poet who writes a book of poems entitled *Concrete Days* can say:

... The world totters
when from my past I get
what I need to live in the depths of myself.
Paul Chaulot, *Jours de béton*

Ah! how solid we would be within ourselves if we could live, live again without nostalgia and in complete ardor, in our primitive world.

In short, isn't that opening on the world of which philosophers avail themselves, a reopening upon the prestigious world of original contemplations? But put another way, is this intuition of the world, this *Weltanschauung* anything other than a childhood which dares not speak its name? The roots of the grandeur of the world plunge into a childhood. For man, the world begins with a revolution of the soul which very often goes back to a childhood. A passage by Villiers de L'Isle-Adam will give us an example of this. In 1862 in his book *Isis*, he wrote of his heroine, the dominating woman: 'The character of her mind was self-determining, and by obscure transitions it attained the immanent proportions where the self is affirmed for what it is. The nameless hour, the eternal hour when children cease to look vaguely at the sky and the earth rang for her in her ninth year. From this moment on, what was dreaming confusedly in the eyes of this little girl took on a more fixed glint: one would have said she was feeling the meaning of herself while awakening in our shadows.'

Thus, in 'a nameless hour,' 'the world is affirmed for what it is,' and the soul which dreams is a consciousness of solitude. At the end of Villiers de L'Isle-Adam's account (p. 225), the heroine will be able to say: 'My memory, suddenly damaged in the deep domains of the dream, felt inconceivable memories.' Thus, the soul and the world are both open to the immemorial.

So, like a forgotten fire, a childhood can always flare up again within us. The fire of yesteryear and the cold of today meet in a great poem by Vincent Huidobro:

In my childhood is born a childhood burning like alcohol
I would sit down in the paths of the night
I would listen to the discourse of the stars
And that of the tree.
Now indifference snows in the evening of my soul.
Altaible

These images which arise from the depths of childhood are not really memories. In order to evaluate all their vitality, a philosopher would have to be able to develop all the dialectics that are summed up too quickly in the two words 'imagination' and 'memory.' We are going to devote a short paragraph to pointing up the boundaries between memories and images.

III

When we were gathering together the themes which constituted, in our eyes, the 'psychology' of the house for our book *The Poetics of Space*, we saw the endless play of the dialectics of facts and values, realities and dreams, memories and legends, projects and chimeras. Examined within such dialectics, the past is not stable; it does not return to the memory either with the same traits or in the same light. As soon as the past is situated within a network of human values, within the inner values of a person who does not forget, it appears with the double force of the mind which remembers and the soul which feasts upon its faithfulness. The soul and the mind do not have the same memory. Sully Prudhomme, who has experienced this division, wrote:

O memory, the soul renounces,
Frightened, to conceive you.

It is only when the soul and the mind are united in a reverie by the reverie that we benefit from the union of imagination and memory. In such a union we can say that we are reliving our past. Our past being imagines itself living again.

From then on, in order to constitute the poetics of a childhood set forth in a reverie, it is necessary to give memories their atmosphere of images. In order to make our philosopher's reflections on remembering reverie clearer, let us distinguish a few polemical points between psychological facts and values.

In their psychic primitiveness, Imagination and Memory appear in an indissoluble complex. If they are attached to perception, they are being badly analyzed. The remembered past is not simply a past of perception. Since one is remembered past is not simply a past of perception. Since one is remembering, the past is already being designated in a reverie as an image value. From their very origin, the imagination colors the paintings it will want to see again. For facts to go as far as the archives of the memory, values must be rediscovered beyond the facts. Familiarity is not analyzed by counting repetitions. The techniques of experimental psychology can scarcely hope to undertake a study of the imagination from the point of view of its creative values. In order to relive the *values of the past*, one must dream, must accept the great dilation of the psyche known as reverie, in the peace of a great repose. Then Memory and Imagination rival each other in giving us back the images which pertain to our lives.

In brief, it is the task of the *animus'* memory to tell the facts well in the objectivity of a life's history. But the *animus* is the outside man, the man who needs others in order to think. Who will help us to find the world of the intimate psychological values which is within us? The more I read poets, the more comfort and peace I find in the reveries of memory. Poets help us cherish our *anima* happinesses. Naturally, the poet tells us nothing of our objective past. But by the quality of the imagined life, the poet places a new light within us; in our reveries we paint impressionistic pictures of our past. Poets convince us that all our childhood reveries are worth starting over again.

The triple liaison between imagination, memory and poetry will then have to help us situate - and this is the second theme of our research - that human phenomenon which is a solitary childhood, a cosmic childhood, within the realm of values. If we could develop our outline, it would then be, for us, a matter of awakening within us, through a reading of the poets, and sometimes thanks to nothing more than a poet's image, a state of new childhood, of a childhood which goes farther than the memories of our childhood, as if the poet were making us continue, complete a childhood which was not well finished (*accomplie*), and yet which was ours and which we have doubtless dreamed on many occasions. The poetic documents we shall gather together ought then to return us to the natural, original oneirism which has no preconditions, the very oneirism of our childhood reveries.

These childhoods multiplied in a thousand images are certainly not dated. It would be going against their oneirism to try to fit them into coincidences in order to link them to the little facts of domestic life. Reverie shifts blocks of thoughts without any great worry about following the thread of an adventure. In that it is much different from the dream which always wants to tell us a story.

The history of our childhood is not psychically dated. Dates are put back in afterwards; they come from other people, from elsewhere, from another time than the time lived. Dates come from precisely that time when one is *recounting*. Victor Ségalen, a great dreamer of life, felt the difference between the recounted childhood and the childhood replaced in a dreamed duration: 'One tells a child of some trait of his early childhood; he retains it, and will make use of it later in order to remember, and in turn recite and prolong, through repetition, the artificial duration,' (*Voyage au pays du réel.*) And in another passage, Victor Ségalen intends to rediscover 'the early adolescent' and really meet 'for the first time' with the adolescent he was. If memories are too often repeated, 'that rare phantom' is no longer anything but a lifeless copy. The 'pure memories' endlessly repeated become old refrains of the personality.

How often can a 'pure memory' warm a remembering soul? Can't the 'pure memory' too become a habit? In enriching our monotonous reveries, in revitalizing the 'pure memories' which repeat themselves, we receive great help from the 'variations' offered to us by the poets. The psychology of the imagination must be a doctrine of 'psychological variations.' The imagination is so current a faculty that it stimulates 'variations' even in our memories of childhood. All these poetic variations which come to us in exaltation are just so many proofs of the permanence within us of a nucleus of childhood. If we wish to grasp its essence as a phenomenologist, history hampers us more than it helps us.

Such a phenomenological project of gathering the poetry of childhood reveries in its personal actuality is naturally much different from the very useful objective examinations of the child by psychologists. Even by letting children speak freely, by observing them uncensured while they are enjoying the total liberty of their play, by listening to them with the gentle patience of a child psychoanalyst, one does not necessarily attain the simple purity of phenomenological examination. People are much too well educated for that and consequently too disposed to apply the comparative method. A mother who sees her child as someone *incomparable* would know better. But alas! a mother does not know for very long . . . From the time a child reaches the 'age of reason,' from the time he loses his absolute right to imagine the world, his mother, like all educators, makes it her duty to teach him to be *objective* - objective in the simple way adults believe themselves to be 'objective.' He is stuffed with sociability. He is prepared for his life as a man along the lines of the ideal of stabilized men. He is also instructed in the history of his family. He is taught most of the memories of early childhood, a whole history which the child will always be able to recount. Childhood – that dough! – is pushed into the die so that the child will follow closely in the path of the lives of others.

The child thus enters into the zone of family, social and psychological conflicts. He becomes a premature man. This is the same as saying that this premature man is in a state of repressed childhood.

The questioned child, the child examined by the adult psychologist, who is strong in his consciousness as *animus*, does not surrender his solitude. The solitude of the child is more secret than the solitude of a man. It is often late in life that we discover our childhood and adolescent solitudes in their depths. In the last quarter of life one understands the solitudes of the first quarter by reflecting the solitude of old age off the forgotten solitudes of childhood. The child dreamer is alone, very much alone. He lives in the world of his reverie. His solitude is less social, less pitted against society, than the solitude of men. The child knows a natural reverie of solitude, a reverie which must not be confused with that of the sulking child. In his happy solitudes, the dreaming child knows the cosmic reverie which unites us to the world.

In our opinion, it is in the memories of this cosmic solitude that we ought to find the nucleus of childhood which remains at the center of the human psyche. It is there that imagination and memory are most closely bound together. It is there that the being of childhood binds the real with the imaginary, that it lives the images of reality in total imagination. And all these images of its cosmic solitude react in depth in the being of the child; aside from his being for men, a being for the world is created under the inspiration of the world. That is the being of cosmic childhood. Men pass; the cosmos remains, an ever primitive cosmos, a cosmos that the world's greatest spectacles will not erase in the entire course of life. The cosmicity of our childhood remains within us. In solitude, it reappears in our reveries. This nucleus of cosmic childhood is then like a false memory within us. Our solitary reveries are the activities of a meta-amnesia. It seems that our reveries toward the reveries of our childhood introduce us to a being preconditional to our being, a whole perspective on the *antecedence of being*.

Were we or were we dreaming of being, and now in dreaming on our childhood, are we ourselves?

The antecedence of being is lost in the distance of time, that is, in the distances of our intimate time, in that multiple indetermination

of our births to the psychism, for the psychism is tried out in many
trials. The psychism is endlessly striving to be born. This antecedence
of being and the infinity of the time of slow childhood are correlative. History – always the history of others! – caked onto the limbo of
the psychism obscures all the forces of the personal meta-amnesia.
And yet, psychologically speaking, *limbo* is not a *myth*. It is an
indelible psychic reality. And to help us penetrate into the limbo of
the antecedence of being, a few rare poets will supply us with rays of
light. Rays? Limitless light! Edmond Vandercammen writes:

Ever upstream from myself
I advance, implore and pursue myself
– O harsh law of my poem
In the hollow of a shadow which flees me.
La porte sans mémoire

In quest of the most distant memory, the poet wants a viaticum, a
first value greater than the simple memory of an event from his
history:

Where I thought I was remembering
I wanted only a little salt
To recognize myself and be on my way.

And in another poem going upstream from upstream, the poet can
say: 'Aren't our years mineral dreams?'
If the senses remember, aren't they going to find, within some
archaeology of the perceptible, these 'mineral dreams,' these dreams
of the 'elements,' which attach us to the world in an 'eternal
childhood.'
'Upstream from myself,' says the poet; 'Upstream from upstream,'
says the reverie which looks to go back up to the springs (*sources*) of
the being; those are the proofs of the antecedence of being. Poets
look for this antecedence of being; therefore it exists. Such a
certainty is one of the axioms of a philosophy of the oneirism.
In what beyond are poets not capable of remembering? Isn't early
life a trial for eternity? Jean Follain can write:

While in the fields
of his eternal childhood
the poet walks
and doesn't want to forget anything.
Exister

How vast life is when one meditates upon its beginnings! Isn't
meditating upon an origin dreaming? And isn't dreaming upon an
origin going beyond it? Beyond our history extends 'our incommen-
surable memory' to take an expression which Baudelaire borrowed
from de Quincey.

In order to force the past, when forgetfulness is hemming us in, poets engage us in reimagining the lost childhood. They teach us 'the audacities of the memory.' (Pierre Emmanuel *Tombeau d'Orphée*.) One poet tells us the past must be invented:

Invent. There is no lost feast
At the bottom of memory.
Robert Ganzo, *L'oeuvre Poétique*

And when the poet invents those great images which reveal the intimacy of the world, isn't he remembering?

Sometimes adolescence upsets everything. Adolescence, that fever of time in the human life! The memories are too clear for the dreams to be great. And the dreamer knows very well that he must go beyond the time of fevers to find the tranquil time, the time of the happy childhood inside his own substance. What sensitivity to the boundary between the times of tranquil childhood and the times of agitated adolescence there is in this passage by Jean Follain: 'There were mornings when it rained substance. ... That feeling of eternity which very early childhood carries with it had already disappeared.' (*Chef-lieu.*) What a change there is in life when one falls under the reign of the time which consumes, of the time when the substance of the being has tears'?

One has but to meditate on all the poems we have just quoted. They are very different and yet they all bear witness to an aspiration to cross the line, to go against the current, to rediscover the great calm lake where time rests from its flowing. And this lake is within us, like a primitive water, like the environment in which an immobile childhood continues to reside.

When the poets call us toward this region, we know a tender reverie, a reverie hypnotized by the faraway. It is this tension of childhood reveries which we designate, for lack of a better name, by the term 'antecedence of being.' To catch a glimpse of it, it is necessary to take advantage of the *detemporalization* of the states of great reverie. Thus we believe that one can know states which are ontologically below being and above nothingness. In these states the contradiction between being and non-being fades away. A sub-being (*moins-être*) is trying itself out as being. This antecedence of being does not yet have the responsibility of being. Neither does it have the solidity of the constituted being which believes itself capable of confronting a non-being. In such a state of mind, one feels clearly that logical opposition, with its too bright light, erases all possibility of penumbral ontology. Very much softened keys are necessary to follow, in a dialectic of light and shadow, all the emergences of the human trying itself out at being.

The terms 'life' and 'death' are too approximate. In a reverie, the word 'death' is vulgar. It ought not to be used in a micrometaphysical study of the being which appears and disappears only to reappear, following the undulations of a reverie on being. Besides, if one dies in certain dreams, in reveries or, in other words, in the peaceful oneirism, one does not die. Is it necessary to add that, in a general manner, birth and death are not psychologically symmetrical? In the human being, there are so many forces being born which do not, at their beginnings, know the monotonous fatality of death! One dies only once. But psychologically we are born many times. Childhood flows from so many springs (*sources*) that it would be as futile to try to construct its geography as to write its history. Thus the poet says:

Of childhoods I have so many
That I would get lost counting them.
Alexandre Arnoux, *Petits Poèmes*

All these psychic glimmers from roughed-out births (*naissances ébauchées*) shed light on a cosmos being born, the cosmos of limbo. Glimmers and limbo, there then is the dialectic of the antecedence of the being of childhood. A word dreamer cannot help being sensitive to the softness of speech which puts glimmers (*lueurs*) and limbo (*limbes*) under the influence of two labiates. With the glimmer there is water in the light, and Limbo is aquatic. And we shall always return to the same oneiric certainty: Childhood is a human water, a water which comes out of the shadows. This childhood in the mists and glimmers, this life in the slowness of limbo gives us a certain layer of births. What a lot of beings we have begun! What a lot of lost springs which have, nevertheless, flowed! Reverie toward our past then, reverie looking for childhood seems to bring back to life lives which have never taken place, lives which have been imagined. Reverie is a mnemonics of the imagination. In reverie we re-enter into contact with possibilities which destiny has not been able to make use of. A great paradox is connected with our reveries toward childhood: in us, this dead past has a future, the future of its living images, the *reverie future* which opens before any rediscovered image.

IV

The great dreamers of childhoods are attracted by this beyond of the birth. Karl Philipp Moritz who, in his book *Anton Reiser*, was able to write an autobiography where his dreams (*rêves*) and memories are woven tightly together, haunted these preambles to existence. He says that the ideas of childhood are perhaps the imperceptible bond which attaches us to former states, at least if what is now our I has existed once before under other conditions.

Our childhood would then be the Lethe where we had drunk in order not to dissolve in the former and future All, to have a suitably limited personality. We are placed in a sort of labyrinth; we do not find the thread which would show us the way out and, doubtless, it is essential that we do not find it. That is why we attach the thread of History to the place where the thread of our (personal) memories breaks, and when our own existence escapes us, we live in that of our ancestors.

The child psychologist will be quick to label such reveries 'metaphysical.' For him they will be entirely futile since they are not common to everyone or since the maddest of dreamers would not dare to speak them. But the fact is there; this reverie has taken place. It has received the dignity of writing from a great dreamer, a great writer. And these madnesses and futile dreams, these aberrant pages find readers whom they captivate. After having quoted Moritz, Albert Béguin adds that Carl Gustav Carus, a doctor and psychologist, said that 'for observations of this depth, he would give all the memories with which literature is flooded.'

The labyrinth dreams evoked by Moritz's reverie cannot be explained by lived experiences. They are not formed with corridor anxieties. It is not with experiences that the great dreamers of childhood pose the question: Where do we come from? Perhaps there is an exit toward clear consciousness, but where was the entry to the labyrinth? Didn't Nietzsche say: 'If we wish to outline an architecture which conforms to the structure of our soul . . ., it would have to be conceived in the image of the Labyrinth.' (*Aurore.*) A soft-walled labyrinth through which, wending his way, slips the dreamer. And from one dream to the other, the labyrinth changes.

A 'night of time' is within us. The one which we 'learn' through prehistory, through history, through the line of 'dynasties' could never be an experienced 'night of time.' What dreamer will ever be able to understand how one makes a millenium out of ten centuries? May we be left then to dream without numbers about our youth, about our childhood, about Childhood. Ah! how faraway are those times! How ancient is our intimate millenium! the one which is ours, within us, very close to engulfing the before-us? When one dreams in depth, he is never finished beginning. Novalis has written: 'Aller wirklicher Anfang ist ein zweiter Moment.' (Every effective beginning is a second moment.)

In such a reverie toward childhood, the depth of time is not a metaphor borrowed from spatial measurement. The depth of time is concrete, concretely temporal. Dreaming with a great dreamer of childhood like Moritz is sufficient to make one tremble before this depth.

When, at the pinnacle of age, at the end of age, one sees such reveries, he draws back a bit, for he recognizes that *childhood is the well of being*. Dreaming this way about unfathomable childhood which is one archetype, I am well aware that I am taken by another archetype. The well is an archetype, one of the gravest images of the human soul.

That black and distant water can mark a childhood. It has reflected an astonished face. Its mirror is not that of the fountain. A narcissus can take no pleasure there. Already in his image living beneath the earth, the child does not recognize himself. A mist is on the water; plants which are too green frame the mirror. A cold blast breathes in the depths. The face which comes back in this night of the earth is a face from another world. Now, if a memory of such reflections comes into a memory, isn't it the memory of a before-world?

A well marked my early childhood. I only approached it with my hand tightly clasped in my grandfather's hand. Who was afraid then, the grandfather or the child? And yet the curb was high. It was in a garden which was soon to be lost ... But a dull evil has remained with me. I know what a well of being is. And since one must tell everything when he is evoking his childhood, I must admit the well of my greatest terrors was always the well of my goose game. In the middle of the softest evenings, I was more afraid of it than of the skull and crossed tibias.

V

What a tension of childhoods there must be, held in reserve at the bottom of our being, for a poet's image to make us suddenly relive our memories, reimagining our images by starting from well assembled words. For the poet's image is a spoken image; it is not an image which our eyes see. One feature of the spoken image is sufficient for us to read the poem as the echo of a vanished past.

In order to restore, it is necessary to beautify. The poet's image gives our memories a halo once again. We are far from having an exact memory (*mémoire*) which could keep the memory (*souvenir*) pure by framing it. For Bergson, it seems that pure memories are framed images. Why would one remember having learned a lesson on a garden bench? As if his goal were to fix a point in history! It would at least be necessary, since he is in a garden, to retell the reveries which distracted our schoolboy attention. The pure memory can only be recovered in reverie. It does not come at a given moment to help us in active life. Bergson is an intellectual who does not know himself. By a fatality of his own time, he believes in the *psychic fact*, and his doctrine of memory remains, all things considered, a doctrine of the utility of memory. Completely involved in developing a practical psychology, Bergson did not encounter the fusion of memory and reverie.

And yet, how often the pure memory, the useless memory of the useless childhood, comes back to nourish reverie as a benefit of the non-life which helps us live an instant on the edge of life. In a dialectical philosophy of repose and act, of reverie and thought, the memory of childhood tells clearly enough the utility of the useless! It gives us an ineffectual past in real life but one which is suddenly dynamized in that life, imagined or reimagined, which is beneficial reverie. In the growing-old age, the memory of childhood returns us to the delicate sentiments, to that 'smiling regret' of the great Baudelairean atmospheres. In the 'smiling regret' which the poet experiences, we seem to realize the strange synthesis of regret and consolation. A beautiful poem makes us pardon a very ancient grief.

To live in this atmosphere of another time, we must desocialize our memory and, beyond memories told, retold and recounted by ourselves and by others, by all those who have taught us how we were in the first childhood, we must find our unknown being, the sum total of all the unknowable elements that make up the soul of a child. When reverie goes so far, one is astonished by his own past, astonished to have been that child. There are moments in childhood when every child is the astonishing being, the being who realizes the *astonishment of being*. We thus discover within ourselves an *immobile childhood*, a *childhood without becoming*, liberated from the gearwheels of the calendar.

Then, the time of men no longer reigns over memory any more than the time of saints, those journeymen of everyday time who mark the life of the child only by the first names of his relations; but it is the time of the four divinities of the sky, the seasons. The pure memory has no date. It has a *season*. The season is the fundamental mark of memories. What sun or what wind was there that memorable day? That is the question which gives the right tension of reminiscence. Then the memories become great images, magnified, magnifying images. They are associated with the universe of a season, a season which does not deceive and which can well be called the *total season*, reposing in the immobility of perfection. Total season because all its images speak the same values, because you possess its essence with one particular image such as that dawn which arose out of the memory of a poet:

What dawn, torn silk
In the blue of the heat
Has arisen remembered?
What movements of colors?
Noël Ruet, 'Le bouquet de sang', *Cahiers de Rochefort*

Winter, autumn, sun, the summer river are all roots of total seasons. They are not only spectacles through sight, they are soul values, direct, immobile, indestructible psychological values. Experienced in the memory, they are *always beneficial*. They are lasting benefits. For me summer remains the bouquet season. Summer is a bouquet, an eternal bouquet which could not wilt. For it always takes on the youth of its symbol; it is an offering, very new, very fresh.

The seasons of memory are beautifying. When one goes off dreaming to the bottom of their simplicity, into the very center of their value, the seasons of childhood are the seasons of the poet.

These seasons find the means to be singular while remaining universal. They circle in the sky of Childhood and mark each childhood with indelible signs. Thus our great memories lodge within the zodiac of memory, of a cosmic memory which does not need the precisions of the social memory in order to be psychologically faithful. It is the very memory of our belonging to the world, to a world commanded by the dominating sun. With each season there resounds in us one of the dynamisms of our entry into the world, that entry into the world which so many philosophers bring up at any time and for any reason. The season opens the world, worlds where each dreamer sees his being blossom. And the seasons, armed with their original dynamism, are the seasons of Childhood. Later, the seasons can make a mistake, develop badly, overlap, or fade. But during our childhood, they never make a mistake with signs. Childhood sees the World illustrated, the World with its original colors, its true colors. The great *once-upon-a-time* (*autrefois*) which we relive by dreaming in our memories of childhood is precisely the world of the *first time.* All the summers of our childhood bear witness to 'the eternal summer.' The seasons of memory are eternal because they are faithful to the colors of the *first time*. The cycle of exact seasons is a major cycle of the imagined universes. It marks the life of our illustrated universes. In our reveries we see our illustrated universe once more with its *childhood colors*.

VI

Every childhood is prodigious, naturally prodigious. It is not that it lets itself be impregnated, as we are tempted to believe, by the ever so artificial fables which are told to it and which serve only to amuse the ancestor doing the telling. What a lot of grandmothers take their grandson for a little fool! But the child being born malicious stirs up the mania for storytelling, the eternal repetitions of romancing old age. The child's imagination does not live from these fossile fables, these fossiles of fables. It is in his own fables. The child finds his fables in his reverie, fables which he tells no one. Then the fable is

life itself: 'I have lived without knowing that I was living my fable.'
This great line is found in a poem entitled 'I am sure of nothing.'
(Jean Rousselot, *Il n'y pas d'exil.*) The *permanent child* alone can
return the fabulous world to us. Edmond Vandercammen appeals to
childhood to 'sweep closer to the sky:'

The sky is waiting to be touched by a hand
 Of fabulous childhood
- Childhood, my desire, my queen, my cradlesong -
 By a breath of the morning.
Faucher plus près du ciel

Besides, how could we tell our *fables* when, precisely, we speak of
them as 'fables'? We hardly know what a *sincere fable* is any more.
Grown-ups write children's stories too easily. Thus they make
childish fables. To enter into the fabulous times, it is necessary to be
serious like a dreaming child. The fable does not amuse; it enchants.
We have lost the language of enchantment. Thoreau wrote: 'It seems
that we only languish during maturity in order to tell the dreams of
our childhood, and they vanish from our memory before we were
able to learn their language.' (*Walden.*)

In order to rediscover the language of fables, it is necessary to
participate in the existentialism of the fabulous, to become body and
soul an admiring being and replace perception of the world with
admiration. Admiration in order to receive the qualities of what is
perceived. And even in the past, to admire the memory. When
Lamartine returned to Saint-Point in 1849, at a site where he was
about to relive the past, he wrote: 'My soul was nothing but a canticle
of illusions.' (*Les foyers du peuple.*) Confronted with witnesses to the
past, with objects and sites which recall memories and make them
precise, the poet discovers the union of the poetry of memory and the
truth of illusions. Childhood memories relived in reverie are really
'canticles of illusions' at the bottom of the soul.

10 A paradigm of guilt — *Oedipus Rex*
Donald Morano

In the *Poetics* Aristotle refers specifically to *Oedipus Rex* and Oedipus' ability to arouse the spectator's pity and fear because Oedipus has committed patricide and incest in ignorance. The Greek word *hamartia*, which in the Christian era was translated into Latin *peccatum*, does not - as recent scholarship has rather conclusively and unanimously established - have the connotation of sin in classical Greek. It is much closer in meaning to an error in judgment because of ignorance. However, to make such a sharp distinction between moral and intellectual categories is not being true to classical Greek thought. For Plato, particularly in his earlier Socratic dialogues, knowledge and virtue are synonymous. Knowing what one should do is tantamount to guaranteeing one's doing it. Oedipus' fault was his ignorance, the concealment to himself of his own lineage and therefore of his true self. In the play, no dilemmas of right and wrong have to be probed; Oedipus does not vacillate in his objectives; Oedipus is simply the searcher after truth. He will unmask the cause of the plague; he will bring to light the guilty one.

According to Martin Heidegger, truth for the classical Greeks is *aletheia*, disclosure, unconcealedness - a term for truth which only in the Greek language contains a privative '*a*' as a prefix and which, as a privative, suggests most vividly the image of truth as that which is violently wrested away and uncovered. There is a *paideia* - one is converted from the shadowy existence of the cave to the radiant brilliance of the sunlight.

The tragic irony of *Oedipus Rex* is that Oedipus who could be so brilliant about the riddle of the Sphinx should be so blind about his own fate; that Oedipus who traveled to Delphi to learn whether the Corinthian rulers were his natural parents should forget his original question when informed of the ominous prophecy about himself;

Source: Donald V. Morano, *Existential Guilt*, Assen (Netherlands), Van Gorcum (1973).

that Oedipus who would spurn the fulfillment of the prophecy with apparently devastating logic by exiling himself from Corinth should bring about its fulfillment precisely by that exile; that Oedipus who was willing to sacrifice so much (home, family, and the right to a throne) to avoid the dire prophecy, should be so precipitous and rash in cutting down an old man and marrying a woman much older than himself, despite the very prophecy; that Oedipus who enjoyed great prestige for his wisdom and understanding should be so blind before the condemnation of blind Tiresias, and finally, that Oedipus who damned the public defiler responsible for the plague should suffer the damnation prescribed by his very decree in the lucidity of his physical blindness.

There is no doubt that if Oedipus had only known who his real parents were, he would have avoided the guilt resulting from his unwitting acts. Certainly we may be more willing to accept Oedipus' fate because of his impetuosity in deciding not to return to Corinth, in killing Laius, in marrying Jocasta, in vitriolically interrogating Tiresias, in accusing Creon of inciting Tiresias to speak his words of warning to Oedipus. But yet, Oedipus' impetuosity, his hauteur, his overweening pride – all characteristics lumped together under the notion of *hybris* – are ultimately irrelevant to his fate. *Moira* (fate) is impersonal, irresistible, irreversible, and usually inscrutable, at least to humans. What is decreed for Oedipus, who, as all men, never chose to be born and who, personally, had always shown the greatest respect towards the gods, invoking them and heeding their words, results from an invicible ignorance, since *moira* must have its say. What makes Oedipus such a compellingly tragic hero is that he is an outstanding man, victimized by an irresistible fate. *A fortiori*, his struggling actually brings about his downfall. We pity Oedipus and fear for our own human condition. Sophocles ends the play with the chorus' lugubrious air:

Call no man fortunate that is not dead.
The dead are free from pain.

Thus it would seem that man, according to Sophocles, is powerless to protect himself against *moira*, that man with his limited intellect, despite all dedication and all conscientiousness and despite even extraordinary human perspicacity and brilliance, is powerless to grasp his situation in the world, to grasp *moira* – that man is condemned to suffer for his unwitting and preordained sacrileges.

Oedipus delivers no pleas of innocence because of ignorance. On the contrary, he feels polluted and criminal in his total being, violently striking out his eyes to punish himself, his guilt-feelings are so overwhelming. The logic seems to run: Man is a fallible creature and therefore he is guilty of whatever he suffers. There is no question of strictly merited punishment. The very nature of tragedy is the deplorable suffering of great-souled men. Man's lot, it would seem, leaves for him only the ideal of *amor fati*, the love of fate. However, the individual's fate is not an isolated one. As Sophocles suggests, man's personal lot has repercussions for all society. For, through Oedipus' suffering the breath of a salutary breeze does drive away the plague at Thebes.

In a sense nothing happens during *Oedipus Rex*; the entire perspective of the play is retrospective; we have no plot development; all we have is denouement. The murder of Laius and Oedipus' marriage of Jocasta and the resulting plague have occurred before the drama opens. Oedipus conceives no new projects; he is obsessed with one intent – we might even say he is monomaniacal – holding to one all-consuming quest; to expose the murderer of the king and thus rid the city of defilement. *Oedipus Rex* is a monody; it is a puzzle in which the solution is precontained, so that by a rigorous application of logic the conclusion ineluctably follows from the premises. Every word and gesture dovetails in explicating more and more explicitly for Oedipus his own guilt. Concentric circles of evidence move in upon him until he cannot escape them. Time is a dead weight; Thebes waits anxiously, hovering, in a death watch for a release from its plague. Thebes does not need Oedipus' decision but his comprehension (in the literal sense of gathering together, of getting a hold on, the evidence).

11 Toys

Roland Barthes

French toys: one could not find a better illustration of the fact that the adult Frenchman sees the child as another self. All the toys one commonly sees are essentially a microcosm of the adult world; they are all reduced copies of human objects, as if in the eyes of the public the child was, all told, nothing but a smaller man, a homunculus to whom must be supplied objects of his own size.

Invented forms are very rare: a few sets of blocks, which appeal to the spirit of do-it-yourself, are the only ones which offer dynamic forms. As for the others, French toys *always mean something*, and this something is always entirely socialized, constituted by the myths or the techniques of modern adult life: the Army, Broadcasting, the Post Office, Medicine (miniature instrument-cases, operating theatres for dolls), School, Hair-Styling (driers for permanent-waving), the Air Force (Parachutists), Transport (trains, Citroëns, Vedettes, Vespas, petrol-stations), Science (Martian toys).

The fact that French toys *literally* prefigure the world of adult functions obviously cannot but prepare the child to accept them all, by constituting for him, even before he can think about it, the alibi of a Nature which has at all times created soldiers, postmen and Vespas. Toys here reveal the list of all the things the adult does not find unusual: war, bureaucracy, ugliness, Martians, etc. It is not so much, in fact, the imitation which is the sign of an abdication, as its literalness: French toys are like a Jivaro head, in which one recognizes, shrunken to the size of an apple, the wrinkles and hair of an adult. There exist, for instance, dolls which urinate; they have an oesophagus, one gives them a bottle, they wet their nappies; soon, no doubt, milk will turn to water in their stomachs. This is meant to prepare the little girl for the causality of house-keeping, to 'condition' her to her future role as mother. However, faced with this world

Source: Roland Barthes, *Mythologies*, tr. Annette Lavers, Jonathan Cape (1972), Reprinted Paladin (1973).

of faithful and complicated objects, the child can only identify himself as owner, as user, never as creator; he does not invent the world, he uses it: there are, prepared for him, actions without adventure, without wonder, without joy. He is turned into a little stay-at-home householder who does not even have to invent the mainsprings of adult causality; they are supplied to him ready-made: he has only to help himself, he is never allowed to discover anything from start to finish. The merest set of blocks, provided it is not too refined, implies a very different learning of the world: then, the child does not in any way create meaningful objects, it matters little to him whether they have an adult name; the actions he performs are not those of a user but those of a demiurge. He creates forms which walk, which roll, he creates life, not property: objects now act by themselves, they are no longer an inert and complicated material in the palm of his hand. But such toys are rather rare: French toys are usually based on imitation, they are meant to produce children who are users, not creators.

The bourgeois status of toys can be recognized not only in their forms, which are all functional, but also in their substances. Current toys are made of a graceless material, the product of chemistry, not of nature. Many are now moulded from complicated mixtures; the plastic material of which they are made has an appearance at once gross and hygienic, it destroys all the pleasure, the sweetness, the humanity of touch. A sign which fills one with consternation is the gradual disappearance of wood, in spite of its being an ideal material because of its firmness and its softness, and the natural warmth of its touch. Wood removes, from all the forms which it supports, the wounding quality of angles which are too sharp, the chemical coldness of metal. When the child handles it and knocks it, it neither vibrates nor grates, it has a sound at once muffled and sharp. It is a familiar and poetic substance, which does not sever the child from close contact with the tree, the table, the floor. Wood does not wound or break down; it does not shatter, it wears out, it can last a long time, live with the child, alter little by little the relations between the object and the hand. If it dies, it is in dwindling, not in swelling out like those mechanical toys which disappear behind the hernia of a broken spring. Wood makes essential objects, objects for all time. Yet there hardly remain any of these wooden toys from the Vosges, these fretwork farms with their animals, which were only possible, it is true, in the days of the craftsman. Henceforth, toys are chemical in substance and colour; their very material introduces one to a coenaesthesis of use, not pleasure. These toys die in fact very quickly, and once dead, they have no posthumous life for the child.

Constraining the child to order

In social theory, just as in practical social life, we select our most deeply held principles of relevance and structure our worlds around them. The most persistent tension within any form of social organization is the pull between the interests of the individual and the interests of the collective. Whichever polarity gains the ascendence and becomes the sacred symbol for that community will inevitably place constraints upon the other. Theories that are dedicated to solidarity and integration necessarily impel the child into that order, and social agencies that are committed to the purity of the norm will exercise control upon that which is viewed as differentiated and therefore pathological.

12 The socialization of the child and the internalization of social value-orientations

Talcott Parsons

The term socialization in its current usage in the literature refers primarily to the process of child development. This is in fact a crucially important case of the operation of what are here called the mechanisms of socialization, but it should be made clear that the term is here used in a broader sense than the current one to designate the learning of *any* orientations of functional significance to the operation of a system of complementary role-expectations. In this sense, socialization, like learning, goes on throughout life. The case of the development of the child is only the most dramatic because he has so far to go.

However, there is another reason for singling out the socialization of the child. There is reason to believe that, among the learned elements of personality in certain respects the stablest and most enduring are the major value-orientation patterns and there is much evidence that these are 'laid down' in childhood and are not on a large scale subject to drastic alteration during adult life. There is good reason to treat these patterns of value-orientation, as analyzed in terms of pattern variable combinations, as the core of what is sometimes called 'basic personality structure' and they will be so treated here. Hence in discussing certain highlights of the socialization of the child, primary emphasis will be placed on this aspect of socialization in more general terms.

Before proceeding it may be emphasized that the socialization of the child is a case of socialization in the strict sense of the above definition, not of social control. What has sometimes been called the 'barbarian invasion' of the stream of new-born infants is, of course, a critical feature of the situation in any society. Along with the lack of biological maturity, the conspicuous fact about the child is that he has yet to learn the patterns of behavior expected of persons in his statuses in his society. Our present discussion is not concerned with

Source: Talcott Parsons, *The Social System*, Routledge (1951).

the fact that children, having learned these patterns, tend very widely to deviate from them, though this, of course, happens at every state, but with the process of acquisition itself on the part of those who have not previously possessed the patterns.

As a mechanism of the social system, the combination of motivational processes in question must be conceived as a set of processes of action in roles which, on the basis of known facts about motivational process, analytical and empirical, tend to bring about a certain result, in the present case the internalization of certain patterns of value-orientation. This result is conceived to be the outcome of certain processes of interaction in roles.

In order to analyze the processes then, it is necessary to have two classes of information available. First we must have knowledge of the processes or mechanisms of learning from the point of view of the actor who is in the process of being socialized. Secondly, we must have in mind the relevant features of the interacting role system, which place the *socializee*, if the term may be permitted, in a situation which favors the relevant learning process. The assumption is that mechanisms of socialization operate only so far as the learning process is an integral part of the process of interaction in complementary roles. Thus not only the socializing agents *but the socializee* must be conceived as acting in roles. At the instant of birth, perhaps, the infant does not do so. But almost immediately a role is ascribed to him which includes expectations of his behavior. The behavior of adults toward him *is not* like their behavior toward purely physical objects, but is contingent on his behavior and very soon what are interpreted to be his expectations; thus '*the baby is expecting* to be fed.' It is only when this mutuality of interaction has been established that we may speak of the socialization process. Purely physical care of the infant in which he has no role but is merely a passive object of manipulation is, if it ever exists, not socialization.

In *Values, Motives and Systems of Action* five cathectic-evaluative mechanisms of learning were distinguished and systemically related to one another. All of these are relevant to the present context and what they are and how related must be briefly reviewed here. In the background stand the cognitive mechanisms of discrimination and generalization. The five are reinforcement-extinction, inhibition, substitution, imitation and identification. The first three do not necessarily involve orientation to social objects, while the last two do.

Reinforcement-extinction is the name given for the most general relation between the gratifying-depriving features of the outcome of a behavioral process, and the strength of the tendency to repeat it under appropriate conditions. The broad law is that in general the receipt of gratifications will tend to strengthen the pattern while that of deprivations will tend to weaken it. This generalization should, of course, be carefully interpreted in the light of the many different meanings in the content of gratifications and deprivations and the complex interrelations of need-dispositions in the personality system as well as the significance of many variations in the conditions. A simple 'hedonistic' interpretation is clearly inadequate.

The second mechanism is inhibition, which means simply the process of learning to refrain from carrying out the action motivated by a given need-disposition, in the presence of an appropriate opportunity for gratification, regardless of what happens to the 'affect' involved. There is a fundamental sense in which inhibition is the obverse of, and inherently linked with, learning itself. For unless complete extinction of previous need-dispositions were immediately given with every new step of learning, learning would be impossible, for the attachment to the old pattern would be unbreakable. Inhibition is thus in one direction the proess of breaking through motivational inertia.

The third general mechanism is substitution, which means the process of transferring cathexis from one object to another. Substitution obviously involves inhibition, in the form of renunciation of cathexis of the *old* object, but in addition it involves the capacity to transfer, to 'learn' that the new object can provide gratifications which are more or less equivalent to the old. Thus in the most general terms 'progress' in learning means, first, at least enough reinforcement to prevent extinction of motivations, second, capacity to inhibit the need-dispositions which block new orientations, and third, capacity to accept new objects, to substitute.

Closely connected with these cathectic-evaluative mechanisms are the primarily cognitive mechanisms of discrimination and generalization. Discrimination is the very first condition of the construction of an object-world, and must continue to operate throughout all learning processes. Generalization on the other hand, by providing awareness of the common attributes of classes of objects, is an indispensable condition of substitution, and of higher levels of organization of an orientation system. Above all, generalization is essential to the cathexis of classes of objects and even more of abstract categories and cultural objects, i.e., symbols, as such, hence to any process of successive substitutions building up to these cathexes, including processes of symbolization. Probably the acquisition of at all generalized patterns of value-orientation involves this mechanism deeply.

Imitation is the process by which *specific* items of culture, specific bits of knowledge, skill, symbolic behavior, are taken over from a social object in the interaction process. In one sense then it may be conceived as a process of short cutting the process of independent learning, in that alter is able to show a shorter and easier way to learn than ego could find by himself. Of course imitation presumably must prove rewarding in some sense if the act to be learned is to be reinforced. But above all imitation does not imply any continuing relation to the 'model,' or any solidarity attachment.

Identification, on the other hand, means taking over, i.e., internalizing, the *values* of the model. It implies that ego and alter have established a reciprocal role relationship in which value-patterns are shared. Alter is a *model* and this is a *learning process*, because ego did not at the beginning of it possess the values in question. Identification may be subclassified according to the type of values and the nature of the attachment to alter. The most important variations would be according to whether it was a specific or a diffuse attachment and whether it was an affective or love attachment or a neutral or esteem attachment. In any case this is obviously the most important of the learning mechanisms for the acquisition of value patterns.

We may now turn to the features of the interaction process itself, as a complementary role structure, which are important for the socializing effect of the operation of the learning processes just reviewed. The socializing effect will be conceived as the integration of ego into a role complementary to that of alter(s) in such a way that the common values are internalized in ego's personality, and their respective behaviors come to constitute a complementary role-expectation-sanction system.

The first point to mention is that, prior to and independent of any identification, alter as an adult has certain control of the situation in which ego acts, so that he may influence the consequences of ego's actions. Put in learning terms, he may use these to reinforce the tendencies of ego's behavior which fit his own expectations of how ego should behave, and operate to extinguish those which are deviant. Corresponding to the *learning* mechanisms of reinforcement-extinction, then, we may speak of *socialization* mechanisms of *reward-punishment*, the particular and specific orientations to ego's behavior which tend to motivate him to conformity and dissuade him from deviance from alter's functioning as a model either for imitation or for identification.

However, rewards and punishments obviously operate to induce inhibitions and substitutions. The simplest motivation for an inhibition presumably is learning that gratification of a need-disposition will bring deprivational consequences. So far as these consequences have been imposed by a social object contingent on ego's action they constitute punishments. For substitution, on the other hand, presumably a combination of rewards and punishments is, if not indispensable in all cases, at least an optimum; namely the punishment of continued retention of the old object, combined with rewarding of cathexis of the new.

Secondly, alter may operate not only as a reinforcing-extinguishing agent but as a model for imitation. In addition to imposing contingent consequences on ego's specific acts he may hold up a model, which in turn becomes the focus of reinforcement-extinction processes, however actively they may or may not be carried out by alter's own action. In this case we may say that alter as an active model adopts the role of a 'teacher' and because the term fits directly, we may speak of *socialization by 'instruction'* as the implementation of the mechanism of imitation by the socializing agent. In the learning context the term imitation emphasizes what happens when *there is* a model for imitation. In the socialization context the fact that a model of a given type *is provided* to 'instruct' ego is just as much the focus of attention. Thus attention is directed to the specific role of *alter* as well as to ego's learning processes as such.

Finally, the mechanism of learning (generally *in addition* to the others in a complex process) may be identification. For identification to take place there must develop a further feature of the interaction relationship of ego and alter. In addition to what alter *does* in the sense of his overt discrete acts with their reward-punishment significance, and to what he *offers* in the sense of patterns for imitation, alter's *attitudes* toward ego become the crucial feature of the socialization process. We have seen at a number of points how crucial this step in the integration of an interactive sytem is. Indeed it is in this way that we have defined an *attachment*, namely an orientation to alter in which the paramount focus of cathective-evaluative significance is in alter's attitudes. Overt acts thereby come to be interpreted mainly as 'expressions' of these attitudes, that is, as signs, or even more as symbols of them.

When a reciprocal attachment has been formed ego has acquired a 'relational possession.' He acquires a 'stake' in the security of this possession, in the maintenance of alter's favorable attitudes, his receptiveness-responsiveness, his love, his approval or his esteem, and a need to avoid their withdrawal and above all their conversion into hostile or derogatory attitudes.

The generalizations about motivational processes which are summed up in what is called the mechanism of identification apparently imply the extremely important generalization, we may perhaps say theorem, that value-orientation patterns can *only* be internalized from outside through reciprocal attachments, that is, through ego becoming integrated in a reciprocal and complementary role relative to alter which reaches the level of organization and cathectic sensitivity which we call that of attachment and a common value pattern involving loyalty. The third of the basic classes of mechanisms of socialization, then, we may call the *mechanisms of value-acquisition* with all the implications as to the nature of the process, not only within the personality of ego, but in terms of his interaction with alter, which have been outlined above.

This sketch of the significance of the process of identification is extremely elementary and leaves many crucial problems unsolved. The stress has been placed on the building up of a pattern of values common to ego and to alter, ego being considered as acquiring the values from alter through identification. This leaves open, however, several crucial problems concerning the processes of differentiation of such a value-system. Above all the roles of ego and alter are generally complementary and not identical. There is, therefore, an element of *common value* but equally an element of *differential applicability* of the common value element to ego and to alter. Ego as a small child is clearly not expected to behave exactly as alter as an adult does. Furthermore, ego and alter may be of opposite sex, thus introducing a further differentiation.

On this basis we may distinguish the following elements in the value-patterns acquired by ego from alter through identification; a) the common value-orientation in sufficiently general terms to be applicable both to ego's role and to alter's and hence, presumably more broadly still, e.g., to the family as a whole, etc. This would take the form of allegations that such and such things are right or wrong, proper or improper, in rather general terms; b) alter's expectations –in value-orientation terms for *ego's* behavior in his role, e.g. differentiated from alter's by age and possibly by sex and perhaps otherwise; and c) the complementary expectations for the definition of alter's role.

There is still a fourth element involved in the possible differentiation from the roles of either ego or alter of third parties, e.g., the father if alter is the mother, and finally a fifth in that ego's role is not static but expected to change in the process of his 'growing up' – so that a valuation relative to his own future is very much part of his value-acquisition. The complex problems involved in these differentiations will be briefly touched upon in the subsequent discussion but their analysis can at best only be begun.

Of course many features of the actual process of socialization of the child are obscure, especially the factors responsible for differences in outcome, and for pathologies. However, using the above conceptual scheme it will be worthwhile to attempt a brief sketch of some of the highlights which at least can provide the points of departure for some hypotheses, if not the codification of established knowledge. It should be remembered that our concern here is with the acquisition of value-orientation patterns, and factors which may be responsible for the internalization of different types of value-orientation pattern. Hence our primary focus will be on mechanisms of value-acquisition through identifications.

There are throughout two terms to the analysis, namely the role of the socializing agent and of the socializee. In the latter case there are three primary classical attributes of the infant, his *plasticity*, which is simply a name for his capacity to learn alternative patterns, his *sensitivity*, which may be interpreted to be a name for his capacity to form attachments in the above sense, and his *dependency*. The last is, given the first two, the primary 'fulcrum' for applying the leverage of socialization. The infant, as an organism, is helpless and dependent on others for the most elementary gratifications of food, warmth and other elements of protection.

The socializing agent is, therefore, inherently in a position to begin the process of socialization by being the agent of rewards and, implicitly at first, then explicitly, of punishments. The beginning orientation of the infant very soon must include awareness of the role of the adult in this most elementary sense. It is, then, the securing of the leverage of the infant's motivation to secure the specific rewards of being fed, kept warm, etc. and avoid the corresponding deprivations which constitute the first beginning of his *playing a role* as distinguished from being merely an object of care. Certain elements of this care come to be expected to be contingent on conformity with alter's expectations, starting with respect to such responses as crying, smiling, or coming to get something (after learning to walk).

13 Childhood

Emile Durkheim

Childhood, in the strict etymological sense, is the age when the man to be cannot yet speak (from the Latin *in-fans*, not speaking). But common practice has increasingly been inclined to extend the period to which this word is applied; it should, says Littré, extend 'from birth to approximately the age of seven'; but he adds that in popular usage it extends 'a little further than that, to the age of thirteen or fourteen'. *The Dictionnaire de l'Académie* has 'to the age of twelve or thereabouts'.

From the point of view which concerns us, it is useful to make a clear distinction between these two interpretations, for they correspond to two quite different periods of education. On the one hand, 'early childhood', including only the first three or four years, to which, in recent times, 'child psychology' or the study of the early phenomena of the small child's physical, intellectual, and moral life has turned its attention; and on the other hand, the 'second period of childhood' or childhood in the more usual and general sense of the word, which interpretation leaves aside the very special questions of the physiology and psychology of early childhood and refers to the normal period of education and instruction.

In this article, we shall deal only with the second of these subjects, in other words, we shall just discuss childhood in the usual sense of the word.

First, we have to ask ourselves what the characteristics of childhood and the natural laws of that period of life are, and consequently, the quite general conditions that the science of education must satisfy.

All the distinctive features of childhood, and in particular those which education must take account of, derive from the definition of childhood itself. The essential function of this age, the role and pur-

Source: *Durkheim: Essays on Morals and Education*, ed. W.F.F. Pickering, Routledge (1979).

pose assigned to it by nature, may be summed up in a single word: it is the period of *growth*, that is to say, the period in which the individual, in both the physical and moral sense, does not yet exist, the period in which he is made, develops and is formed. What is needed then for growth to take place? What does this phenomenon necessarily suppose in the person where it occurs? two conditions are assumed, which are always the same in all domains and in the most diverse forms: on the one hand weakness and on the other, mobility. These are, one might say, two aspects of the same situation: the person who grows finds himself in a sort of unstable and constantly changing equilibrium; he grows because he is incomplete, because he is weak, because there is still something he lacks. And he grows because deep in his nature there is a force for change, for transformation or rather formation and rapid assimilation which permits him to undergo constant modification until he attains full development.

In everything the child is characterized by the very instability of his nature, which is the law of growth. The educationalist is presented not with a person wholly formed – not a complete work or a finished product – but with a *becoming*, an incipient being, a person in the process of formation. Everything in child psychology and in educational theory derives from the essential characteristic of this age, which is sometimes manifest in the negative form – as the weakness and imperfection of the young person – and at other times in the positive form as strength and need for movement.

What is the child from the physical point of view? He is the puniest of beings, a small body that the merest blow can break, that the slightest illness imperils, a collection of muscles, nerves and organs which are, so to speak, made of milk and which only form, develop and increase in strength by their being placed in a wonderful environment of careful attention, of consideration, of favourable circumstances and protective influences. Physical childhood is essentially weakness itself from birth to well beyond the age of twelve mentioned by the *Dictionnaire de l'Académie*. The child cannot fend for itself and begins and continues to grow only through the ceaseless intervention of the parents or their substitutes. Yet on the other hand, what rapidity of growth, what marvels there are in the development of this weak little body which unfolds its limbs, takes shape, hardens and grows though no man can say how, which changes before one's very eyes and is constantly in process of renewal! There is in all of this a power of movement, of growth and development whose ceaseless progress, intensity and inexhaustible exuberance baffle the imagination.

And if we turn to the mental aspect, the same two characteristics are apparent. Whichever stage in the period of childhood is chosen for consideration, one is always confronted with an intelligence which is at one and the same time so weak and fragile, so newly-formed and delicately constituted, endowed with such limited faculties and acting, as it were, in such a miraculous way, that one cannot help trembling with fear, when one gives the matter thought, for the safety of this delightful but fragile mechanism. And at the same time, the mechanism is never still; from one day to the next it generates, so to speak, new parts; it never stops. Do not ask it to come to rest; rather than remain idle it runs to no purpose at all; it is capable of everything except rest and inertia. It is fickle, changeable, capricious, full of disappointments and pleasant surprises.

Lastly, the moral aspect evinces the same weakness and mobility. The child's expressions of will are the faintest of impressions and are scarcely traces. As a rule, neither good nor evil is very deep-rooted in his nature; he is incapable of great and sustained effort; good resolutions are no sooner made than forgotten. But, at the same time, what eagerness greets every novelty! This diminutive *conscience* is a veritable kaleidoscope. The most varied mental states, the most contradictory passions and attitudes follow one another in succession; laughter gives way to tears, playful submissiveness to stubborn resistance, outbursts of tenderness to explosions of anger. These passions and enthusiasms wane just as quickly as they are aroused. Nothing is ever definitive. Everything is continually made and unmade.

It is the duty of the educationalist to bear in mind this dual character of the child whom he undertakes to train in every aspect of that process. Whether it is the senses, the intelligence or the will which is concerned, he knows that the most fragile of organisms has been placed in his hands, an organism which is scarcely formed and which is so tender and soft that he must always beware of exhausting its strength and of interfering with its growth by wishing to hasten it. And, as it is important throughout this period to discover what the precise needs are that correspond to it, what powers lie at the child's disposal, and the exact level and true extent of his faculties, the first law of teaching is to adapt the education the child receives as closely as possible to the level of his capabilities. In the most rigorously ideal conditions, the tutor should ask himself, as he embarks on each exercise, each moral or intellectual lesson: has my pupil really reached this stage? might I not be over or under-estimating his present capabilities? Without taking this concern too far, one may say that nothing is of more benefit to the tutor than frequently to call to mind the weakness of childhood, the allowances he should make for it and the progress which, taking everything into consideration, the very child who seems to be making the least progress, has already achieved, though this may not be apparent. So much for the first of the two points of view we have distinguished.

The second is no less important, though the attitude it implies is somewhat more complex and tricky.

On the one hand, it is plainly evident that one must take into account the child's acutely felt need for movement which, to varying degrees, subsists until adolescence. Any attempt at brutal repression of this tendency would incur the risk of extinguishing the flame which must be kindled. It would choke the keen and joyous impulses of a young life, of a strength which is as yet ill-balanced though powerful, in its weakness, by virtue of its very mobility. One must, for the sake of the child, beware of the fatigue which nullifies all efforts, its own as well as its tutor's. And fatigue does not occur only when too much is demanded of the child's faculties, but also when their free development is inhibited. This is not all, for one can get the child to work harder and apply himself more by learning how to yield to this highly imperious natural need of his, by making frequent changes of subject, by ending the lesson at the precise moment attention wanes and by allowing the pupil some degree of initiative, freedom and movement. He should set about his work with the same wholeheartedness he puts into play, with all his being, with that plenitude of activity, that passion and vigour which never tire him so long as they are expended freely, spontaneously and naturally. One can only hope to obtain this result from the sort of educational system which makes special allowances for all the child's pleasures, such as varied activity, free movement and unhindered development.

But on the other hand, one should not lose sight of the fact that this lack of continuity and equilibrium is a state which cannot last: it has to be outgrown. The child must learn to regulate and co-ordinate his actions; he must not remain the victim of circumstances, dependent on the sudden shifts of his mood and the incidents of life outside him; let him learn to control himself, to contain and master himself and formulate his own principles; let him acquire the taste for discipline and order in his conduct.... Self-control, the power to contain, regulate and overcome oneself is one of the essential characteristics of the individual. In this respect a veritable metamorphosis is required. The state that has to be created appears to be at the opposite pole from the one which we set out with.

Happily, nature is of such richness that it provides us with the very instruments of action this transformation requires; we need only learn to apply them. We obtain the remedy from the same source as the trouble.

Whilst the child is a sort of anarchist, ignorant of all rules, restraints and consequences, he is also a little traditionalist, even a stick-in-the-mud. If he is made to repeat a movement several times over, he will repeat it *ad infinitum*. The stories he knows best and which he has heard the most often are those he clamours for most enthusiastically; he does not tire of hearing them again. He refuses to eat with a different knife and fork from those he is accustomed to and to sleep in any other bed than his own. He would sooner go without food or sleep. Though, in some ways, he seems enamoured of novelties and changes, he would also appear to have a true horror of all change and novelty. These two sentiments, however contradictory, are each effects of one and the same cause: his instability. It is precisely because he never ceases changing that every state, movement or idea which happens to be repeated a certain number of times assumes, by virtue of this repetition, a power – a force of action which cannot be resisted because it has nothing to counterbalance it. Other states have no hold over him, just because they are fleeting and superficial. Hence any state which succeeds in acquiring some fixity, however tenuous it may be, tends of itself to be repeated, and becomes a need which can easily be tyrannical unless care is taken. *For this reason, it is very easy to make the child acquire habits.*

The power which habit has over him as a result of the instability of his psychic life allows such instability to be corrected and contained. The taste for regular habits is already an early form of the taste for order and continuity. It is like an initiation into moral life and can begin very early; for almost as soon as he is born it is advisable to make him acquire set habits in all that concerns the principal circumstances of his existence. If this first seed is nurtured with prudence and wisdom, the child's life will gradually and progressively cease to present the contradictory spectacle of extreme mobility which alternates with an almost manic routine. Its fleeting and mobile aspects will become fixed; it will become regularized and thoroughly ordered. Admittedly, this somewhat mechanical order does not in itself possess any great moral value, but it paves the way for a superior quality of order. The taste for regularity is not yet respect for rule and duty, but it is on the way to becoming so. And, moreover, . . . it is possible and relatively easy to impart to the child the sentiment of moral authority and discipline, which constitutes the second stage in the formation of character and will. So nature does in fact place in our hands the means necessary for transcending it.

14 The rise of the child-saving movement

Anthony Platt

Studies of crime and delinquency have, for the most part, focused on their psychological and environmental origins. Correctional research has traditionally encompassed the relationship between prisoners and prison-management, the operation of penal programs, the implementation of the 'rehabilitative ideal' and, in recent years, the effectiveness of community-based corrections. On the other hand, we know very little about the social processes by which certain types of behaviour come to be defined as 'criminal' or about the origins of penal reforms. If we intend rationally to assess the nature and purposes of correctional policies, it is of considerable importance to understand how laws and legislation are passed, how changes in penal practices are implemented, and what interests are served by such reforms.

This paper analyzes the nature and origins of the reform movement in juvenile justice and juvenile corrections at the end of the nineteenth century. Delinquency raises fundamental questions about the objects of social control, and it was through the child-saving movement that the modern system of delinquency-control emerged in the United States. The child-savers were responsible for creating a new legal institution for penalizing children (juvenile court) and a new correctional institution to accommodate the needs of youth (reformatory). The origins of 'delinquency' are to be found in the programs and ideas of these reformers, who recognized the existence and carriers of delinquent norms.

Images of delinquency

The child-saving movement, like most moral crusades, was characterized by a 'rhetoric of legitimization', built on traditional values

Source: *Annals of the American Academy*, January 1969, 381, 21-38.

and imagery. From the medical profession, the child-savers borrowed the imagery of pathology, infection, and treatment; from the tenets of Social Darwinism, they derived their pessimistic views about the intractability of human nature and the innate moral defects of the working class; finally, their ideas about the biological and environmental origins of crime may be attributed to the positivist tradition in European criminology and to anti-urban sentiments associated with the rural Protestant ethic.

American criminology in the last century was essentially a practical affair. Theoretical concepts of crime were imported from Europe, and an indiscriminating eclecticism dominated the literature. Lombrosian positivism and Social Darwinism were the major sources of intellectual justification for crime workers. The pessimism of Darwinism, however, was counter-balanced by notions of charity, religious optimism, and the dignity of suffering which were implicit components of the Protestant ethic.

Before 1870 there were only a few American textbooks on crime, and the various penal organizations lacked specialized journals. Departments of law and sociology in the universities were rarely concerned with more than the description and classification of crimes. The first American writers on crime were physicians, like Benjamin Rush and Isaac Ray, who were trained according to European methods. The social sciences were similarly imported from Europe, and American criminologists fitted their data to the theoretical framework of criminal anthropology. Herbert Spencer's writings had an enormous impact on American intellectuals, and Cesare Lombroso, perhaps the most significant figure in nineteenth-century criminology, looked for recognition in the United States when he felt that his experiments had been neglected in Europe.

Although Lombroso's theoretical and experimental studies were not translated into English until 1911, his findings were known by American academies in the early 1890's, and their popularity, like that of Spencer's works, was based on the fact that they confirmed popular assumptions about the character and existence of a 'criminal class'. Lombroso's original theory suggested the existence of a criminal type distinguishable from noncriminals by observable physical anomalies of a degenerative or atavistic nature. He proposed that the criminal was a morally inferior human species, characterized by physical traits reminiscent of apes, lower primates, and savage tribes. The criminal was thought to be morally retarded and, like a small child, instinctively aggressive and precocious unless restrained. It is not difficult to see the connection between biological determinism in criminological literature and the principles of 'natural selection'; both of these theoretical positions automatically justified the 'eradication of elements that constituted a permanent and serious danger'.

Nature versus nature

Before 1900, American writers were familiar with Lombroso's general propositions but had only the briefest knowledge of his research techniques. Although the emerging doctrines of preventive criminology implied human malleability, most American penologists were pre-occupied with the intractability of the 'criminal classes'. Hamilton Wey, an influential physician at Elmira Reformatory, argued before the National Prison Association in 1881 that criminals were 'a distinct type of human species', characterized by flat-footedness, asymmetrical bodies, and 'degenerative physiognomy'.

Literature on 'social degradation' was extremely popular during the 1870's and 1880's, though most such 'studies' were little more than crude polemics, padded with moralistic epithets and preconceived value judgments. Richard Dugdale's series of papers on the Jukes family, which became a model for the case-study approach to social problems, was distorted almost beyond recognition by anti-intellectual supporters of hereditary theories of crime. Confronted by the evidence of Darwin, Galton, Dugdale, Caldwell and many other disciples of the biological image of man, correctional professionals were compelled to admit that 'a large proportion of the unfortunate children that go to make up the great army of criminals are not born right'. Reformers adopted the rhetoric of Darwinism in order to emphasize the urgent need for confronting the 'crime problem' before it got completely out of hand. A popular proposal was the 'methodized registration and training' of potential criminals, 'or these failing, their early and entire withdrawal from the community'.

The organization of correctional workers through national representatives and their identification with the professions of law and medicine operated to discredit the tenets of Darwinism and Lombrosian theory. Correctional workers did not think of themselves merely as custodians of a pariah class. The self-image of penal reformers as doctors rather than guards and the domination of criminological research in the United States by physicians helped to encourage the acceptance of 'therapeutic' strategies in prisons and reformatories. As Arthur Fink has observed:

The role of the physician in this ferment is unmistakable. Indeed, he was the dynamic agent.... Not only did he preserve and add to existing knowledge - for his field touched all borders of science - but he helped to maintain and extend the methodology of science.

Perhaps what is more significant is that physicians furnished the official rhetoric of penal reform. Admittedly, the criminal was 'pathological' and 'diseased', but medical science offered the possibility of miraculous cures. Although there was a popular belief in the existence of a 'criminal class' separated from the rest of mankind by a 'vague boundary line', there was no good reason why this class could not be identified, diagnosed, segregated, changed, and controlled.

By the late 1890's, most correctional administrators agreed that hereditary theories of crime were over-fatalistic. The superintendent of the Kentucky Industrial School of Reform told delegates to a national conference on corrections that heredity is 'unjustifiably made a bugaboo to discourage efforts at rescue. We know that physical hereditary tendencies can be neutralized and often nullified by proper counteracting precautions'. E R L Gould, a sociologist at the University of Chicago, similarly criticized biological theories of crime for being unconvincing and sentimental. 'Is it not better', he said, 'to postulate freedom of choice than to preach the doctrine of the unfettered will, and so elevate criminality into a propitiary sacrifice?'

Charles Cooley was one of the first sociologists to observe that criminal behaviour depended as much upon social and economic circumstances as it did upon the inheritance of biological traits. 'The criminal class,' he said, 'is largely the result of society's bad workmanship upon fairly good material'. In support of this argument, he noted that there was a 'large and fairly trustworthy body of evidence' to suggest that many 'degenerates' could be converted into 'useful citizens by rational treatment'.

Urban disenchantment
Another important influence on nineteenth-century criminology was a disenchantment with urban life – an attitude which is still prevalent in much 'social problems' research. Immigrants were regarded as 'unsocialized', and the city's impersonality compounded their isolation and degradation. 'By some cruel alchemy,' wrote Julia Lathrop, 'we take the sturdiest of European peasantry and at once destroy in a large measure its power to rear to decent livelihood the first generation of offspring upon our soil.' The city symbolically embodied all the worst features of industrial life. A member of the Massachusetts Board of Charities observed:

Children acquire a perverted taste for city life and crowded streets; but if introduced when young to country life, care of animals and plants, and rural pleasures, they are likely to be healthier in mind and body for such associations.

Programs which promoted rural and primary group concepts were encouraged because slum life was regarded as unregulated, vicious, and lacking social rules. Its inhabitants were depicted as abnormal and maladjusted, living their lives in chaos and conflict. It was consequently the task of social reformers to make city life more wholesome, honest and free from depravity. Beverley Warner told the National Prison Association in 1898 that philanthropic organizations all over the country were

making efforts to get the children out of the slums, even if only once a week, into the radiance of better lives.... It is only by leading the child out of sin and debauchery, in which it has lived, into the circle of life that is a repudiation of things that it sees in its daily life, that it can be influenced.

Although there was a wide difference of opinion among experts as to the precipitating causes of crime, it was generally agreed that criminals were abnormally conditioned by a multitude of biological and environmental forces, some of which were permanent and irreversible. Biological theories of crime were modified to incorporate a developmental view of human behavior. If, as it was believed, criminals are conditioned by biological heritage and brutish living conditions, the prophylactic measures must be taken early in life. Criminals of the future generations must be reached. 'They are born to crime,' wrote the penologist Enoch Wines in 1880, 'brought up for it. They must be saved.'

Maternal justice

The 1880's and 1890's represented for many middle-class intellectuals and professionals a period of discovery of the 'dim attics and damp cellars in poverty-stricken sections of populous towns' and of 'innumerable haunts of misery throughout the land'. The city was suddenly discovered to be a place of scarcity, disease, neglect, ignorance, and 'dangerous influences'. Its slums were the 'last resorts of the penniless and the criminal'; here humanity reached its lowest level of degradation and despair.

The discovery of problems posed by 'delinquent' youth was greatly influenced by the role of feminist reformers in the child-saving movement. It was widely agreed that it was a woman's business to be involved in regulating the welfare of children, for women were considered the 'natural caretakers' of wayward children. Women's claim to the public care of children had some historical justification during the nineteenth century, and their role in child-rearing was considered paramount. Women were regarded as better teachers than men and were also more influential in child-training at home. The fact that public education also came more under the direction of women teachers in the schools increased the predominance of women in the raising of children.

Child-saving was a predominantly feminist movement, and it was regarded even by antifeminists as female domain. The social circumstances behind this appreciation of maternalism were women's emancipation and the accompanying changes in the character of traditional family life. Educated middle-class women now had more leisure time but a limited choice of careers. Child-saving was a reputable task for women who were allowed to extend their housekeeping functions into the community without denying antifeminist stereotypes of woman's nature and place. 'It is an added irony,' writes Christopher Lasch in his study of American intellectualism,

that the ideas about women's nature to which some feminists still clung, in spite of their opposition to the enslavement of woman in the home, were these very deep clichés which had so long been used to keep her there. The assumption that women were morally purer than men, better capable of altruism and self-sacrifice, was the core of the myth of domesticity against which the feminists were in revolt.... (F)eminist and antifeminist assumptions seemed curiously to coincide.

Child-saving may be understood as a crusade which served symbolic and status functions for native, middle-class Americans, particularly feminist groups. Middle-class women at the turn of the century experienced a complex and far-reaching status revolution. Their traditional functions were dramatically threatened by the weakening of domestic roles and the specialized rearrangement of famly life. One of the main forces behind the child-saving movement was a concern for the structure of family life and the proper socialization of young persons, since it was these concerns that had traditionally given purpose to a woman's life. Professional organizations - such as settlement houses, women's clubs, bar associations and penal organizations - regarded child-saving as a problem of women's rights, whereas their opponents seized upon it as an opportunity to keep women in their proper place. Child-saving organizations had little or nothing to do with militant supporters of the suffragette movement. In fact, the new role of social worker was created by deference to antifeminist stereotypes of a 'woman's place'.

A woman's place

Feminist involvement in child-saving was endorsed by a variety of penal and professional organizations. Their participation was usually justified as an extension of their housekeeping functions so that they did not view themselves, nor were they regarded by others, as competitors for jobs usually performed by men. Proponents of the 'new penology' insisted that reformatories should resemble home life, for institutions without women were likely to do more harm than good to inmates. According to G E Howe, the reformatory system provided 'the most ample opportunities for woman's transcendent influence'.

Female delegates to philanthropic and correctional conferences also realized that correctional work suggested the possibility of useful careers. Mrs W P Lynde told the National Conference of Charities and Correction in 1879 that children's institutions offered the 'truest and noblest scope for the public activities of women in the time which they can spare from their primary domestic duties'. Women were exhorted by other delegates to make their lives meaningful by participating in welfare programs, volunteering their time and services, and getting acquainted with less privileged groups. They were told to seek jobs in institutions where 'the woman-element shall pervade . . . and soften its social atmosphere with motherly tenderness'.

Although the child-savers were responsible for some minor reforms in jails and reformatories, they were more particularly concerned with extending governmental control over a whole range of youthful activities that had previously been handled on an informal basis. The main aim of the child-savers was to impose sanctions on conduct unbecoming youth and to disqualify youth from enjoying adult privileges. As Bennett Berger has commented, 'adolescents are not made by nature but by being excluded from responsible participation in adult affairs, by being rewarded for dependency, and penalized for precocity'.

The child-saving movement was not so much a break with the past as an affirmation of faith in traditional institutions. Parental authority, education at home, and the virtues of rural life were emphasized because they were in decline at this time. The child-saving movement was, in part, a crusade which, through emphasizing the dependence of the social order on the proper socialization of children, implicitly elevated the nuclear family and, more especially, the role of women as stalwarts of the family. The child-savers were prohibitionists, in a general sense, who believed that social progress depended on efficient law enforcement, strict supervision of children's leisure and recreation, and the regulation of illicit pleasures. What seemingly began as a movement to humanize the lives of adolescents soon developed into a program of moral absolutism through which youth was to be saved from movies, pornography, cigarettes, alcohol, and anything else which might possibly rob them of their innocence.

Although child-saving had important symbolic functions for preserving the social prestige of a declining elite, it also had considerable practical significance for legitimizing new career openings for women. The new role of social worker combined elements of an old and partly fictitious role – defenders of family life – and elements of a new role – social servant. Social work was thus both an affirmation of cherished American values and an instrumentality for women's emancipation.

Juvenile court

The essential preoccupation of the child-saving movement was the recognition and control of youthful deviance. It brought attention to, and thus 'invented', new categories of youthful misbehaviour which had been hitherto unappreciated. The efforts of the child-savers were institutionally expressed in the juvenile court, which, despite recent legislative and constitutional reforms, is generally acknowledged as their most significant contribution to progressive penology.

The juvenile-court system was part of a general movement directed towards removing adolescents from the criminal-law process and creating special programs for delinquent, dependent, and neglected children. Regarded widely as 'one of the greatest advances in child welfare that has ever occurred', the juvenile court was considered 'an integral part of total welfare planning'. Charles Chute, an enthusiastic supporter of the child-saving movement, claimed:

No single event has contributed more to the welfare of children and their families. It revolutionized the treatment of delinquent and neglected children and led to the passage of similar laws throughout the world.

The juvenile court was a special tribunal created by statute to determine the legal status of children and adolescents. Underlying the juvenile-court movement was the concept of *parens patriae* by which the courts were authorized to handle with wide discretion the problems of 'its least fortunate junior citizens'. The administration of juvenile justice differed in many important respects from the criminal-court processes. A child was not accused of a crime but offered assistance and guidance; intervention in his life was not supposed to carry the stigma of criminal guilt. Judicial records were not generally available to the press or public, and juvenile-court hearings were conducted in relative privacy. Juvenile-court procedures were typically informal and inquisitorial. Specific criminal safeguards of due process were not applicable because juvenile proceedings were defined by statute as civil in character.

The original statutes enabled the courts to investigate a wide variety of youthful needs and misbehavior. As Joel Handler has observed, 'the critical philosophical position of the reform movement was that no formal, legal distinctions should be made between the delinquent and the dependent or neglected'. Statutory definitions of

'delinquency' encompassed (1) acts that would be criminal if committed by adults; (2) acts that violated county, town, or municipal
ordinances; and (3) violations or vaguely defined catch-alls – such as
'vicious or immoral behavior', 'incorrigibility' and 'truancy' – which
'seem to express the notion that the adolescent, if allowed to
continue, will engage in more serious conduct'.

The juvenile-court movement went far beyond a concern for
special treatment of adolescent offenders. It brought within the
ambit of governmental control a set of youthful activities that had
been previously ignored or dealt with on an informal basis. It was not
by accident that the behaviour selected for penalizing by the child-
savers – sexual licence, drinking, roaming the streets, begging,
frequenting dance halls and movies, fighting, and being seen in
public late at night – was most directly relevant to the children of
lower-class migrant and immigrant families.

The juvenile court was not perceived by its supporters as a revolutionary experiment, but rather as a culmination of traditionally
valued practices. The child-saving movement was 'antilegal', in the
sense that it derogated civil rights and procedural formalities, while
relying heavily on extra-legal techniques. The judges of the new
court were empowered to investigate the character and social life of
the predelinquent as well as delinquent children; they examined
motivation rather than intent, seeking to identify the moral reputa-
tion of problematic children. The requirements of preventive
penology and child-saving further justified the court's intervention in
cases where no offense had actually been committed, but where, for
example, a child was posing problems for some person in authority
such as a parent or teacher or social worker.

The personal touch

Judges were expected to show the same professional competence as
doctors and therapists. The sociologist Charles Henderson wrote:

A careful study of individuals is an essential element in wise procedure. The study
must include the physical, mental and moral peculiarities and defects of the children
who come under the notice of the courts. Indeed we are likely to follow the lead of
those cities which provide for a careful examintion of all school children whose
physical or psychical condition is in any way or degree abnormal, in order to prevent
disease, correct deformity and vice, and select the proper course of study and
discipline demanded by the individual need.

Juvenile court judges had to be carefully selected for their skills as
expert diagnosticians and for their appreciation of the 'helping'
professions. Miriam Van Waters, for example, regarded the juvenile
court as a 'laboratory of human behaviour' and its judges as 'experts
with scientific training' and specialists in 'the art of human relations'.

It was the judge's task to 'get the whole truth about a child' in the same way that a 'physician searches for every detail that bears on the condition of a patient'.

The child-savers' interest in preventive strategies and treatment programs was based on the premise that delinquents possess innate or acquired characteristics which predispose them to crime and distinguish them from law-abiding youths. Delinquents were regarded as constrained by a variety of biological and environmental forces, so that their proper treatment involved discovery of the 'cause of the aberration' and application of 'the appropriate corrective or antidote'. 'What the trouble is with the offender,' noted William Healy, 'making him what he is, socially undesirable, can only be known by getting at his mental life, as it is an affair of reactive mechanisms.'

The use of terms like 'unsocialized', 'maladjusted' and 'pathological' to describe the behaviour of delinquents implied that 'socialized' and 'adjusted' children conform to middle-class morality and participate in respectable institutions. The failure empirically to demonstrate psychological differences between delinquents and non-delinquents did not discourage the child-savers from believing that rural and middle-class values constitute 'normality'. The unique character of the child-saving movement was its concern for predelinquent offenders – children who occupy the debatable ground between criminality and innocence – and its claim that it could transform potential criminals into respectable citizens by training them in 'habits of industry, self-control and obedience to law'. This policy justified the diminishing of traditional procedures in juvenile court. If children were to be rescued, it was important that the rescuers be free to provide their services without legal hindrance. Delinquents had to be saved, transformed and reconstituted. 'There is no essential difference', said Frederick Wines, 'between a criminal and any other sinner. The means and methods of restoration are the same for both.'

The reformatory system

It was through the reformatory system that the child-savers hoped to demonstrate that delinquents were capable of being converted into law-abiding citizens. The reformatory was initially developed in the United States during the middle of the nineteenth century as a special form of prison discipline for adolescents and young adults. Its underlying principles were formulated by Matthew Davenport Hill, Alexander Maconchie, Walter Crofton and Mary Carpenter. If the United States did not have any great penal theorists, it at least had energetic penal administrators who were prepared to experiment with new programs. The most notable advocates of the reformatory plan in the United States were Enoch Wines, Secretary of the New York Prison Association; Theodore Dwight, the first Dean of Columbia Law School; Zebulon Brockway, Superintendent of Elmira Reformatory in New York; and Frank Sanborn, Secretary of the Massachusetts State Board of Charities.

The reformatory was distinguished from the traditional penitentiary by its policy of indeterminate sentencing, the 'mark' system, and 'organized persuasion' rather than 'coercive restraint'. Its administrators assumed that abnormal and troublesome individuals could become useful and productive citizens. Wines and Dwight, in a report to the New York legislature in 1867, proposed that the ultimate aim of penal policy was reformation of the criminal, which could only be achieved by placing the prisoner's fate, as far as possible, in his own hand, by enabling him, through industry and good conduct to raise himself, step by step, to a position of less restraint; while idleness and bad conduct, on the other hand, keep him in a state of coercion and restraint. But, as Brockway observed at the first meeting of the National Prison Congress in 1870, the 'new penology' was toughminded and devoid of 'sickly sentimentalism. . . . Criminals shall either be cured, or kept under such continued restraint as gives guarantee of safety from further depredations'.

Reformatories, unlike penitentiaries and jails, theoretically repudiated punishments based on intimidation and repression. They took into account the fact that delinquents were 'either physically or mentally below the average'. The reformatory system was based on the assumption that proper training can counteract the impositions of poor family life, a corrupt environment, and poverty, while at the same time toughening and preparing delinquents for the struggle ahead. 'The principle at the root of the educational method of dealing with juvenile crime', wrote William Douglas Morrison, 'is an absolutely sound one. It is a principle which recognizes the fact that the juvenile delinquent is in the main, a product of adverse individual and social conditions.'

The reformatory movement spread rapidly through the United States, and European visitors crossed the Atlantic to inspect and admire the achievements of their pragmatic colleagues. Mary Carpenter, who visited the United States in 1873, was generally satisfied with the 'generous and lavish expenditures freely incurred to promote the welfare of the inmates, and with the love of religion'. Most correctional problems with regard to juvenile delinquents, she advised, could be remedied if reformatories were built like farm schools or 'true homes'. At the Massachusetts Reform School, in

Westborough, she found an 'entire want of family spirit', and, in
New York, she complained that there was no 'natural life' in the
reformatory. 'All the arrangements are artificial', she said; 'instead
of the cultivation of the land, which would prepare the youth to seek
a sphere far from the dangers of large cities, the boys and young men
were being taught trades which will confine them to the great
centers of an over-crowded population.' She found similar conditions
in Philadelphia where 'hundreds of youth were there congregated
under lock and key', but praised the Connecticut Reform School for
its 'admirable system of agricultural training'. If she had visited the
Illinois State Reformatory at Pontiac, she would have found a
seriously overcrowded 'minor penitentiary' where the inmates were
forced to work ten hours a day manufacturing shoes, brushes, and
chairs.

To cottage and country
Granted the assumption that 'nurture' could usually overcome most
of nature's defects, reformatory-administrators set about the task of
establishing programs consistent with the aim of retraining delinquents for law-abiding careers. It was noted at the Fifth International Prison Congress, held in Paris in 1895, that reformatories
were capable of obliterating hereditary and environmental taints. In
a new and special section devoted to delinquency, the Congress
proposed that children under twelve years:

should always be sent to institutions of preservation and unworthy parents must be
deprived of the right to children.... The preponderant place in rational physical
training should be given to manual labor, and particularly to agricultural labor in the
open air, for both sexes.

The heritage of biological imagery and Social Darwinism had a
lasting influence on American criminology, and penal reformers
continued to regard delinquency as a problem of individual adjustment to the demands of industrial and urban life. Delinquents had to
be removed from contaminating situations, segregated from their
'miserable surroundings' instructed and 'put as far as possible on a
footing of equality with the rest of the population'.
The trend from congregate housing in the city to group living in
the country represented a significant change in the organization of
penal institutions for young offenders. The family or cottage plan
differed in several important respects from the congregate style of
traditional prisons and jails. According to William Letchworth, in
an address delivered before the National Conference of Charities and
Correction in 1886:

A fault in some of our reform schools is their great size. In the congregating of large numbers, individuality is lost.... These excessive aggregations are overcome to a great extent in the cottage plan.... The internal system of the reformatory school should be as nearly as practicable as that of the family, with its refining and elevating influences; while the awakening of the conscience and the inculcation of religious principles should be primary aims.

The new penology emphasized the corruptness and artificiality of the city; from progressive education, it inherited a concern for naturalism, purity, and innocence. It is not surprising, therefore, that the cottage plan also entailed a movement to a rural location. The aim of penal reformers was not merely to use the countryside for teaching agricultural skills. The confrontation between corrupt delinquents and unspoiled nature was intended to have a spiritual and regenerative effect. The romantic attachment to rural values was quite divorced from social and agricultural realities. It was based on a sentimental and nostalgic repudiation of city life. Advocates of the reformatory system generally ignored the economic attractiveness of city work and the redundancy of farming skills. As one economist cautioned reformers in 1902:

Whatever may be said about the advantages of farm life for the youths of our land, and however much it may be regretted that young men and women are leaving the farm and flocking to the cities, there can be no doubt that the movement city-ward will continue ... There is great danger that many who had left home (that is reformatory), unable to find employment in agricultural callings, would drift back to the city and not finding there an opportunity to make use of the technical training secured in the institution, would become discouraged and resume their old criminal associations and calling.

The 'new' reformatory suffered, like all its predecessors, from overcrowding, mismanagement, 'boodleism', under-staffing, and inadequate facilities. Its distinctive features were the indeterminate sentence, the movement to cottage and country, and agricultural training. Although there was a decline in the use of brutal punishments, inmates were subjected to severe personal and physical controls: military exercise, 'training of the will', and long hours of tedious labour constituted the main program of reform.

Summary and conclusions

The child-saving movement was responsible for reforms in the ideological and institutional control of 'delinquent' youth. The concept of the born delinquent was modified with the rise of a professional class of penal administrators and social servants who promoted a developmental view of human behavior and regarded most delinquent youth as salvageable. The child-savers helped to create special judicial and correctional institutions for the processing and management of 'troublesome' youth.

There has been a shift during the last fifty years or so in official policies concerning delinquency. The emphasis has shifted from one emphasizing the criminal nature of delinquency to the 'new humanism' which speaks of disease, illness, contagion, and the like. It is essentially a shift from a legal to a medical emphasis. The emergence of a medical emphasis is of considerable significance, since it is a powerful rationale for organizing social action in the most diverse behavioral aspects of our society. For example, the child-savers were not concerned merely with 'humanizing' conditions under which children were treated by the criminal law. It was rather their aim to extend the scope of governmental control over a wide variety of personal misdeeds and to regulate potentially disruptive persons. The child-savers reforms were politically aimed at lower-class behavior and were instrumental in intimidating and controlling the poor.

The child-savers made a fact out of the norm of adolescent dependence. 'Every child is dependent,' wrote the Illinois Board of Charities in 1899, 'even the children of the wealthy. To receive his support at the hands of another does not strike him as unnatural, but quite the reverse.' The juvenile court reached into the private lives of youth and disguised basically punitive policies in the rhetoric of 'rehabilitation'. The child-savers were prohibitionists, in a general sense, who believed that adolescents needed protection from even their own inclinations.

The basic conservatism of the child-saving movement is apparent in the reformatory system which proved to be as tough-minded as traditional forms of punishment. Reformatory programs were unilateral, coercive, and an invasion of human dignity. What most appealed to correctional workers were the paternalistic assumptions of the 'new penology', its belief in social progress through individual reform, and its nostalgic preoccupation with the 'naturalness' and intimacy of a preindustrial way to life.

The child-saving movement was heavily influenced by middle-class women who extended their house-wifely roles into public service. Their contribution may also be seen as a 'symbolic crusade' in defense of the nuclear family and their positions within it. They regarded themselves as moral custodians and supported programs and institutions dedicated to eliminating youthful immorality. Social service was an instrumentality for female emancipation, and it is not too unreasonable to suggest that women advanced their own fortune at the expense of the dependency of youth.

This analysis of the child-saving movement suggests the importance of (1) understanding the relationship between correctional reforms and related changes in the administration of criminal justice, (2) accounting for the motives and purposes of those enterprising groups who generate such reforms, (3) investigating the methods by which communities establish the formal machinery for regulating crime, and (4) distinguishing between idealized goals and enforced conditions in the implementation of correctional reforms.

Implications for corrections and research

The child-saving movement illustrates a number of important problems with the quality and purposes of correctional research and knowledge. The following discussion will draw largely upon the child-saving movement in order to examine its relevance for contemporary issues.

Positivism and progressivism

It is widely implied in the literature that the juvenile court and parallel reforms in penology represented a progressive effort by concerned reformers to alleviate the miseries of urban life and to solve social problems by rational, enlightened, and scientific methods. With few exceptions, studies of delinquency have been parochial and inadequately descriptive, and they show little appreciation of underlying political and cultural conditions. Historical studies, particularly of the juvenile court, are, for the most part, self-confirming and support an evolutionary view of human progress.

The positivist heritage in the study of social problems has directed attention to (1) the primacy of the criminal actor rather than the criminal law as the major point of departure in the construction of etiological theory, (2) a rigidly deterministic view of human behavior, and (3) only the abnormal features of deviant behavior. The 'rehabilitative ideal' has so dominated American criminology that there have been only sporadic efforts to undertake sociological research related to governmental invasion of personal liberties. But, as Francis Allen has sugested:

Even if one's interests lie primarily in the problems of treatment of offenders, it should be recognized that the existence of the criminal presupposes a crime and that the problems of treatment are derivative in the sense that they depend upon the determination by law-giving agencies that certain sorts of behavior are crimes.

The conservatism and 'diluted liberalism' of much research on delinquency results from the fact that researchers are generally prepared to accept prevailing definitions of crime, to work within the premises of the criminal law, and to concur at least implicitly with those who make laws as to the nature and distribution of a 'criminal' population. Thus, most theories of delinquency are based on studies of convicted or imprisoned delinquents. As John Seeley has observed in another context, professional caution requires us 'to *take* our problems rather than *make* our problems, to accept as constitutive of our "intake" what is held to be "deviant" in a way that concerns people in that society enough to give us primary protection'. Money, encouragement, co-operation from established institutions, and a market for publication are more easily acquired for studies of the socialization or treatment of delinquents than for studies of how laws, law-makers, and law-enforcers, contribute to the 'registration' delinquency.

Law and its implementation have been largely dismissed as irrelevant topics for inquiry into the 'causes' of delinquency. According to Herbert Packer, it is typical that the National Crime Commission ignored the fundamental question of: 'What is the criminal sanction good for?' Further research is needed to understand the dynamics of the legislative and popular drive to 'criminalize'. Delinquency legislation for example, as has been noted earlier, was not aimed merely at reducing crime or liberating youth. The reform movement also served important symbolic and instrumental interests for groups who made hobbies and careers out of saving children.

Policy research
Correctional research in this country has ben dominated by persons who are intimately concerned with crime and its control. The scholar-technician tradition in corrections, especially with regard to delinquency, has resulted in the proliferation of 'agency-determined' research whereby scholarship is catered to institutional interests. Much of what passes under the label of 'research' takes the form of 'methods engineering', produced in the interest of responsible officials and management. It is only rarely, as in Erving Goffman's study of 'total institutions', that sympathetic consideration is given to the perceptions and concerns of subordinates in the correctional hierarchy.

There are many historical and practical reasons why corrections has been such a narrow and specialized field of academic interest. First, corrections has been intellectually influenced by the problematic perspective of scholar-technicians, which limits the scope of 'research' to local, policy issues. In the last century especially, penology was the exclusive domain of philanthropists, muckrakers, reformers, and missionaries. Secondly, the rise of the 'multiversity' and of federal-grant research has given further respectability to applied research in corrections, to the extent that social science and public policy are inextricably linked. Nevertheless, such research is minimal when compared, for example, with that done under the auspices of the Defense Department. It is quite true, as the National Crime Commission reports, that research in corrections has been unsystematic, sporadic, and guided primarily by 'intuitive opportunism'. Thirdly, it should be remembered that correctional institutions are politically sensitive communities which resist intrusions from academic outsiders unless the proposed research is likely to serve their best interests. Research which undermines policy is generally viewed as insensitive and subversive, aside from the fact that it helps to justify and harden administrators' suspicions of 'intellectuals'. The lack of critical research is, no doubt, also due to the reluctance of scholars to address the specific problems faced by those charged with the perplexing task of controlling and rehabilitating offenders.

Politics and corrections

Correctional institutions have been generally regarded as distinct, insulated social organizations. Their relationship to the wider society is viewed in a bureaucratic, civil-service context, and their population is defined in welfare terms. Prisons and their constituency are stripped of political implications, seemingly existing in an apolitical vacuum. Corrections as an academic specialization has focused on the prison community to the neglect of classical interest in the relationship between political decision-making and social policies. As Hans Matick has observed:

There is very little appreciation ... that this 'contest between good and evil', and the whole 'drama of crime', is taking place within the larger arena of our political system and this, in part, helps to determine public opinion about the nature of crime, criminals and how they are dealt with.

As the gap between social deviance and political marginality narrows, it becomes increasingly necessary to examine how penal administrators are recruited, how 'new' programs are selected and implemented, and how local and national legislatures determine correctional budgets. The crisis caused by white racism in this country also requires us to appreciate in what sense prisons and jails may be used as instrumentalities of political control in the 'pacification' of black Americans. Similarly, it furthers our understanding of 'delinquency' if we appreciate the motives and political interests of those reformers and professionals who perceive youth as threatening and troublesome.

Faith in reform

The child-saving movement further illustrates that corrections may be understood historically as a succession of reforms. Academics have demonstrated a remarkably persistent optimism about reform, and operate on the premise that they can have a humanitarian influence on correctional administration. As Irving Louis Horowitz has observed, to the extent that social scientists become involved with policy-making agencies, they are committed to an elitist ideology:

They come to accept as basic the idea that men who really change things are at the top. Thus, the closer to the top one can get direct access, the more likely will intended changes be brought about.

There is little evidence to support this faith in the ultimate wisdom of policy- makers in corrections. The reformatory was not so much an improvement on the prison as a means of extending control over a new constituency; probation and parole became instruments of supervision rather than treatment; halfway houses have become a means of extending prisons into communities rather than democratically administered sanctuaries; group therapy in prisons has justified invasion of privacy and coercive treatment on the dubious grounds that prisoners are psychologically unfit; community-based narcotics programs, such as the nalline clinic, disguise medical authoritarianism in the guise of rehabilitation. Nevertheless, the optimism continues, and this is nowhere more apparent than in the National Crime Commission's Task Force Report on Corrections, which reveals that, in Robert Martinson's words, correctional policy consists of 'a redoubling of efforts in the face of persistent failure'.

Finally, we have neglected to study and appreciate those who work in corrections. Like the police and, to an increasing extent, teachers and social workers, correctional staffs are constrained by the ethic of bureaucratic responsibility. They are society's 'dirty workers', technicians working on people. As Lee Rainwater has observed.

The dirty-workers are increasingly caught between the silent middle class, which wants them to do the dirty work and keep quiet about it, and the objects of that dirty work, who refuse to continue to take it lying down.... These civilian colonial armies find their right to respect from their charges challenged at every turn, and often they must carry out their daily duties with fear for their physical safety.

Correctional workers are required to accommodate current definitions of criminality and to manage victims of political expediency and popular fashion – drug users, drunks, homosexuals, vagrants, delinquents and 'looters'. They have minimal influence on lawmakers and rarely more than ideological rapport with law enforcers. They have no clear mandate as to the purpose of corrections, other than to reduce recidivism and reform criminals. They have to live with the proven failure of this enterprise and to justify their role as pacifiers, guards, warehouse-keepers and restrainers. They are linked to a professional system that relegates them to the lowest status in the political hierarchy but uses them as a pawn in electoral battles. They are doomed to annual investigations, blue-ribbon commissions, ephemeral research studies, and endless volumes of propaganda and muckraking. They live with the inevitability of professional mediocrity, poor salaries, uncomfortable living conditions, ungrateful 'clients', and tenuous links with established institutions. It is understandable that they protect their fragile domain from intrusive research which is not supportive of their policies.

15 Madness is childhood

Michel Foucault

The absence of constraint in the nineteenth-century asylum is not unreason liberated, but madness long since mastered.

For this new reason which reigns in the asylum, madness does not represent the absolute form of contradiction, but instead a minority status, an aspect of itself that does not have the right to autonomy, and can live only grafted onto the world of reason. Madness is childhood. Everything at the Retreat is organized so that the insane are transformed into minors. They are regarded 'as children who have an overabundance of strength and make dangerous use of it. They must be given immediate punishments and rewards; whatever is remote has no effect on them. A new system of education must be applied, a new direction given to their ideas; they must first be subjugated, then encouraged, then applied to work, and this work made agreeable by attractive means.' For a long time already, the law had regarded the insane as minors, but this was a juridical situation, abstractly defined by interdiction and trusteeship; it was not a concrete mode of relation between man and man. Minority status became for Tuke a style of existence to be applied to the mad, and for the guards a mode of sovereignty. Great emphasis was placed on the concept of the 'family' which organized the community of the insane and their keepers at the Retreat. Apparently this 'family' placed the patient in a milieu both normal and natural; in reality it alienated him still more: the juridical minority assigned to the mad-man was intended to protect him as a subject of law; this ancient structure, by becoming a form of coexistence, delivered him entirely, as a psychological subject, to the authority and prestige of the man of reason, who assumed for him the concrete figure of an adult, in other words, both domination and destination.

Source: Michel Foucault, *Madness and Civilization*, tr. Richard Howard, Tavistock (1967).

The child at work and play

As we get older we can only license play through playing with children; in this context children are all *joie de vivre*. This adult sense of play treats the activity as essentially diverting and non-serious; in this way the margin between play and work marks out the rules of the adult and child communities. Child's play becomes a threat when it begins to encroach upon adult interests. Children, however, are not rule breakers; they do not know our rules. We can begin to see their play not simply as diversion or copy, but rather as the serious work of acting through a structure of exclusive rules, albeit distant from our own. Their day to day worlds are organized and the principle of that organization is playfulness.

16 The lore and language of schoolchildren

Iona Opie and Peter Opie

The scraps of lore which children learn from each other are at once more real, more immediately serviceable, and more vastly entertaining to them than anything which they learn from grown-ups. To a child it can be a 'known fact' that the Lord's Prayer said backwards raises the devil, that a small knife-wound between the thumb and forefinger gives a person lock-jaw, that a hair from the head placed on the palm will split the master's cane. It can be a useful piece of knowledge that the reply to 'A pinch and a punch for the first of the month' is 'A pinch and a kick for being so quick'. And a verse a child hears the others saying,

Mister Fatty Belly, how is your wife?
Very ill, very ill, up all night,
Can't eat a bit of fish
Nor a bit of liquorice.
O-U-T spells out and out you must go
With a jolly good clout upon your ear hole spout,

may seem the most exciting piece of poetry in the language.

Such a verse, recited by 8-year-olds in Birmingham, can be as traditional and as well known to children as a nursery rhyme; yet no one would mistake it for one of Mother Goose's compositions. It is not merely that there is a difference in cadence and subject-matter, the manner of its transmission is different. While a nursery rhyme passes from a mother or other adult to the small child on her knee, the school rhyme circulates simply from child to child, usually outside the home, and beyond the influence of the family circle. By its nature a nursery rhyme is a jingle preserved and propagated not by children but by adults, and in this sense it is an 'adult' rhyme. It is a rhyme which is adult approved. The schoolchild's verses are not intended for adult ears. In fact part of their fun is the thought,

Source: Iona Opie and Peter Opie, *The Lore and Language of Schoolchildren*, Oxford University Press (1959).

usually correct, that adults know nothing about them. Grownups have outgrown the schoolchild's lore. If made aware of it they tend to deride it; and they actively seek to suppress its livelier manifestations. Certainly they do nothing to encourage it. And the folklorist and anthropologist can, without travelling a mile from his door, examine a thriving unselfconscious culture (the word 'culture' is used here deliberately) which is as unnoticed by the sophisticated world, and quite as little affected by it, as is the culture of some dwindling aboriginal tribe living out its helpless existence in the hinterland of a native reserve. Perhaps, indeed, the subject is worthy of a more formidable study than is accorded it here. As Douglas Newton has pointed out: 'The world-wide fraternity of children is the greatest of savage tribes, and the only one which shows no sign of dying out.'

Continuity

No matter how uncouth schoolchildren may outwardly appear, they remain tradition's warmest friends. Like the savage, they are respecters, even venerators, of custom; and in their self-contained community their basic lore and language seems scarcely to alter from generation to generation. Boys continue to crack jokes that Swift collected from his friends in Queen Anne's time; they play tricks which lads used to play on each other in the heyday of Beau Brummel; they ask riddles which were posed when Henry VIII was a boy. Young girls continue to perform a magic feat (levitation) of which Pepys heard tell ('One of the strangest things I ever heard'); they hoard bus tickets and milk-bottle tops in distant memory of a love-lorn girl held to ransom by a tyrannical father; they learn to cure warts (and are successful in curing them) after the manner which Francis Bacon learnt when he was young. They call after the tearful the same jeer Charles Lamb recollected; they cry 'Halves!' for something found as Stuart children were accustomed to do; and they rebuke one of their number who seeks back a gift with a couplet used in Shakespeare's day. They attempt, too, to learn their fortune from snails, nuts, and apple-parings – divinations which the poet Gay described nearly two and a half centuries ago; they span wrists to know if someone loves them in the way that Southey used at school to tell if a boy was a bastard; and when they confide to each other that the Lord's Prayer said backwards will make Lucifer appear, they are perpetuating a story which was gossip in Elizabethan times.

The same continuity obtains in their games and play songs. When the Birmingham 8-year-olds chant about 'Mister Fatty Belly' they are perpetuating a verse with a lineage going back to schooldays under the Regency.

Apparent uniformity of the lore

The fact that schoolchild lore continues to thrive in a natural manner amongst unselfconscious adherents, and that we have been able to watch it functioning in a number of widely separated communities, has enabled us to obtain a picture of the state of traditional lore over the country as a whole. Thus it has shown that traditional lore exists everywhere; that as many, if not more, traditional games are known to city children as to country children; and that children with homes and backgrounds as different from each other as mining community and garden suburb share jokes, rhymes, and songs, which are basically identical. Conscious as we were of the economy of human invention, and the tenacity of oral tradition (the two elements without which there would be no folklore), we were not prepared for quite the identity of ritual and phraseology which has been revealed throughout the land in children's everyday witticisms, and in the newer of their self-organized amusements.

The faithfulness with which one child after another sticks to the same formulas even of the most trivial nature is remarkable. A meaningless counting-out phrase such as 'Pig snout, walk out', sometimes adapted to 'Boy Scout, walk out', or a tag for two-balls like 'Shirley Temple is a star, S-T-A-R', is apparently in use throughout England, Scotland, and Wales. If, in the vicinity of Westminster, a visitor hears for the first time children skipping to the simple chant,

Big Ben strikes one,
Big Ben strikes two,
Big Ben strikes three,

he may well suppose that the words are the just-for-the-minute invention of a particularly unimaginative local child. Yet this formula is repeated all over London, down side-streets behind the Victorian mansions of Kensington, in the bustle of Hackney, in Manor Park, and outside London in Croydon, Enfield, and Welwyn. Travelling farther afield it will be found in use at Scunthorpe in Lincolnshire, at Cwmbran in Monmouthshire, in Edinburgh, in Glasgow, and, in fact, apparently everywhere.

Speed of oral transmission

Since, through our collaborators, it has been possible to keep an eye on several widely separated places simultaneously, we have, on occasion, been afforded glimpses of oral transmission in actual operation. The speed with which a newly made-up rhyme can travel the length and breadth of the country by the schoolchild grapevine seems to be little short of miraculous. Some idea of the efficiency of oral transmission càn be obtained by the following verses which are topical, or which are parodies of newly published songs, and can consequently be dated, although for test purposes it is, unfortunately, best to study specimens which are of a scurrilous or indelicate nature for with these there is, in general, less likelihood of dissemination by means other than word-of-mouth.

A notorious instance of the transmission of scurrilous verses occurred in 1936 at the time of the Abdication. The word-of-mouth rhymes which then gained currency were of a kind which could not possibly, at that time, have been printed, broadcast, or even repeated in the music halls. One verse, in particular, made up one can only wonder by whom,

Hark the Herald Angels sing,
Mrs. Simpson's pinched our king,

was on juvenile lips not only in London, but as far away as Chichester in the south, and Liverpool and Oldham in the north. News that there was a constitutional crisis did not become public property until around 25 November of that year, and the king abdicated on 10 December. Yet at a school Christmas party in Swansea given before the end of term, Christmas 1936, when the tune played happened to be 'Hark the Herald Angels Sing', a mistress found herself having to restrain her small children from singing this lyric, known to all of them, which cannot have been composed much more than three weeks previously.

Wear and repair during transmission

The previous section has shown how quickly a rhyme passes from one schoolchild to the next, and illustrates a further difference between school lore and nursery lore. In nursery lore a verse or tradition, learnt in early childhood, is not usually passed on again until the little listener has grown up, and has children of his own, or even grandchildren. The period between learning a nursery rhyme and transmitting it may be anything from twenty to seventy years. With the playground lore, however, a rhyme may be excitedly passed on within the very hour it is learnt; and, in general, it passes between children who are the same age, or nearly so, since it is uncommon for the difference in age between playmates to be more than five years. If, therefore, a playground rhyme can be shown to have been current for a hundred years, or even just for fifty, it follows that it has been retransmitted over and over again; very possibly it has passed along a chain of two or three hundred young hearers and tellers, and the wonder is that it remains alive after so much handling, let alone that it bears resemblance to the original wording.

In most schools there is a wholly new generation of children every six years; and when a rhyme such as 'Little fatty doctor, how's your wife?' can be shown to be more than 130 years old it may be seen that it has passed through the keeping of not less than twenty successive generations of schoolchildren, and been exposed to the same stresses that nursery lore would meet only after 500 years of oral conveyance. This, in itself, makes schoolchild lore of peculiar value to the student of oral communication, for the behaviour and defects of oral transmission can be seen in operation during a relatively short period, much as if the phenomenon had been placed in a mechanical stresser to speed up the wear and tear.

Thus we find that variations, even apparently creative ones, occur more often by accident than by design. Usually they come about through mishearing or misunderstanding, as in the well-known hymnal misapprehension:

Can a woman's tender care
Fail towards the child she-bear?

A line in the song 'I'm a knock-kneed sparrow' quickly becomes 'I'm a cockney sparrow'. 'Calico breeches', no longer familiar to youth today, become 'comical breeches'. 'Elecampane' becomes 'elegant pain'. 'Green gravel, green gravel' becomes by association 'Greengages, greengages'. And the unmeaning 'Alligoshee, alligoshee', in the marching game, is rationalized to 'Adam and Eve went out to tea'.

Thus, it may be seen, oral lore is subject to a continual process of wear and repair, for folklore, like everything else in nature, must adapt itself to new conditions if it is to survive. An old rustic prognostication about magpies, for instance, is now commonly repeated by city children (who probably would not recognize a magpie even if they saw one) when telling fortunes with bus tickets. The lyrics of certain obsolescent singing games have obtained a new lease of life by being speeded up and sung while skipping. Cigarette cards, which have become scarce, are being replaced in flicking games by milk- bottle tops, known as 'flying saucers'. The bonfires of Hallowe'en have been postponed five days to become part of the effigy burning on Guy Fawkes Night. And a ribald rhyme of sixty years ago such as 'Lottie Collins has no drawers' is now chanted in honour of a modern idol, Miss Diana Dors.

The children themselves often have a touching faith in the novelty of their oral acquisitions. Of the rhyme,

House to let, apply within,
Lady turned out for drinking gin,

which we have collected from twenty-four places in the British Isles, also from South Africa, Australia, and the United States, and which was recorded as traditional in 1892 (G. F. Northall, *English Folk-Rhymes*, p. 306) an Alton girl remarked: 'Here's one you won't know because it's only just made up.'

Children are, in fact, prone to claim the authorship of a verse when they have done no more than alter a word in it, for instance substitute a familiar name for a name unknown to them; and they tend to be passionately loyal to the presumed genius of a classmate, or of a child who has just left their school, who is credited with the invention of each newly heard composition. The unromantic truth, however, is that children do not 'go on inventing games out of their heads all the time', as Norman Douglas believed; for the type of person who is a preserver is rarely also creative, and the street child is every bit as conservative as was George VI with his lifelong preference for the hymns he sang in the choir at Dartmouth. The nearest the normal child gets to creativeness is when he stumbles on a rhyme, as we have overheard: an 8-year-old, playing in some mud, suddenly chanted 'Stuck in the muck, stuck in the muck', whereupon his playmates took up the refrain, 'Stuck in the muck, stuck in the muck'. A 10-year-old added:

It's a duck, it's a duck,
Stuck in the muck, stuck in the muck,

and the group echoed this too, and went on chanting it, spasmodically, with apparent satisfaction, for above an hour, so that it seemed certain that we were in at the birth of a new oral rhyme. But when we asked them about it a week later they did not know what we were talking about. The fact is that even a nonsense verse must have some art and rhythm in it if it is to obtain a hold on a child's mind, although exactly what the quality is which gives some verses immortality is difficult to discover.

Where, then, do the rhymes come from? the origins of only a few can be traced, but these few may be indicative. The popular verse,

Sam, Sam, the dirty man,
Washed his face in a frying pan;
He combed his hair with a donkey's tail,
And scratched his belly with a big toe nail,

known throughout Britain in a multitude of versions (this one is from a 13-year-old boy in Pontefract) is a relic of a once famous song 'Old Dan Tucker' composed by the black-faced minstrel Daniel Decatur

Emmett, of 'Dixie' fame, and printed in 1843. Similarly Nellie Bligh who 'shuts her eye' ('because she cannot shut her ears'), or who catches a fly and ties it to a pin, was the heroine of a mid-nineteenth-century nigger minstrel song by Stephen Foster.

If the uniformity of schoolchild lore, to which we have so far been witness, was the whole story it would of course only be necessary to study one locality to know what goes on in every locality; and no matter how comprehensive and virile the lore was found to be, if it was the same everywhere, it would confirm the apprehensions of those who suppose that standardized education, mass entertainment, and national periodical literature have already subverted local traditions and characteristics. Happily our tale is not yet complete. Two distinct streams of oral lore flow into the unending river of schoolchild chant and chatter, and these two streams are as different from each other as slang and dialect. The slangy superficial lore of comic songs, jokes, catch phrases, fashionable adjective, slick nicknames, and crazes, in short that noise which is usually the first that is encountered in playground and street, spreads everywhere but, generally speaking, is transitory. The dialectal lore flows more quietly but deeper; it is the language of the children's darker doings: playing truant, giving warning, sneaking, swearing, snivelling, tormenting, and fighting. It belongs to all time, but is limited in locality. It is so timeworn indeed that it cannot be dated, and words of which Shakespeare would have known the meaning, as 'cog', 'lag', and 'miching', are, in their particular districts, still common parlance; while the language which children use to regulate their relationships with each other, such as their terms for claiming, securing precedence, and making a truce, vary from one part of the country to another, and can in some instances be shown to have belonged to their present localities not merely for the past two or three generations, but for centuries.

Conflicting as are the characteristics of these two types of lore, the one rapidly spreading from place to place and having a brief existence, the other having a prolonged existence but rarely spreading, it is not impossible to see how they subsist together. When a child newly arrives in a district any slang expression he knows, any jokes or tricks, or any new skipping or 'dipping' rhymes he brings with him, are eagerly listened to, and if found amusing, are added to the local repertoire, and may eventually supplant similar pieces of lore already known. But the local children, while willing to enlarge their store of jokes and rhymes, will not consciously brook any alteration to what they already know. The new child must learn, and very quickly does so, the 'legislative' language of his new playmates. He must learn the local names for the playground games, and the expressions used while playing them. Unless he does this, he will not merely be thought peculiar, he will not be understood.

17 The everyday world of the child
Matthew Speier

1. A new look at the empirical content of childhood socialization

Sociology considers the social life of the child as a basic area of study in so-called institutional analyses of family and school, for example. What is classically problematic about studying children is the fact of cultural induction, as I might refer to it. That is, sociologists (and this probably goes for anthropologists and psychologists) commonly treat childhood as a stage of life that builds preparatory mechanisms into the child's behavior so that he is gradually equipped with the competence to participate in the everyday activities of his cultural partners, and eventually as a bona fide adult member himself. This classical sociological problem has been subsumed under the major heading of socialization. In studying the organization of culture and society it seems quite natural to inquire into the process by which a new entrant acquires the status of a member in the eyes of others in his surrounding cultural milieu (unlike those entrants who arrive as adults, as 'strangers' or immigrants, tourists and the like, the child enters upon the scene with a clean slate, because the process takes place without the underlay of previous cultural experience).

The classical formulation of the problem of socialization has centered on treatments of the child's entry and incorporation into culture as a *developmental process*. Its working paradigm has been to ask questions about child development, such as the general one: How does the child internalize the norms, values, attitudes, etc., of others in his society? Traditional anthropological ethnography has asked in addition: How does the child develop particular skills in social and economic ways of life? Psychologists have focused on maturational growth and on personality development. Lately,

Source: *Understanding Everyday Life*, ed. Jack Douglas, Routledge and Kegan Paul (1970).

researchers from all these disciplines have become interested in the development of language skills.

I would like to propose an approach that differs sharply from the developmental one found in the classical formulations of socialization research. This approach sets aside questions of development yet retains the substantive interests of adult-child interaction central to the study of socialization.

I propose a simple definition of socialization that if acceptable to developmentally oriented research would imply the investigation of a hidden frame of analysis altogether: *socialization is the acquisition of interactional competences*. We can readily admit to the fact that children acquire 'a sense of social structure,' to use Cicourel's phrase. That is, for the child to develop from a newborn entrant to a participating member in social arrangements around him, he must undergo a learning process over the course of growing up through successive stages of life. However, to study this implicitly recognized acquisition process, presupposes a good knowledge of the features of interactional competences that are acquired. That is, what in fact are children developmentally acquiring? An investigation of the concrete features of competent interaction is nothing more or less than a study of what children normally and routinely do in their everyday activities, and as such it is not a study at all in the development of competence but a study in descriptive interactional analysis. It is my firm belief that no investigation of acquisition processes can effectively get underway until the concrete features of interactional competences are analyzed as topics in their own right. Without this preliminary step, which deliberately refrains from treating the topic of development, discussions of social competence must necessarily remain too vague and abstract to be of any direct use in empirical socialization research.

The target phenomena I propose to examine, interactions and concerted activities, are not customarily the subject of childhood socialization research. I refer to those sorts of interactions and activities that are *naturally situated* in the stream of everyday life. Naturalistic interactions and activities regularly take place by means of one very dominant mode of human communication, namely, talk. The centrality of talk in the everyday organization of human activity . . . is perhaps the major contribution by so-called ethnomethodologists to the history of modern sociology, a discipline that has remained oddly sluggish in recognizing the central role of speech in the organization of group life.

Talk and its conversational properties (including, where necessary, accompanyng nonspoken aspects of interaction such as gestures, facial organization, and ecological spacing) therefore comprise an altogether new set of empirical dimensions in the study of childhood social organization. It can easily be shown how investigators of childhood socialization have regularly relied on the speech communications of cultural participants in making inferences about 'childrearing practices,' though the speech practices themselves are never treated explicitly as analytic topics in their own right, directly relevant to the abstractions that are constructed about organized native knowledge presumably underlying children's and parents' situated courses of action.

This new direction in childhood socialization encourages the generation of topical analyses dealing with problems in how children talk to other children and how they talk with parents and other adults. These constitute, in part, problems in conversational analysis. . . . Unlike past researchers who have only noted in passing the most general significance of language (as in symbolic interactionism), this new direction in studying speech as the living performance of language has emphasized the *methods* participants use when building talk and practical activity around each other. By methods is meant what others have alluded to as the *procedural basis* for everyday interactions, or, as Turner puts it, our enterprise consists of 'the uncovering of members' *procedures* for doing activities,' talking or 'doing things with words' being a major component of those procedures.

Our task in research, then is to gather 'samples' (and at this point no sampling rules can be evinced) of concrete instances of natural interactions involving children. What can we explicate about the formal properties of those conversational procedures, for example, that we find participants using in the concrete instance coming before our analytic scrutiny?

The reader accustomed to the conventional paradigm in childhood socialization will not find hypothetical inquiries about 'socialization influences and aims,' nor problems in the social-structural basis for the child's 'internalization of norms,' etc. He will find, instead, that that interactional orientation to childhood organization will supply a frame of reference that precludes the posing of such abstract problems, and that in fact such problems as are found in the classical formulations will be dissolved and replaced by a whole new set of analytic considerations. In searching out the procedural properties of children's conversational interactions, a vast variety of studies in childhood social organization could be attempted, encompassing parent-child interactions in everyday household activity, adult-child interactions in other families' homes, in public places, in schools, or interactions exclusively among children themselves. Children's exclusive contacts constitute problems of study in what might be called the organization of 'children's culture,' and as such open up a wholly new sociological domain.

In this reformulated context for studying children's everyday activity the notion of development takes on a new shape. The temporal scale is vastly reduced to interactional units of *occasioned and situated activity*. The focus now is upon developing sequences of interaction from one moment to the next, rather than upon stages of development in the child's life; on the way interactants build a social scene and build a conversation together, episodically, beginning with procedures for opening and entering into copresent interactions, next for sustaining them around practical purposes using conversational resources for so doing, and finally for terminating the interaction or shifting into new activities or situations along natural junctures. The notion of development, then, enters into the analysis of interactional sequences moving naturally through time as participants do and say things methodically together. Children presumably have sufficient competence to cooperate in interactional development over a great variety of social circumstances. As interactants they must be able to employ conversational procedures with those they routinely encounter in everyday life. What conversational resources are available to children and to their interlocutors when routine interactions arise and take shape? That is, how are such procedures for interacting employed resourcefully by participants as they go about their talking and acting and their everyday practical achievements?

In the discussion that follows I will attempt to demonstrate how a concrete instance of data in the child's everyday life can be analyzed so as to yield some key issues in the organization of childhood activity.

II. Treating an instance as an opening gambit

I will open with an analysis of a piece of data from the study of children's everyday activities. From it I hope to generate a few important issues that I will take up in more detail in the sections following this one. These issues will center on the analysis of interactional development as a sequence of conversation, and on the nature of some of the conversational resources used by participants in that sequence. I take it that the instance is typical of a mundane routine that children confront in daily life, namely, calling on their friends. Children's contacts often involve and sometimes require the intervention of adults. This is a point about the organization of childhood to keep in mind when examining the instance I am about to present.

The following complete event took place in an encounter between a neighborhood child and a household mother. I was a guest in this home and at the time of the interaction was alone in a bedroom whose window was situated in a favorable position to overhear and record the entire sequence. It lasted for about one minute. The ecological arrangement is very important for an interpretation of the data. This house, on a street of private attached homes in San Francisco, has a front gate off the street that is always locked and that leads onto a tunnel or passage that has a staircase at the far end going up to the front door of the house. The staircase turns and a caller at the front gate at street level cannot see the front door one flight above. To gain entry a caller must always ring the bell at the gate first. This is a standard architectural arrangement for many homes in this city. It structures an interaction between caller and door-answer in such a way that neither party can see the other unless the answerer descends the staircase and turns the corner to look down the passageway at the caller. The entire passage and staircase are actually outdoors. The following transpired:

1. Caller: (Boy rings bell and waits for an answer to his ring.)
2. Mother: Who's there?
3. Caller: Can your son come out?
4. Mother: What?
5. Caller: Can your son come out?
6. Mother: What do you want?
7. Caller: Can your son come out?
8. Mother: (pause) Who is it?
9. Caller: Jerry. Can your son come out?
10. Mother: Oh - No he can't come right now. (Closes the front door.)
11. Caller: When do you think he could come out?
12. Mother: (Silence, since mother has not heard, having closed the door before the boy spoke utterance 11.)
13. Caller: (leaves)

I want to make the following points about this piece:

1 One of the features of family arrangements consists of an ecological containment of members inside the confines of a physical setting, commonly thought of as a residence. Family members therefore carry on their household activities in a home territory. In this instance we find that home territories have entrance points, such as doors and front gates. Those who are bona fide residents of the territory have the right of free passage into their own homes and in fact need not knock or ring to ask permission to be granted entry. In the case at hand, adults have keys, and others wishing entry, such

as household children, ring, wait for voice identification, and without further question get passage by means of an electric button pressed by the door answerer. This does *not* constitute asking for and receiving permission where household members are concerned but merely requests clearance, a form of mechanical security to control the entry of *out-siders*. In other words it is an inconvenience to children of the house who may not own a key to the gate, the price paid for such security measures in big cities. But where nonhousehold members are concerned, entry does indeed involve the granting of permission to come in through the front door (guests are treated as temporary household members and therefore the simple clearance pattern of ring-voice identification-entry applies).

2 A child wishing to call on another child must attend to this problem of entering another home territory (whether gates, locks, closed front doors, or some other physical arrangements exist). Now as far as conversational interaction or a state of talk goes, *the child must be prepared to identify himself as a caller and likewise the person on whom he is calling*. He must therefore have at his disposal the conversational resources to make such relevant identifications as necessary conditions, perhaps, for paying a visit to another child or getting him to come out to play.

3 As the data shows, the opening of the interaction is founded upon the principle of getting an adequate identification from the caller *as a second step in the sequence*, the first being the summoning of a household member by the bell-ring. The structural parallel is to that of the opening sequences of telephone calls, as analyzed by Schegloff. Where in telephoning activity the answerer speaks first after hearing the ring summon him, so too in the household entry situation in our data. But unlike the telephoning interaction, here the answerer provides a question that calls for explicit identification from the caller: 'Who's there?' Unlike the telephone answerer, who cannot know where the caller is located, the door-bell answerer knows precisely his location and thereby presumably his most general intention: to speak to some member of the house and possibly to gain entry.

4 Now the boy caller in the data hears the mother's call for an identification, but rather than supplying it with an *identification term* he relies on voice recognition to do this identificational work. But it does not. His question, moreover, is his reason for being there. Instead of identifying himself in the terms of reference carried within his utterance, he offers an identification of the one he is calling on, the thirteen-year-old boy of the house: 'Can your son come out?'

5 What can be gathered from this question? The caller could have made an identification by using the boy's first name (*FN*), but instead he has selected a term from an altogether different set of possible calling terms. He uses what I might call a *relational term*, that is one of a number of such terms applying to members of a unit of social membership called 'family.' The selection of 'your son' is interactionally viable because the caller has performed an analysis of his interlocutor, the mother of the house. Hearing (not seeing) her as the mother, because either he is familiar with her voice or he assumes any woman's voice will typically be that of the mother of the house, he transforms his own identification term for his friend, a *FN*, used to address him, into relational terms for the benefit of the answerer. In other words, when a child talks to another child's mother he can refer to his friend in terms of his relationship to her as her son. Now another consideration about this selection procedure suggests itself, namely, that when a neighborhood child doesn't in fact know the name of a boy on the block he has played with in the past, he can formulate an identification using familial relationships in households. This is a conversational resource to accomplish the purpose of his call. Perhaps he just wants *someone* to play with.

6 The mother's failure to make voice identification leads her to ask the boy to repeat his first utterance. After he does, she still cannot identify him, so she then goes on to inquire about the purpose of his call: 'What do you want?' The caller repeats himself for the third time, still waiting at the front gate and out of sight, and the mother calls once more for an identification of the caller. This is preceded by a brief pause in which she appears to be scrutinizing the voice for familiarity. It brings the boy's identification: 'Jerry. Can your son come out?' He selects *FN*, but he doesn't employ a parallel term for the rest of his utterance, and continues to identify the boy of the house in family-relationship terms. I cannot prove it, but I would speculate that he does not know the *FN* of the boy of the house.

7 The mother then grasps fully the purpose of the call and what its interactional consequences might be, that her son is being asked to go outside and play. However, at that moment she knows that her son is playing with another child in the house, and also that he has not discerned the occasion of the caller's visit. This raises the next interesting point for our discussion. Instead of relaying the matter to her son, she instead tells the caller herself that he can't come out. Two aspects of this suggest themselves for consideration of the nature of adult interventions in children's contacts and on the nature of children's rights. On the one hand, this mother has the entitlement, as does presumably any mother, to make decisions about contacts between her child and other children. On the other hand, she does not feel obligated to inform her son of the event *before closing it off* on her own. Finally, she does not show obligation to the caller to provide for future contacts by saying 'Come back later,' for example. So, in no sense has she assigned herself the responsibility of being a go-between in a fully developed way. Her intervention then might be characterized in terms of the parental rights she typically exercises to *answer for or talk for* her child. In this this way we see that a child has restricted rights as a speaker, given that we do indeed find in many different situations that parents enforce their entitlements to speak for their own children. Needless to say, the restriction of rights to speak is intimately connected to the restrictions on responsibilities, such as the child's presumed responsibility to take appropriate courses of action or to make suitable interactional decisions where other children are concerned. By talking for her son, a mother can practice interactional control over household activity.

8 Finally, the sequence terminates when the caller places a question designed to provide for future contact, and, recognizing that the answerer has retreated inside the house, leaving only silence, he takes leave of the front gate, never having gained entry.

18 The work of little children
Norman K Denzin

Societies and people organize themselves into interacting moral orders: families and schools, rich people and poor people, the educated and the uneducated, the child and the adult. Relationships between them are grounded in assumptions which justify the various social evaluations. Thus, it is taken as right and proper that the rich should have more privileges than the poor, or that children cannot engage in adult activities. These assumptions are institutionalised and routinely enforced, so that those people who are judged to be less competent are kept in their place. In this article, I want to look at some of the ideologies that surround the adult-child relationship. I shall present data from an on-going field study of young children in 'pre-school', in recreational areas and in families, which challenge the view of children that is taken for granted, at least in America.

Childhood is conventionally seen as a time of carefree, disorganized bliss. Children find themselves under constant surveillance. They are rewarded and punished so that proper standards of conduct can be instilled in their emergent selves. The belief goes that they enjoy non-serious, play-directed activities. They avoid work and serious pursuits at all costs. It is the adult's assignment to make these non-serious selves over into serious actors. In America, this belief lasts at least until the child enters the world of marriage and gainful employment.

There is a paradox in these assumptions. Even if a child or adolescent wants to take part in serious concerns he may find himself excluded. Thus, when the state of California recently passed a law, along the lines already adopted in Britain, giving the vote to 18 year olds, members of the Assembly refused to accord them drinking privileges, and one argument held that eighteen year olds were not yet competent enough to incur debts and assume adult responsibilities (like signing contracts).

Source: *New Society*, January 1971, 12-14.

The paradox extends beyond exclusion. Even when children go so far as to act in adult-like ways, these actions are usually defined as unique, and not likely to occur again unless an adult is there to give guidance and direction. This assumption serves to justify the position of the educator. If children could make it on their own, there would be no place for the teacher. This fact is best seen in American pre-schools, where instructors assume that little children have short attention or concentration spans. The belief is quite simple. If left to their own ingenuity, little children become bored. Time structures must be developed, so that the child does not become bored. In California, these timetables typically go as follows:

9-9.15: Hang up coats and say 'Good morning' to other children.

9.15-10: Play inside on solitary activities (painting, puzzles, toys).

10-10.30: Go outside for group activities on swing, in sandbox, dancing, making things.

10.30-11: Juice and biscuit time in small groups around tables.

11-11.20: Quiet time: small groups around instructors where instructor reads a story.

11.20-11.30: Get coats and jackets and prepare to be picked up by parents.

11.30: Session over; instructors relax and have coffee and cigarettes.

When there are clashes over timetable – if, for example, a child refuses to come in for juice and biscuits – an instructor will be dispatched to inform him that it is time to come in.

These timetables are revealing and serve several functions. They tell the instructor what he will be doing at any given moment. They give instructors control over the children. They state that children, if left on their own, could not organize their own actions for two and a half hours.

Another paradox is evident. Although children are systematically informed of their incompetence, and rewarded for the quality of their non-serious conduct, adults appear to assume that something important is happening at these early ages. In fact, it is something so serious that normal, everyday adults cannot assume responsibility for what occurs. As rapidly as possible, the child is taken from the family setting and placed in any number of child-care, educational and baby-sitting facilities.

My interviews with, and observations of, 100 American parents, who delivered their children to a co-operative and experimental pre-school, revealed two assumptions. Firstly, the school was a cheap and effective baby-sitter. The parents had no fears for their child's safety when he was there. Second, if the child was an only child, or if the parents lived in a neighbourhood where there were no other playmates, the pre-school would expand and cultivate the child's skill at getting on with other children. These parents feared that their child would appear later in kindergarten, and not know how to interact with other children. Because pre-schools do not formally assess how a child is doing, the parents felt fairly safe. They transferred the function of looking after their child's sociability from themselves to a neutral party – the pre-school teacher.

The school, then, gave the parents a year to get the child ready for his first encounter with formal education. The task of the pre-school was to shape up the child's speech and to teach him or her how to be polite and considerate to others. A side function was to give painting, say, which many parents defined as too messy for their homes. Economically stable families with several children were less likely to send their child to the pre-school. Brothers and sisters performed the sociability function of the pre-school.

Let me now note a final paradox. Observers like Iona and Peter Opie – in their *Lore and Language of Schoolchildren* and their *Children's Games in Street and Playground* – have found that, when left on their own, children produce complex societies and social orders.

The fact that many children's games are often spontaneously produced, yet are passed on from generation to generation, and that their songs and stories are made to fit special selves, must indicate the child's ability to be a serious, accountable actor.

An example from the Opies' study of children's games reveals the serious character of play. Here the game is 'playing school':

'The most favourite game played in school is Schools.' says an Edinburgh nine year old. 'Tommy is the headmaster. Robin is the schoolteacher, and I am the naughty boy. Robin asks what are two and two. We say they are six. He gives us the belt. Sometimes we run away from school and what a commotion! Tommy and Robin run after us. When we are caught we are taken back and everyone is sorry.'

In their attendant analysis of this game, the Opies observe:

Clearly, playing Schools is a way to turn the tables on real school: a child can become a teacher, pupils can be naughty, and fun can be made of punishments. It is noticeable, too, that the most demure child in the real classroom is liable to become the most talkative when the canes are make-believe.

Urie Bronfenbrenner's recent study of child-rearing practices in the Soviet Union shows, too, that Russians take the games of their young children quite seriously. Such games are used to instill self-reliance and collective respect on the part of the child. Here is one instance:

Kolya started to pull at the ball Mitya was holding. The action was spotted by a junior staff member who quickly scanned the room and then called out gaily: 'Children, come look! See how Vasya and Marusya are swinging their teddy bear together. They are good comrades.' The two offenders quickly dropped the ball to join the others in observing the praised couple, who now swung harder than ever.

Bronfenbrenner notes that such co-operation is not left to chance. From pre-school on, Soviet children are encouraged to play co-operatively. Group games and special toys are designed to heighten this side of self-development.

The point I want to make is that when they are left on their own, young children do not play, they work at constructing social orders. 'Play' is a fiction from the adult world. Children's work involves such serious matters as developing languages for communications; presenting and defending their social selves in difficult situations; defining and processing deviance; and construction rules of entry and exit into emergent social groups. Children see these as serious concerns and often make a clear distinction between their play and their work. This fact is best grasped by entering those situations where children are naturally thrown together and forced to take account of one another.

Many specialists have assumed that young children lack well-developed self-conceptions. My observations show, on the contrary, that as early as four a child can stand outside his own behaviour and see himself from another's perspective. I carried out intensive interviews with fifteen four year olds. These revealed support for the general hypothesis that a person's self-concept reflects the number of people he interacts with. The more friends a child had, or the larger his network of brothers and sisters, the more elaborate his self-conception.

Keith, who was four years seven months old at the time of the interview, described himself as follows:

1 My name is Keith -.
2 I am a boy who plays at a nursery school.
3 If I was asked 'What do you like to play best?' I would say 'I like to dance to my favourite records'! (*What are your favourite records?*) 'Yummy, Yummy'; 'Bonnie and Clyde.'
4 If someone asked me, 'Where do you live?' I'd say, '(Name of street).'
5 If someone said, 'Do you know how to do cartwheels?' I'd say 'No.'
6 If someone said, 'What kind of picture can you draw?' I'd say 'I can draw my favourite things. I like to draw a man's head.' (*Why?*) 'Because so much can be added to it. I'd put hair, a chin, eyes, a forehead, a nose, a mouth, and a chin on it.'

Keith was a leader of the boys' group at the pre-school, had nine good friends, and was one of a family that had two other children. Nancy, on the other hand, was an isolate, having only four acquaintances at school. However, her family also had two other children.

Her low integration in the social network of the school is reflected in the fact that she could only give two self-descriptions:

1 I'm at school.
2 I live in (name of city).

As extremes, Keith and Nancy point to a basic feature of life at the pre-school. Insofar as a child is a member of the social life of the pre-school, the more adult-like will be his, or her, behaviour. The social life of the school, then, makes the child into a small adult.

Name games – which take many forms – reveal another side of the child's serious self. Children may reverse or switch names. On a Hallowe'en afternoon, I saw three girls, all aged four, who were sitting around a table mixing pumpkin muffins, systematically assign to themselves and all newcomers the name of the child next to them. The rule was quite simple. Each child was assigned every name in the group but their own. One girl resisted and said: 'That's a mistake! My name isn't Kathy. I'm Susan.' Kathy replied: 'We know your name isn't mine, silly; we're just pretending. We don't mean it.'

There was a clear separation of play, fantasy and serious activity in this eposide. Each girl knew her name. The sequence merely solidified their self-identity. Martha Wolfenstein, in a study of children's humour, has observed that inevitably some child will find these games disturbing, refusing to accept the identity that goes with the new name. Probably such children are not yet firmly committed to the identity designated by their proper name.

Name calling is another game. Here, the child's proper name is dropped and replaced by either a variation on that name, or by an approving/disapproving term. Martha Wolfenstein noted names like 'Heinie', 'Tits', 'Freeshow', 'Fuckerfaster', and 'None-of-your-business'. In name-calling games the child's real identity is challenged. He or she is singled out of the group and made a special object of abuse or respect. (Parenthetically, it must be noted that adults also engage in such games. Special names for sports and political figures are examples.)

A more severe game is where the child has his name taken away. The other children simply refuse to interact with him. By taking away his name, they effectively make him a non-person, or non-self. In nameless games the child may be referred to as a member of a social category (young child, honkie, brat, dwarf). In these moments his essential self, as a distinct person, is denied.

The Opies have described another name game, which is called 'Names', 'Letters in Your Name' or 'Alphabet'. Here, a child calls out letters in the alphabet, and contestants come forward every time a letter contained in their name is called.

All of these name games reflect the importance children assign to their social lives. A name is a person's most important possession simply because it serves to give a special identity.

In pre-schools, the children are continually constructing rules to designate group boundaries. In those schools where sexual lines are publicly drawn, boys and girls may go so far as to set off private territories where members of the opposite sex are excluded. One observer working with me noted boys and girls in a four-year-old group, carrying posters stating that they were 'Boys' or 'Girls'. On another occasion I observed the creation of a 'Pirate Club' which denied entry to all females and all males who did not have the proper combination of play money for paying their membership dues. This group lasted for one hour. At juice and biscuit time, it was disbanded by the instructor and the boys were made to sweep out their tree house. Adult entry into the club seemed to reduce its interest for the boys.

The study of early childhood conversations reveals several similarities to adult speech. Like adults, young children build up special languages. These languages are silent and gestural. What a child says with his eyes or hands may reveal more than his broken speech. As children develop friendships, 'private' terms and meanings will be employed. To grasp the conversations of young children, it is necessary to enter their language communities and learn the network of social relationships that bind them together. Single words can have multiple meanings. 'Baby' can cover a younger brother or sister, all small children, or contemporaries who act inappropriately. To understand what the word 'baby ' means for the child, it is necessary to (a) understand his relationship to the person called a baby, (b) the situation where he uses the word, and (c) the activity he is engaging in at the moment.

Neologisms are especially crucial in the development of new relationships. The involved children attempt to produce a word that outsiders cannot understand. Its use sets them off from the other children; it serves to give a special designation to the newly formed relationship. I observed two girls, aged three, who had suddenly discovered one another. Within an hour they had developed the word 'Buckmanu'. With smiles on their faces they came running inside the pre-school, holding hands and singing their new word. After several repetitions of 'Buckmanu' they came over for juice, and a mother asked them what they were saying. They ignored her and suddenly switched the word to 'Manubuck'. And then, with precision and correct enunciation, they said, 'Manuel bucked us off!' Manuel was the name of a pre-school instructor. They had taken one of his actions (playing horseback) and his name, and forged the two into a new word. Once they revealed the name to the mothers, they ceased using it.

19 The play of little children

Gregory P. Stone

Physical educators too often have a restricted view of play, exercise, and sport, asking only how such activities contribute to the motor efficiency and longevity of the organism. Yet, the symbolic significance of recreation is enormous, providing a fundamental bond that ties the individual to his society. Indeed, many of society's forms - its myths and legends - endure only in play. Play is recreation, then, because it continually re-creates the society in which it is carried on. Social psychology, concerned as it is with the meaningful aspects of human life, is well suited to the analysis of play as a symbolic process.

Social psychologists have long recognized the significance of play for preparing young children to participate later on in adult society. But social psychology, when viewed against the backdrop of history, is very young. Furthermore, there is a disquieting tendency for many social science disciplines to lose their sense of history and develop what they conceive to be universal propositions based on observations made in quite spatially and temporally delimited milieux. This article is primarily designed to place the play of children in historical perspective and, then, to set forth some functions of contemporary child's play, reserving judgment about the universality of such functions. It is hoped that the very tentativeness with which such assertions are set forth will inspire the curiosity of others and encourage them to extend the spatial and temporal focus of their studies of childhood. Play, like other collective enterprises, is a collective representation: it *re*presents the arrangements of the society and historical era in which it is carried on.

Historical emergence of children and child's play

In an extraordinary work (Ariès, 1962), Philippe Ariès asks the

Source: *Quest* (1965), IV, 23-31.

seemingly naive question: where do children come from? He is not, of course, concerned with the biological origins of infants, but with the historical origins of the social *identity*, 'child.' Although the classical Greek civilization (and those it influenced directly) had distinguished children socially from babes and adults if only as objects of aesthetic appreciation, children did not emerge as social entities in the subsequent history of Western civilization until the early seventeenth century.

France as an early source of children
Prior to the seventeenth century there were babes and adults in Western civilization, but no in-betweens. Babes were swaddled; adults attired; children were, in fact, *homunculi.* There was no distinctive dress to differentiate them, and expectations directed toward them were not age-specific. The elaborate record of the life of Louis XIII kept by his doctor, Heroard, amazes us today. The Dauphin was betrothed by his first birthday. At seventeen months, he was singing and playing the violin. By the age of two years, he was dancing various kinds of dances. At three and a half, he was reading, and he was writing at four. It must be emphasized here that the child, Louis, was not thought of as particularly brilliant. Such activities were merely expected of the little people we call children today. Nor was this seemingly precocious activity necessarily confined to children of royalty and aristocracy, although such intricate play forms were undoubtedly concentrated in that estate. Paintings of the period, as well as earlier paintings, show the children of commoners and peasants freely participating in what we think of today as adult settings, e.g., taverns and wine shops.

It is not as though there were no play at that time. Louis had his hobby horse, tops, and balls. Rather, play permeated all segments of the society. Ariès chides the contemporary historian Van Marle for his amazement upon discovering that the games played by grown-ups were no less childish than those played by children, retorting, 'Of course not: they were the same'. Festivals were another matrix of community-wide play in medieval Europe. Despite the fact, however, that play was general in the society, its unanticipated consequences were probably different for children and adults as they are today. Certainly some child's play provided young people with a vehicle for anticipatory socialization, permitting them to rehearse roles they would enact or encounter in later life, as in military play. Then as now, the play of children pulled them into the larger society. Adult play, on the other hand, undoubtedly released the players at times from everyday social demands and obligations. That adults and children played the same games makes such differences difficult to verify.

If play was general in the society of medieval Europe, attitudes toward play were not. In fifteenth and sixteenth century France, the Catholic clergy took a dim view of play, unless it followed the performance of work, and this view was subsequently adopted by police and other authorities. Yet, play could not be suppressed by such moralizers in a society where play was general in the population and work did not have the significance it was to acquire with industrialization. The only enforceable suppression of play was accomplished in universities where clergy were recruited and trained, and there is evidence to suggest that this was not very effective. Possibly for this very reason, the Jesuits assimilated the play of the larger society in the seventeenth century. Play was redefined as educational and incorporated in college curricula. At the end of the eighteenth century, emerging nationalism provided a further legitimation of play. Play was conceived as a way of preparing young people for military service. The inclusion of play forms in military training programs is a frequent mode of legitimation. Thus, boxing or 'prize-fighting' became legal in the United States in 1917 when it became an integral part of the U.S. Army's physical training program.

As play acquired the approval of the moral custodians of seventeenth and eighteenth century French society, childhood also became established as a separate social identity in the human biography, and play became rather more of a childish thing. Ariès interprets this emergence of the child in the social morphology as one consequence of the rise of an entrepreneurial stratum in European society. As work moved to the center of social arrangements, play became increasingly relegated to childhood, and *pari passu*, children were established as identifiable social beings. This may have been the case with France, but play and children were to have a more painful birth in the Protestant nations.

Play in the history of England and America
Protestantism provided a religious justification for the tremendous expansion of work in the emerging industrial societies. Work was the key to the gates of the Protestant heaven: by your works are ye known. In contrast to the relegation of play to childhood in seventeenth and eighteenth century France, play had been generally suppressed in England by the end of the eighteenth century. In particular, the legislated inclosures of open areas deprived much of the population of play space. Play was further suppressed by legislation in English towns which, for example, forbade children

from playing with tops in the streets or running races on the roads. When Wesley drew up the rules for his school at Kingswood, no time was set aside for play, because, in his view, 'he who plays as a boy will play as a man'.

In America, the status of play in the seventeenth and eighteenth century is less clear. We do know, of course, that child labor persisted in the United States into the twentieth century. Tocqueville thought that the Americans of his time were so wrapped up in work that they could not enjoy play: 'Instead of these frivolous delights, they prefer those more serious and silent amusements which are like business and which do not drive business wholly out of their minds.' On the other hand, Green has observed that play was smuggled into many areas of earlier American life in the guise of work, as in quilting parties and barn-raisings, and, by the end of the nineteenth century, Bryce was impressed by the 'brighter' life afforded the factory workers in New England through their 'amusements than that of the clerks and shopkeepers of England'. The picture is, at best, a confused one. Moreover, what seemed 'serious and silent' to a Frenchman may well have seemed 'bright' to an Englishman.

Probably, however, there was no overall moral consensus on the value of work and play. In a very careful study, Miyakawa has shown that there were sharp regional differences and, within regions, denominational differences. In nineteenth century Ohio, Presbyterians led a gayer life than Methodists, and, in Connecticut, the Congregationalists did not hesitate to dance and enjoy musical entertainment. Even on the frontier, 'at least some German, Swedish, and other continental settlers had occasional songfests, plays, dances, and music'. Miyakawa's observations, given the relatively high social status of Presbyterian and Congregational denominations, permit the inference that play was looked upon with favor in the higher socio-economic strata of nineteenth century America. At this status level, as Veblen has shown, we find a leisure class straining to shed the trappings of work, and I would offer the general hypothesis that play is introduced into the bleak ages of any society by high status circle and spread throughout the society as a consequence of the emulation carried on in lower status circles and aggregates. Once this is accomplished, the moral 'character' of the society is transformed. Yet, the mere emulation of play styles is not a sufficient explanation for the spread of play in society. It is a necessary condition.

Ariès may well be correct in his assertion that the emergence of an entrepreneurial stratum in France established the identity of child and cloaked that identity with distinctive play forms, but in England and America it is a very different matter. It required a social movement *against the excesses of capitalism,* in the Protestant countries, to release children from the bonds of work and confer the privileges of play. The movement had its inception in the reformist and revolutionary thought of the mid-nineteenth century and persisted until the twentieth. Indeed, Ritchie and Kollar maintain that, for the United States, the 'institutionalization of children's play and games is largely a twentieth century phenomenon'. It is even possible that this institutionalization was not formally secured until the formulation of the Children's Charter of the 1930 White House Conference on Child Health and Protection which proclaimed: 'With the young child, his work is his play and his play is his work'.

Implications for the social psychology of play
Children and child's play, then, emerged much later on the social scene in the Protestant than in the Catholic countries. As I have pointed out elsewhere, this difference persists today in contrasting Protestant and Catholic attitudes toward gaming or gambling. Nevertheless, the fact remains that children and child's play have not always been with us, particularly as we know them today. Thus, when we speculate upon the social significance of child's play, we may well be developing hypotheses that have relevance only for a particular and relatively recent era of Western civilization. I have often wondered whether or not this is the best any social scientist can do – to dramatize effectively his own socio-historical era. As Marx, Veblen, and Freud effectively dramatized the industrial era, so have Mills, Riesman, and Harry S. Sullivan effectively dramatized the era that Walter Rostow calls high mass consumption. This may well be the case because of the interaction between the social scientist and his subject matter. The very publication of social science theory and research alters the behavior it attempts to explain. For example, the incorporation of Keynesian economics into national fiscal policy introduced a political variable into business cycle theory, and nothing has altered sexual attitudes more than the dissemination of Freudian theory, with the result that contemporary psychoanalysts, such as Allen Wheelis, are confounded by the presence of disorders which defy explanation in classical Freudian terms.

Differentiation and integration of the child's self through play

It is the task of society to make the lives of its members meaningful. This is accomplished by bringing little children into a meaningful communication with adults and one another, and, at the same time, by establishing their selves as objects so they can refer the other objects of their worlds to such established selves, thereby imbuing these worlds with significance. Play has a major part in the accomplishment of these tasks.

The play of mother and child

Meaning only exists in communication, and it is established when one's own symbols call out in the other about the same symbolic responses as they call out in himself. (Thus, this article can only be meaningful if readers respond to these words about the way that I have responded. Failing this, the article is nonsense!) This seems to be accomplished very early by the infant when it takes over the response patterns of the mothering one as its own. It may be that babbling is a kind of playing with noise, but we shall never know, for we cannot ask the babbler. Nevertheless, in the course of babbling, the infant may hit upon a word-like sound which is then re-presented by the mothering one as a word, together with an appropriate response pattern. 'Baa,' for example, may be re-presented as 'ball' as the round object is grasped and held up before the babbling baby, In time, the infant takes over the response pattern: 'ball' *means* grasping the round object.

Too, in this early stage of the development of meaning, the infant is often a plaything, while the mothering one is the player. In time, both the child and the mothering one are mutually players and playthings:

As actions become possible for him and as words take on meanings, the child is increasingly able to respond to the play actions of his mother with play actions of his own. Thus, for example, he uses his hands to play 'peek-a-boo' and 'patty cake.' (Ritchie and Kollar, 1964).

Such commonalty of responses establishes a rudimentary domestic universe of discourse which can serve as a base from which a vast social symbolism can be elaborated.

Child's play as drama

'Play' has several meanings, among which *drama* must be included, and drama is fundamental for the child's development of a conception of self as an object different from but related to other objects – the development of an *identity*. To establish a separate identity (many identities depend for their establishment and maintenance on counter-identities, e.g., man-woman, parent-child, teacher-student), the child must literally get outside himself and apprehend himself from some other perspective. Drama provides a prime vehicle for this. By taking the role of another, the child gains a reflected view of himself as different from but related to that other.

Thus, we find little children playing house, store, or school in which they perform the roles of parent, merchant, or teacher, gaining a reflected view of their own identities from the perspective of those identities whose roles they perform. Indeed, in playing house, it is difficult to recruit a child to play the role of child or baby. Such a role has no implication for the building of his own identity. A doll, therefore, is better suited to the role.

We may note an additional consequence of such drama. In the examples cited, the child prepares himself for the subsequent enactment of such roles in later life or for communication with those who will be performing such roles. Merton speaks of such drama as anticipatory socialization. However, not all childhood drama is of this anticipatory character. Many of the roles the child performs are fantastic, in the sense that the child can not reasonably be expected to enact or encounter such role performances in later life. I have in mind such identities as cowboy and Indian, creatures from outer space, or pirate. In much fantastic drama, incidentally, we can detect an additional function of child's play. Fantastic drama often serves to maintain and keep viable the past of the society – its myths, legends, villains, and heroes. This is also true of toys and other items of the technology of child's play. As one example, the jousting tournament disappeared in the sixteenth century and was replaced by the quintain and the unhooking of a ring by a galloping horseman. The latter persists today in the merry-go-round. This function of child's play has inspired Ariès to remark that 'children form the most conservative of human societies'.

Fantastic drama seems more to characterize the play of male children in our society than that of female children. Thus, the dramatic play of children in our society may function more to prepare little girls for adulthood than little boys. This observation, however, may not necessarily be confined to contemporary American society and its recent past. In discussing the dress of children in eighteenth century France, Ariès points out: 'the attempt to distinguish children was generally confined to boys ... *as if childhood separated girls from adult life less than it did boys*'. It may well be that the drama fo childhood makes it difficult for boys to establish an early well-founded conception of adult life and, consequently, hinders their assumption of an adult identity. In contrast, such drama may facilitate the transition of female children to adulthood. However, once boys do become men (in the social psychological sense), given the sexual arrangements of our society, they have a relatively easy time of it, while the problems of females begin when girls become women!

Children differ, too, according to their *knowledge* of the roles they perform in childhood drama. Although he was not always consistent, Mead presumed an 'open awareness' of the roles performed in drama. There are at least two reasons why such an assumption can not be maintained. First, the details of the role performance may not be objectively accessible to the young actor. For example, a colleague, Duane Gibson of Michigan State University, noticed a boy and girl playing house in a front yard. The little girl was very busy sweeping up the play area, rearranging furniture, moving dishes about, and caring for baby dolls. The boy, on the other hand, would leave the play area on his tricycle, disappear to the back of the (real) house, remain for a brief while, reappear in the play area, and lie down in a feigned sleep. The little girl had a rather extensive knowledge of the mother role, but, for the boy, a father was one who disappeared, reappeared, and slept, *ad infinitum!* Second, nuances of the role performance may be deliberately concealed from children. We tend to conceal domestic difficulties from children, e.g., financial troubles. Should a child overhear such a discussion, we play it down, encouraging the child not to worry about it.

Finally, in this discussion of childhood drama, we ought to acknowledge that one child's fantasy is another child's reality. The probability that the roles children enact in their dramas will be assumed or encountered in adult life is very much restricted by their position in the various orders of stratification – income, prestige, and accessibility to political office –, their rural or urban residence, their 'race' or ethnicity, or their sex. It is, in short, anticipatory for the boy to play the role of baseball player, but not for the girl.

We have very few empirical studies of childhood play and, particularly, drama. When we do conduct them, then, we ought to realize the complex nature of drama. Is it anticipatory or fantastic? Is knowledge of the dramatized role accessible to the young performer? Is it probable that the actor will, in later life, enact or encounter the role performance that he is dramatizing? Above all, how is recruitment into the adult roles that the drama of childhood represents organized by larger social arrangements? When such questions are answered, we will have far better knowledge of precisely how childhood drama provides children with identities, casting them in the character of meaningful objects.

Obviously, as Mead insisted, drama is not a sufficient source of identity, for it provides the young actor with many parts and scripts, and these are often unrelated. The development of an integrated self requires the playing of team games in which one can generalize the related team positions and adapt his own behavior to the generalized expectations of the entire team. Such games occur later in childhood and are beyond the scope of this article. However, one final form of play found in early childhood will be considered here, namely, tests of poise.

Childish tests of poise

It is not enough only to establish an identity for one's self; it must be established for others at the same time. Identities are *announced* by those who appropriate them and *placed* by others. Identities must always be validated in this manner to have reality in social interaction. Usually such announcements are silent, accomplished by clothing, the posturing of the body, painting of the face, sculpting of the hair, the manipulation of props, or the physical location of the self on the scene of action. For these reasons, child's play demands costume and body control, and it is facilitated by props and equipment (toys) appropriate to the drama. Moreover, as Huizinga has remarked, play spaces are usually clearly marked off, and one's location within them communicates to other players and on-lookers the part he is playing. Thus, child's play demands the assembly, arrangement, and control of spaces, props, equipment, clothing, and bodies, as well as other elements. If crucial elements are missing, if they become disarranged, or if control over them is lost, the play is spoiled, and the drama can not be carried off. Loss of control over these elements is literally embarrassing and may be equated to loss of poise.

We know that much of the drama of childhood replicates the interaction of the larger society in which it occurs. Indeed, it is almost trite to observe that society *is* drama. In everyday interaction, we must always announce to others who we are and be poised or prepared for the upcoming communication. This requires the assembly, arrangement, and control of a host of objects and demands considerable skill, for the staging of social interaction is an intricate affair, a highly complex juggling and balancing act.

Much childhood play takes the form of deliberately perpetrating loss of poise with the unintended but highly important consequence of preparing the child for the maintenance of self-control in later life. Thus, everywhere we find little children spinning about inducing dizziness, pushing and tripping one another, disarranging clothing, teasing, playing pranks, or bringing play to a sudden halt by depriving the players of some crucial item ('I'm going to take my ball and go home'). Indeed, a technology has developed to facilitate such play and is found in playgrounds, amusement parks, and carnivals.

All this is well known, but I have the distinct impression that such play is viewed almost exclusively as contributing to body control or motor efficiency. Playful tests of poise reach out beyond the body to include clothing and grooming. Pranks can be perpetrated by disturbing any element essential to the staging process – furniture, equipment, locations, and a host of other objects and arrangements. The analysis of such play, then, ought to take into account the development of body control and coordination, but the emphasis ought to be on its symbolic significance in relation to the other elements of staging essential to the silent definition of situations in everyday life.

Conclusions

This article has placed the play of little children in the context of social symbolism. It has shown how playing with children, childhood drama, and childish pranks function to prepare little children for their meaningful participation in adult society. Such play, however, is not always functional. Some childhood drama may militate against later social participation because of its relative inappropriateness, and I suppose some pranks may be so severe as to have unforeseen traumatic effects. In any case, the play of little children demands extensive scientific investigation. However, any propositions formulated as a consequence of such research may not have universal validity. Both children and child's play, like all other social beings, are creatures of history.

Comparative approaches to childhood

When we compare social phenomena from culture to culture our intentions might be twofold; either to demonstrate the variety of forms or to work reductively and to distil the common elements. The former tends to weaken our attachment to the surface structure of our own culture and the latter tends to reaffirm a commitment to a singular version of human being. Cross-culturally children vary immensely in terms of their degree of responsibility, the expectations held of them, their level of dependency, need for care, life expectation and more generally the nature of their relationship with adults.

20 The necessity and significance of comparative research in developmental psychology

Jean Piaget

Developmental psychology can be described as the study of the development of mental functions, in as much as this development can provide an explanation, or at least a complete description, of their mechanisms in the finished state. In other words, developmental psychology consists of making use of child psychology in order to find the solution to general psychological problems.

From this point of view, child psychology constitutes an irreplaceable instrument of psychological enquiry, as many people these days are increasingly coming to suspect, but there is less often an awareness that it could play an almost equally important role in the field of sociology. Comte rightly holds that one of the most important phenomena of human societies is the formative action of each generation on the following one, and Durkheim reached a conclusion which favoured a collective origin of moral opinions, legal norms and even logic itself; but there is only one experimental method for verifying hypotheses such as these: namely the study of the progressive socialization of the individual, in other words the analysis of his development in terms of the specific or general social influences which he undergoes while his character is being formed.

All comparative research dealing with differing civilizations and social environments raises from the outset the problem of distinguishing those factors peculiar to the spontaneous and internal development of the individual from the specific group or cultural factors of the particular society which provides his environment. This delimitation, which is inescapable, can lead to some unexpected results. In the field of affective psychology for example, the early Freudian doctrines provided a model of an endogenous process of development of the individual, so endogenous that the different stages which were proposed (in particular the stage of the so-called 'Oedipal' reactions) were presented as being essentially due to the

Source: Jean Piaget, *Psychology and Epistemology*, tr. P.A. Wells, Penguin (1972).

successive manifestations of one and the same 'instinct', in other words of internal propensities which owed nothing to society as such. On the other hand, we are aware that a sizeable group of contemporary psychoanalysts known as 'culturalists' (Fromm, Horney, Kardiner, Glover, etc., together with anthropologists such as Benedict and Mead) currently support the hypothesis of a close dependence of the various Freudian complexes, particularly of the Oedipal propensities, upon the surrounding social environment.

Factors in development

In the realm of cognitive functions, the only area with which we shall be concerned in the following discussion, the chief advantage of comparative research is likewise that it allows us to separate out the individual from the group factors in development. However, it is still advisable first to introduce some necessary distinctions regarding the factors to be considered.

1. Biological factors

In the first place there exist biological factors associated with the 'epigenetic system' (interactions between genome and physical environment during growth) and manifesting themselves in particular through the maturation of the nervous system. These factors, which are almost certainly not susceptible to social influences, play a part which is still poorly understood, but their importance is probably none the less decisive in the development of cognitive functions, and it is therefore essential to bear in mind the possibility of this influence. In particular, the development of an 'epigenotype' implies, from the biological point of view, the presence of stages which exhibit a 'sequential' character (each being necessary to the following one in an established order), of 'creodes' (channels or paths necessary to the development of each individual sector of the whole), and of a 'homeorhesis' (dynamic equilibrium such that a deviation with respect to the creodes is more or less compensated for, with a tendency to return to the normal channel). These are characteristics which until now we have believed to be present in the development of the operations and logico-mathematical structures of intelligence; and, if the hypothesis is correct, this would naturally presuppose a certain degree of constancy or uniformity in development, whatever the social environments within which the individual is formed. Reversals in the succession of stages, or profound modifications in their character between environments, would prove, on the other hand, that these basic biological factors do not play a part in the cognitive development of the individual. There is here, therefore, a fundamental problem of the first order whose solution requires extensive comparative research.

2. Factors in the equilibration of actions

However, examination of the development of intellectual operations in the many culturally sophisticated countries where the study of our stages has been undertaken reveals immediately that psychobiological factors are far from being the only ones at work. If, indeed, only one continuous action played a part in the internal maturation of the organism and the nervous system, the stages would not just be sequential, but also linked to relatively constant chronological dates, as is the co-ordination of vision and prehension at about four to five months, the appearance of puberty, and so on. In fact, depending on the individuals and their family, school or social environments we find in children from the same town advances or retardations which are often considerable. These are not inconsistent with the sequential order (which remains constant), but indicate that other factors must be added to the epigenetic mechanisms.

A second group of factors must now be introduced whose possible relationships with social life are to be borne in mind, but which in principle draw attention once again to the activities peculiar to behaviour in general in its psychobiological as much as in its group aspects: these are the factors of equilibration in the sense of autoregulation and thus in a sense which is more closely akin to homeostasis than to homeorhesis. Individual development is, in fact, a function of a multitude of activities in terms of exercise, experience, action on the environment, and so on. Particular or increasingly general relationships therefore occur continually among these activities.

This general interrelating of activities, then, presupposes multiple systems of autoregulation or equilibration, which will be the result of circumstances as much as of epigenetic potential. The operations of intelligence can themselves be considered as superior forms of these adjustments, and this indicates both the importance of the equilibration factor and its relative independence with respect to preformed biological structures.

But here too, even if the factors of equilibration can be thought of as extremely general and relatively independent of particular social environments, the hypothesis requires verification by comparative studies. In particular, processes of equilibration of this kind are observed in the formation of concepts of conservation, whose stages show (in the environments studied) not just sequential succession but the elaboration of compensatory systems whose intrinsic characteristics are extremely typical of these adjustments through successive degrees. But are these specific stages to be found everywhere? If the answer is yes, then we would have, if not yet a verification of the hypothesis, then at least a more or less favourable indication. If the answer is no, it would, on the other hand, be the sign of cultural and educational influences both specific and variable.

3. Social factors in inter-individual co-ordination

Turning now to social factors, it is appropriate to introduce an essential and no less important distinction concerning these in the area of psychobiology, namely between epigenetic potentialities and effective adjustments or equilibrations which appear or are formed in the course of behavioural activities. This distinction is one between general social (or inter-individual) interactions or relationships common to all societies, and particular cultural or educational traditions or rearing practices which vary from one society to another or from one restricted social environment to another.

Whether we study children in Geneva, Paris, New York or Moscow, in the mountains of Iran or the heart of Africa, or on an island in the Pacific, we observe everywhere certain ways of conducing social exchanges between children, or between children and adults, which act through their functioning alone, regardless of the context of information handed down through education. In all environments, individuals ask questions, work together, discuss, oppose things, and so on; and this constant exchange between individuals takes place throughout the whole of development according to a process of socialization which involves the social life of children among themselves as much as their relationships with older children or adults of all ages. Just as Durkheim invoked general social mechanisms in holding that 'beneath civilisations, there is civilisation', so, in order to deal with relationships between cognitive functions and social factors, it is essential to begin by contrasting 'general patterns' of group activity to particular cultural traditions which are crystallised in a different way in each society. Thus, even if it were the case that our stages and our results were to be found in all societies studied, this would still prove nothing more than that these convergent developments are of a strictly individual nature: since it is evident that children everywhere benefit from social contacts from the most tender age, this would further indicate that there exist certain common processes of socialization which interact with the processes of equilibration discussed above (cf. section 2).

These interactions are so probable, and probably so closely knit, that we can immediately form the hypothesis, which should be confirmed or disproved by future comparative studies, that in the realm of cognitive functions at least, it is quite possible that the general co-ordination of activities, whose progressive equilibration seems to be a constituent of the formation of logical or logico-mathematical operations, concerns actions which are collective or between individuals as well as individual actions. In other words, whether we are concerned with actions executed individually or with actions carried out communally and involving social exchanges, collaborations, oppositions and so on, we would find the same laws of relationship and adjustment resulting in the same final structures of operations or co-operations, in the sense of joint operations. Logic could thus be considered, in the sense of being the final form of equilibrations, as being simultaneously individual and social: individual in so far as it is general or common to all individuals and likewise social in so far as it is general or common to all societies.

4. Factors in the transmission of educational and cultural concepts

On the other hand, over and above this functional and to some extent age-invariant nucleus which is nevertheless susceptible to construction and evolution, characteristic of exchanges between individuals, we must of course consider the factor which is principally age independent, and formed by the cultural traditions and the communications of education which vary from one society to another. It is these differential social pressures which generally come to mind when one speaks of 'social factors', and it is obvious that (to the extent that cognitive processes can vary from one society to another) it is this group of factors as distinct from the preceding group that we should bear in mind, beginning with the various languages, which are capable of exercising a greater or lesser influence, if not on the operations themselves, at least in the detail of conceptualizations (content of classifications, of relations, etc.).

Comparative research in the area of cognitive processes

Once we have admitted this classification into four kinds of factors, according to the general types of relationships between the individual and the social environment, let us attempt to separate out the essential value which would be offered by comparative research as to our knowledge of cognitive processes. The central problem in this respect is that of the nature of intellectual operations and in particular of logico-mathematical structures. Several hypotheses are possible which correspond, among other things, to the four factors previously distinguished, with additional subdivisions where the need arises.

Biological factors and factors in the co-ordination of actions
A first interpretation would be to consider these, if not as innate, at least as resulting exclusively from biological factors of an epigenetic nature (maturation, etc.). Lorenz, one of the founders of contemporary ethology, who believes in the idea of *a priori* forms of knowledge and interprets them in terms of instincts, inclines towards this view.

From the point of view of the comparative data which has become, and which will eventually become available, there are two questions which must be distinguished: will the same developmental stages always be found, taking into account, of course, the possible corrections and improvements to be applied to the overall picture as we know it, and will they always be found at the same average ages? In order to answer these two kinds of questions, it is, moreover, useful and even almost essential to have reference points at our disposal in comparing the evolution of responses to operational tests (conservation, classification and inclusion, serialization, numerical correspondence, etc.) with the evolution, with age, of responses to tests of simple intellectual performance, like those which are generally used to determine an intellectual quotient.

Comparative research is only just beginning, and it would be extremely imprudent to draw conclusions from it so soon, given the material at one's disposal and the great difficulties, both linguistic and otherwise, that arise in replications, not to mention the long initiation necessary for mastery of the test procedures, which are increasingly difficult to use the more closely they relate to operational functioning. But the first studies give an indication of certain results which at least point out a possible line of interpretation, in the event of their being generally applicable.

In Iran, for example, Mohseni questioned children from Teheran who had received schooling, and young illiterates from country areas, by means of conservation tests, on the one hand, and performance tests (Porteus maze, drawing tests etc.) on the other. The three main results obtained on five-to ten-year-old children are as follows: (a) in broad outline, the same stages were found both in town and in country, in Iran and in Geneva (in the order of appearance of conservation of substance, weight and volume, etc.); (b) we observe a systematic displacement of two to three years for operational tests between village and town children, but the actual ages concerned are almost the same in Teheran and in Europe; and (c) the retardation is more considerable, at four years and particularly at five years, for performance tests between village and town children, to the extent that the village children appeared mentally deficient if the operational tests were not taken into account.

Assuming that similar results are obtained elsewhere, one would be led to formulate the following hypotheses:

1 A more general verification of constancy in the order of stages would tend to show their sequential character, in the sense indicated above. So far this constant order seems to be confirmed (in Hong Kong, in Aden, in Martinique, in South Africa), but it is obviously necessary to have still more data at our disposal. To the extent that one could continue to speak of sequential order, there would be an analogy here with epigenetic development in the sense used by Waddington, and consequently a certain probability of intervention of factor 1 mentioned above. But how far can we pursue this analogy? In order to be able to invoke with certainty the concept of biological factors in maturation, we would have to be in a position to establish the existence not only of a sequential order of stages, but of some chronologically fixed average dates of appearance. Mohseni's results show, on the contrary, systematic retardation of stages in the country as compared with town children – which indicates, of course, that factors other than those of maturation are playing a part.

On the other hand, in the field of representation of thought we would perhaps be able to find an important age which is the same everywhere: namely that of the forming of the semiotic or symbolic function, which appears in our environments at approximately one to two years of age (formation of symbolic play, of mental images, etc., and above all, language development). It seems that the principal factor which makes possible this semiotic function is the internalization of imitation. This latter, at the sensory-motor level, already constitutes a kind of representation in act, by virtue of being a motor copy of a model, in such a way that its continuations, at first deferred in imitation, then internalized in imitation, permit the formation of representations in images, and so on. But this process of deferred responses followed by internalization naturally presupposes certain neurological conditions, for example inhibition at the level of certain stages in the realization of action schemas, without carrying them through to completion. A comparative study of the sensory-motor forms of imitation and of the ages of appearance of semiotic functions, taking deferred imitation as its starting-point, would perhaps show certain chronological regularities, not only in the sequential order of stages, but in the more or less fixed dates of formation: in this case, we would be getting even closer to the possible maturational factors which relate to the epigenetic system (intervention of language centres, etc.).

2 The second clear result from Mohseni's research is the fairly general retardation in country children as compared with those from Teheran concerning operational tests (conservation) as much as measures of performance. This retardation thus undoubtedly proves the intervention of factors distinct from those of mere biological maturation. But here we may hesitate between the three groups of factors labelled 2, 3, and 4 above, that is to say the factors of activity and equilibration of actions, the factors of general interaction between individuals, and those of the transmission of educational and cultural concepts. In fact, any of these factors could play a part. Where factor 2 is concerned the author has noted the startling lack of activity in country children who not only have no schools in general but not even any toys, except pebbles or pieces of wood, and whose situation bears witness to a passivity and apathy which are constant enough. We are therefore in the presence at the same time of a weak development of individual patterns of activity (factor 2), activities between individuals (factor 3), and transmission of ideas through education, which is reduced since the children are illiterate (factor 4); and this implies a convergence of these three groups of connected factors. How, then, can they be distinguished?

3 On this point the third result obtained by Mohseni is instructive: in spite of the deplorable situation of the country children, it turns out that their responses to operational tests are superior to their results on measures of performance. Even though they might be considered as mentally deficient or even as imbeciles on the basis of measures of intellectual performance alone, they are only two or three years behind the Teheran schoolchildren on tests of conservation. Here again it is obvious that we could not risk generalizations before being in possession of large quantities of data originating from environments which differ yet again. But, to demonstrate the interest of the problem and the multiplicity of distinct situations which remain to be studied, let us draw attention to the fact that Boisclair, together with Laurendeau and Pinard, has begun to study in Martinique a population of schoolchildren who were in no way illiterate since they were following the French programme of education for primary schools, and who nevertheless showed evidence of a delay of approximately four years in the principal operational tests; in this case, the delay seems to be attributable to the general characteristics of social interactions (factor 3 in liaison with factor 2) more than to a deficiency in education (factor 4).

In the case of Iran, the interesting lead of successes on conservation tests, which are the index of operational mechanisms, over the performance measures used elsewhere, seems to indicate a duality of nature between relationships of a fairly general kind necessary to the functioning of intelligence and more specialized acquisitions relating to particular problems. This would lead, in the event of these results being replicated, to a distinction between factors 2 and 3 considered together (general patterns of activity, whether within or between individuals) and factor 4 (educational procedures): the operational tests, in other words, would give rise to better results because they are linked to the relationships necessary to all intelligence (necessary in as much as they are products of progressive equilibration and not as antecedent biological conditions), while the performance measures would undergo delays of a function of more particular cultural factors, which in this case are particularly lacking.

These are, in broad outline, the various approaches to the problem which could be provided by comparative data of the kind collected by Mohseni. But these are only extremely broad outlines and it behoves us to examine now in more detail the role of social factors within the scope of sections 3 and 4.

Social factors in educational transmission
If operational structures were not explained by the most general laws of behavioural relationships in accordance with the hypothesis which we have developed, it would be necessary to consider some more restricted factors. The two principal factors could be, for example, an educational process by the adult analogous to those which generate moral imperatives, and language itself, in so far as it involves the crystallization of syntax and semantics, which, under their general forms, comprise a system of logic.

(a) The hypothesis that education by the adult has a formative action undoubtedly contains a certain degree of truth, for, even in the perspective of general patterns of activities (material or internalized in operation), the adult, being more advanced than the child, can help him and speed up his development in the course of educational processes either within the family or at school. The question, however, is whether this factor plays an exclusive rôle: this was the view of Durkheim, for whom logic proceeds, like ethics and law, from the total structure of society and imposes itself on the individual, owing to social and above all to educational constraints. Bruner likewise tends towards this view; he has asserted, although thinking of educational processes which are less related to schooling and nearer to the American models of learning, that one can learn anything, at any age, by going about it in an appropriate manner.

Where Durkheim's view is concerned (but not that of Bruner, who emphasizes laboratory experiments rather than comparative studies), some findings, like those which have been observed in Martinique by the Canadian psychologists, seem to indicate that ordinary schooling according to the French programme (which facilitates the comparison), is not enough to ensure normal development of operational structures, since there is in this case a three or four year delay as compared with children from other cultural environments. But here again we must of course be on our guard against over-hasty conclusions: it would still remain, in particular, to separate out family and school influences. All that we would claim is that the comparative method is, on this point as on others, capable of providing the solutions we are looking for.

(b) As for the major problem of language, in its interactions with the development of operations, we are beginning to see more clearly following Sinclair's research on linguistic development in the child, and that of Inhelder and Sinclair on the rôle of language in the learning of operational structures.

We shall limit ourselves, without entering into the details of method and results, to emphasizing the perspectives opened up by Sinclair's research from the comparative point of view. Let us recall, for example, the experiment on two groups of children, the older group possessing structures of conservation in a clear form (together with explicit arguments) and the other, younger, group at a similarly unequivocal level of non-conservation; the subjects from these two groups were asked to describe not the material which was previously used to determine the groups, but certain objects attributed to characters represented by dolls (a short fat pencil, another long thin one, several small balls, a smaller number of larger balls, etc.). It was then established, at a highly significant level, that the language used in the two groups differed as to the expressions of comparison employed: while the subjects without conservation used above all what the linguist Bull has called 'scalars' ('large' and 'small', 'many' or 'few', etc.), the subjects from the operational level made use of 'vectors' ('more' and 'less', etc.). In addition, the structure of expression differed according to binary modes ('this one is longer and thinner') or quaternary ('here it is fat and the other one is thin; here it is long and the other one is short'), and so on. There is thus a close correlation between operativity and language, but in what sense? Learning experiments, which do not directly concern us here, show that by training subjects who are not at the operational stage to use the expressions of older children, only small operational progress is obtained (one out of ten cases); the question still exists moreover of establishing whether we are dealing with the action of language as such, or with the influence of exercises in analysis which are involved in learning, and whether certain aspects of progress would not have taken place (without this learning through development of schemas) as a function of various activities. It seems, therefore, that it is operativity which leads to the structuring of language (preferably within the framework of pre-existing models of language, of course), rather than the converse.

We thus see immediately the great interest which there would be in repeating experiments of this kind as a function of various languages. Sinclair has found the same results in French and English. But it remains to make use of very different languages. In Turkish, for example, there exists only one vector, which corresponds to the French expression 'encore' ('again', 'still'); in order to say 'more' one would say 'many again' and to say 'fewer', 'few again'. It is obvious that in other languages one will find plenty of other combinations. In this case, it would be of great interest to examine the delay in development of operational structures as a function of the language of the subjects and to return to Sinclair's experiments on children of different levels. If the evolution of thought structures remained the same in spite of linguistic variations, this would be a factual datum of some importance which would argue in favour of factors of progressive and autonomous equilibration. Supposing, on the other hand, that there were modifications of operations according to linguistic environments, it would remain to examine closely the meaning of these dependencies, according to the experimental model proposed by Sinclair.

Conclusion

In short, the psychology which we are carrying out in our various environments, characterized by a certain culture, a certain language and so on, remains essentially conjectural in as much as the comparative material necessary as a control has not yet been provided. And, to proceed no further than the field of cognitive functions, the comparative research whose coming has long been awaited does not just concern the child, but development as a whole, including the final adult stages. When Lévy-Bruhl raised the problem of the 'prelogic' appropriate to the 'primitive mentality', he doubtless exaggerated the contradictions, just as his posthumous retraction perhaps exaggerates in the opposite direction the generality of structures; however, there still exists a series of questions as yet unanswered, it seems to us, by the works of Lévi-Strauss: for example, what is the operational level of adults in a tribal organization, concerning technical intelligence (which was completely neglected by Lévy-Bruhl), verbal intelligence, solution of elementary logico-mathematical problems, and so on? It is obviously only by understanding the situation which is that of the adults themselves that developmental data relating to inferior levels of age would assume their full significance. It is in particular quite possible (and this is the impression given by generally known ethnographic works) that in many societies adult thought does not go beyond the level of 'concrete' operations and thus does not reach that of propositional operations which are achieved between twelve and fifteen years in our surroundings: it would thus be of great interest to know whether the previous stages develop more slowly in children in such societies or whether the degree of equilibrium which will not be passed is attained, as with us, at about seven to eight years or only with a slight degree of retardation.

21 Early childhood experience and later education in complex cultures

Margaret Mead

Education in a complex society may be seen as merely an extension of the educational process found in simpler societies, but taking longer, requiring more specialized institutions, and involving progressive absorption into wider or narrower segments of the total society. Or it may be seen as involving, from the very start (from the moment that a rattle is put into an infant's hands, or a set of alphabet blocks is spilled on the floor) a set of assumptions that are different in kind from education in a primitive society. Both approaches have their uses. By taking the former, Hart and Yehudi Cohen have been able to point out striking correspondences between the treatment of the prepubertal and pubertal young, and the initiation ceremonies and educational experiences to which they are subjected. I have used the same approach in discussing such questions as the way in which children learn sex roles or control of impulse. It may be said that where we are concerned with character formation – the process by which children learn to discipline impulses and structure their expectations of the behavior of others – this cross-cultural approach is very valuable. It provides insights into such subjects as conscience formation, the relative importance of different sanctioning systems, sin, shame and pride, and guilt, and into the relationships between independence training and achievement motivation.

It may be argued that the younger the child, the more we are concerned with educational processes that are universal and of fundamental importance throughout life, and least imbued with the specific cultural differences that distinguish a Frenchman from an Egyptian, or an Eskimo from a Bushman or from an American. All infants must be weaned, but only a certain number will ultimately be asked to master calculus or a dead language. All infants must learn to respond with enthusiasm or apathy to adult incentives, but only a

Source: *Anthropological Perspectives on Education*, ed. Murray Wax et al., New York, Basic Books (1971).

certain number, in identified countries and at particular periods, will come to care about the controversies between Stoics and Epicureans, or between fundamentalists and contextualists. So it has been fashionable in many areas in which the relationship between child development and later character has been studied, to concentrate on uniformly present experiences, and to ignore the subtler and more difficult problems of what as well as how the child is learning.

Take, for example, the question of reward and punishment. It is relatively easy to characterize systems of child rearing as using either reward or punishment in certain distinguishable proportions. The reflections of this learning can be followed in later life, and differences can be demonstrated in the school performance of children who act out fear of being wrong, as compared with those who actively seek rewards for being right. Such reflections can also be recognized later in the conformist behavior of the civil servant - secure unless he makes a positive mistake - and in the freer behavior of the politician who must perform in some positive manner if he is to be rewarded by re-election. It is upon the recognition of identifiable sequences such as these that constructs such as David McClelland's achievement motivation are built.

Literacy

But we may ask instead what happens if we stress what a modern society requires its new members to learn, rather than start with the relationship between early disciplines and later learning. For purposes of study, we would then juxtapose two societies - one that required that children learn to read and the other that did not. We would not consider learning to read in terms of motivation, of who taught the child his letters, or whether, while learning, the child had his hands smacked, or had honey put on his tongue. We would say, instead, that learning to read involves first the idea that such a thing as reading exists, that artificial marks that are small, regular, identifiable, and recurrent have meaning. We would note that when someone who can read looks at one book, he utters a particular series of words, while if he looks at another book, he utters a different series of words. Children often learn this elementary fact by associating sequences of words with pictures, and 'read' by reciting a memorized sentence that goes with a particular picture. They may then move to the over-all 'look' of the sentence - whether it is long or short, or contains a certain number of capital letters. The child who does this is not learning to read, but is, in fact, learning an early form of reading badly. He is dependent upon past experience and upon the extraneous and irrelevant likeness between the contours of words but is skipping the stage of learning that is the essence of reading – the arbitrary correspondence between symbols and sounds.

So one child may learn, depending upon the kind of home in which he lives, that there are many, many books, that the pages of each yield different materials, and that if he can learn to decipher these pages he will have a new experience, as compared with another child who learns to repeat, from minor clues, a sentence that an adult has read to him. This fundamental piece of over-all learning is probably determinative of whether individuals will be literate or nonliterate, no matter how much schooling they are exposed to. The history of developing countries – in which education is imposed, often in a different language, on people who own no books and read no newspaper – has demonstrated how it is possible to make a people formally literate, able to read and write simple information, decipher signs, and keep lists and records, although they never read, in the sense that they pick up a written object of unknown content. Sometimes, children from nonreading homes may learn by accident, later in life, that reading is a way of opening a window to something new. These individuals experience a tremendous sense of freedom and enlightenment, comparable in freshness but often greater in intensity to the experience of a child who for the first time reads something new by himself. Elementary education geared to establishing literacy but not reading ability in people who are thought of as 'the masses' or even 'the people,' carries with it a continuation of what the child has learned at home. It strengthens the concept that reading is simply saying what you know is there (for example, whether today is Monday or Tuesday, or if it is the first or the second of the month) instead of being a way of finding out things you don't know, or of reading a new story with an end you don't know.

One of the familiar phenomena of the American scene in the post World War II years, is the terrible boredom that reading parents feel toward Dick and Jane, the reader based on the simple expectation that learning to read is learning to reproduce correctly only what is in the reader.

A terrible degeneration accompanies the shift from teachers who read to teachers who do not read. It is often found in developing countries, as missionaries are phased out in favor of native speakers who never read but can teach competently enough from a text. Teachers who read can teach children what reading is about; teachers who have not learned to read but have only learned to be literate, cannot do this.

So we may usefully compare the infant in a primitive preliterate home, the infant in a literate but nonreading home, and the infant in a reading home. The infant in the primitive home never sees any event that suggests that there is a substitute for the spoken and heard word. If his father wants to send a message to his brother-in-law in the next village, someone has to go and tell him. If it is important to know whether a debt consists of forty dog's teeth or only of thirty, there is a lengthy debate with supporting evidence, and the matter is likely to be clinched by the dictum of whichever participant is most respected or known to have the most accurate memory. There is no way to go back to the event in question except in memory, and people's memories differ. Whether the child will learn that an event actually did occur, and that different people give different versions, some more accurate than others, or simply that the world consists of claims and counterclaims that are designed to promote the purpose of one person rather than another, depends upon the particular culture. This may seem a very small point, but it is perhaps not an accident that those people whose interest in relating past events is simply to validate present purposes, may, when writing comes to them, use it for forgery rather than for records. In contrast, those people who have been deeply concerned over establishing the actuality of an event, take delightedly to the possibilities of script that can provide them with accurate records and cross-checks on the process. This difference between regarding script as accurate and reliable, and regarding it as something to be manipulated, reflecting as it does much earlier attitudes – recurs at many levels of the use of records. It is seen, for example, in the fundamentalist approach to the Scriptures, which is based on an excessive reverence for the written word among people who themselves could read but did not write. It is seen in other peculiar manifestations, such as the willingness of otherwise well-trained scientists to believe that a film, in which they are dependent on the experimenter to identify the subjects, nevertheless is convincing proof that something occurred.

So, in the primitive home, into which the idea of script will penetrate with conquest and community development programs, are already a series of underlying expectancies that will partly shape the ways in which reading and writing will be learned. One of these expectancies will be the amount of curiosity that is cultivated within the particular sociocultural setting. If there is a strong interest in the strange and the unknown, then the groundwork is laid for looking at pictures and later reading books about that which is not known. Or one may find the society in which there is strong genealogical interest. Where writing is done by individuals it is used primarily to preserve the history of the family, the only photographs in which people are interested are those of family members. The intermediate position in which pages of *Life* magazine are pasted sideways on the wall to cover a crack, or as meaningless decorations, are active preparations for the rejection of reading. Probably the single picture pasted sideways is more threatening to the future literacy of children in the family than the differences in abstract and concrete thinking being so heavily emphasized today. The picture pasted sideways means that the symbolic nature of position in space is ignored, and also very often that even the representational quality of the picture is ignored; it becomes a bright red splotch on a gray wall.

The first introduction of a primitive people to script may come in a variety of ways. A government official may come into the village and try to take a census. As people repeat their names, he writes down their responses, often with only the most faulty approximations. But still, since people remember things such as the order in which they gave their names, they can recognize their names the next time the official comes. At this point, another essential piece of learning may occur. Writing is seen as a way in which people can get the better of you, know who you are, relate your past actions to the future, check on whom you married, how many children you have, and where you live. In New Guinea, natives almost invariably responded in this way to attempts at census-taking by the government. It became fashionable to have a 'government name' that was used for no other purpose, and that people remembered only with the greatest difficulty from one governmental visit to the next. Instead of records being considered as a way in which one becomes securely placed in the world, so that over a period of time one's identity becomes firmer and more unassailable, record-keeping is thus turned into a hostile act. This response of the illiterate to the record-keeping abilities of the powers that be is reflected at a higher level in current attitudes toward a central computer. Such concern is constantly expressed as a fear that knowledge of who you are will only be used to do you damage. In New Guinea, the response means that electoral rolls are almost impossible to compile, that savings bank accounts lie dormant because the depositor has not claimed them – in fact, has often forgotten the name under which they were deposited – and that individuals who need treatment for leprosy or tuberculosis may either go unidentified or receive double doses of treatment.

On the other hand, a first experience with writing may be brought by missionaries. If the missionaries refer their power and superior wisdom not to lists of the natives' names, but to lists of other peoples' names and deeds, then the power of the book, as compared with the power of the handmade list or record, can become salient. The aspiring young native will also want to learn to read that book. Indeed, his ability to read it aloud, to read different things from different pages, will give him prestige among his nonliterate fellows. He comes among them clothed in a mantle of external and higher authority, conferred by books that he can vocalize and they cannot. The prestige of all sacred texts, read by the elite, memorized by the humble, and in cases where religion is transplanted from one language group to another, often 'read' in the sense of being pronounced without respect to meaning, can be referred to this experience in which the one who reads has power not shared by those who do not.

The ease with which literacy can be spread, among the children of immigrants or within a class or group to which education was previously unavailable, is partly explained by the obvious power that educated children acquire over their uneducated parents. Any association of reading or writing with increased autonomy and authority can be made attractive. This was so even where the parents were themselves literate, like shtetel Jews. As soon as he was literate, a boy could argue with the elders and be treated with respect, and thus he was permitted the verbal release of aggression which physically had been restrained since childhood. 'And the love of learning was born'.

If we shift from the consideration of a primitive people experiencing script for the first time to children learning from their immediate surroundings what script is about, we find that early learning may be equally determinative. What is a book? One of many, standing on shelves, one of many kinds – some read by Daddy, some by Mommy, some by older siblings, some recent presents, some heirlooms, and some read by Mommy when she was a little girl. What is a book? Something that Daddy is writing and you mustn't disturb him or he won't get that chapter finished. What are those long shiny pieces of paper with printing all over the back that Mommy gives you to draw pictures on, but she says are part of Daddy's book. Why did grandmother look so stern when you knocked that book off the table, and why did she start talking about the way your dead grandfather felt about books? How does writing your name in the front of a book make it your book? What does 'dedicated' mean – so that this book, which is dedicated to you, is somehow more yours than any other book, but nobody reads it to you because you aren't old enough? What is the difference between books with pictures for children and books without pictures for grownups? Why don't grownups need pictures to tell them what Little Red Riding Hood looked like? What tells them? What is a dictionary, and why are Daddy and Mommy always having a kind of fight that ends with one of them going and getting a dictionary, and one looks pleased and one looks angry? What is an engagement book, and what is an address book, and what is the difference between the telephone book Mommy made, and the big one that is printed? And what is printing? How do they make so many copies of the newspaper that are all alike, and yet there is only one copy of each book in the house? Why, if someone gives you a second copy of *When We Were Very Young* does Mommy say, 'Oh, we have that; we'll give it to Jimmy?'

For the child in the home of those who not only read but also write books, a book becomes something that is made by the kind of people you know. A book is something that you yourself might write. In fact, you can begin now, folding pieces of paper together in book form and covering them with imitation letters. Or if you are a little older, write the beginnings of a story, labeled 'Susan Lane, her book.' Children from such homes passionately enter into reading. If they have difficulties, it is because they have serious problems of eye coordination, or deep emotional difficulties, or occasionally because they have gotten so far ahead of themselves that the discrepancy between what they can read and what they can write is unbearably frustrating. Such children have no image of a house that does not contain books, of an adult who does not often have a book in his hand, or of an individuality of which books are not a part. The hazards here are hazards that come from the overevaluation of books. The child whose eyes coordinate more slowly may become frightened and his parents may share his fright. 'Maybe he isn't going to read' is a statement almost equivalent to 'Maybe he isn't going to be human.' The child who wants to learn, but who is held back because his parents have been warned not to attempt to teach their children prematurely, may give up. The bright moment passes, never to be regained. But attitudes toward the importance of reading have been established for good or ill, long before the child goes to school.

It will be by careful detailed ethnographical study of different kinds of homes, of which the two quoted represent extremes, that we should be able to chart, and correct for, children's earliest learnings about reading and writing. Inevitably, experience will be diverse and defective with respect to the goals held up by a society in which reading is absolutely essential. In addition to the kinds of broad learnings that have been sketched in here, there will be many idiosyncratic miscarriages: children to whom letters or numbers come to have a magical significance, children who learn to read secretly and so become unintelligible to those around them, and children who block completely on part of the symbolic process. But these individual early sequences can only be fully identified, allowed for and treated, if the broader cultural outlines associated with class and occupation, region and religion, are better known.

Abstract thought

Much of the current discussion of the relationship between types of thinking displayed by school children in the United States, which distinguishes between abstract and concrete thinking, lacks comparative perspective, and so fails to take into account many significant dimensions. However, when the various explanatory schemes for the development of thought that have evolved within one culture, or that include material from other cultures taken out of context, are subjected to comparative scrutiny, the kind of links between early childhood experience and type of thinking that individuals will display as adults can be distinguished in outline, however lacking we may be in detailed research on their implications.

Whether one follows the classical outlines of Binet, the original schemes of Piaget – or whether one follows the developmental schemes of Gesell and Ilg, it seems clear that we must take into account when, from whom, and in what way children encounter such types of thinking, as, for example, the Binet interpretation of proverbs, the Piaget demand for a recognition of the conservation of matter, or the Gesell-Ilg recognition of mathematical pattern as a recurrent spiraling capacity. Every intellectual capacity that is later tested by achievement, test, or observation is intimately linked with early childhood experience, with the level of education of parent or nurse, with the structure and furnishing of the home, with the content with which the members of the family and the neighborhood are preoccupied, and with the availability of the apparatus and technology on which abstract thought is dependent.

The child who is cared for in infancy and early childhood by individuals of a lower level of education than the child will later be expected to reach, faces a different educational situation than one who is reared from infancy by parents who represent the same level of education to which the child is expected to aspire. Whether it is an explanation of time or space, money, or the telephone, or a recognition of the child's attempt to search for some generalization among dissimilar objects, the highly educated parent or surrogate will meet the child on a different level than will the educated nurse, child nurse, or peasant grandmother. Where the educational level is lower, crude, or folk, concrete explanations may be given that will coexist in the child's mind and interfere with his later learning required by the school. This situation is further complicated by the relative intelligence of nurse and parent, which need not be proportional to their educational level. If the nurse is actually more intelligent, but less literate and less widely experienced than the parent, the child may develop considerable confusion about modes of thought. If the nurse or grandparent is able to draw on a folk level of thinking, rich in imagery and metaphor, while the parent represents the first generation of schooling – arid, disassociated from his or her primary learning – this may lead to the kind of repudiation of the intellectual life in which poverty and immediate existential experience are opposed to the hypocrisy, or aridity of formal learning. The importance to the total character structure of the child, of the nurse who taps a different cultural level, has long been recognized, but the educational consequences for thought remain unexplored. But it surely accounts for the superior achievement of parent-reared children who come from families with several generations of high achievement. They are exposed to highly abstract thinking from earliest childhood as contrasted with (1) children reared by nurses with low levels of literacy; (2) those who grow up with a lower level of thought at home than that encountered in church and school; (3) those who grow up in homes where no abstraction is ever made, and who in many cases are taught by teachers who came from similar homes, and who have only attained a schoolroom acquaintance with educated thought.

High intelligence occurs in all social strata and every ethnic group. A few individuals from primitive tribes or severely disadvantaged groups have risen to great intellectual distinction. But emphasis on these conspicuous exceptions has obscured the equally significant fact that the absence of a nurturing environment stunts and stultifies the mind of a child so that in most cases high natural intelligence is never realized. Early contact between young children and highly intelligent, highly educated adults is the best means we have yet devised for giving children a chance to escape the limitations imposed by uneducated parents and limited homes. This was evidenced in the striking contrast between the style – as expressed in posture, gesture, expression, and responsiveness – of the infants reared in Anna Freud's special residential home for children during World War II, where the children were cared for and taught by highly educated refugees, and that of children of the same class who were cared for by lower-class adults with limited education.

But the failure to make finer discriminations than rural and urban, educated and uneducated, colored and white, professional and nonprofessional, rich and poor, is likely to obscure the issue, especially in the United States. In some ethnic groups – notably Eastern European Jewish groups – parents in the poorest homes, with the simplest occupations and very little formal schooling, may still provide a premium on thinking and exegesis that supports the child in school. Even before he enters school, the child learns the rudiments of analytical thought. On the other hand there are homes in which the father's highly paid occupation and specialized education is never made manifest, or where the children are left to the care of unintelligent and uneducated nurses. In such homes the children are more handicapped than those in a very simple home, where the Bible is read with reverence, and the preacher is expected to discuss Scripture like an educated man. When we are dealing with large populations or with whole ethnic groups in the midst of transition, or with large urban immigrant groups with a given background, it may often be possible to establish some regularities. Such regularities can be discerned in the contrast between the adaptation of Japanese and Chinese immigrant children in California, or between the intellectuality of Eastern European and Middle Eastern Jewish children on the East Coast of the United States. But any attempt to generalize without research into the specific group is dangerous. What we need is more basic research on the one hand, and more devices for assaying the quality of preschool experience on the other.

The consequences of the differences, in the intellectual tone and interest of those who are most in contact with a small child, involve a variety of factors, some cultural, some idiosyncratic, and some familial. On the cultural level it is possible to work out in some detail the consequences for later learning of living in houses constructed without benefit of any precise measurement, without clocks or calendars, or even toys that embody some of the principles on which education is postulated. The house built to specifications – the fine machine tool, the clock and calendar, the thermometer and barometer, the compass and the blender, the thermostat and the television set – all carry a set of messages that can be absorbed in early childhood and later transformed into an interest in mathematics and computers. This can be so even when there is no adult in the home capable of explicitly fostering a child's interest in abstraction. Similarly, the city child learns from plants that mother keeps for show, or father keeps to impress the neighbors, or from herbs growing in the window box, things about a part of the universe that he would not otherwise experience. The regularities in the homes of any group of children can be analyzed for these mute messages that equip them, long before they enter school, for receptivities far beyond the level of the background from which they come. All this learning will be enormously reinforced if at least one adult in the home understands and explains a short-circuit, or the principle upon which the thermostat operates. But the artifacts that are the products of science nevertheless carry their own teaching: the child who comes from housing built on the basis of explicit geometrical knowledge makes a different order of discovery of geometry than the child who comes from a circular thatched dwelling, or from a crazy, sagging hut made of broken pieces of tin. In turn, the child who comes from a squatter's town built partly of thatch and partly of fragments of tin that have been shaped to recognizable geometrical forms learns still something else about pattern as being independent of materials.

Conversely, it is possible for homes to so smother children in words and high-level generalizations that their ability to work from direct perception of shape and size and material may be permanently impaired. High levels of verbal precocity may accompany very rudimentary understanding of basic physical and physiological relationships.

It should be borne in mind that each of the situations with which I have dealt may occur on a cultural, societywide basis. They may be characteristic of particular families, and therefore, incongruent with the over-all cultural emphasis. They may even be attributes of one individual within a family who gives the young child some extraordinarily deviant and unorthodox intellectual exposure. When the familial or individual style deviates from the wider style, the educator has still another element to cope with – the unexpected language of particular children that renders them incomprehensible, unpredictable, and maladjusted in the schoolroom with its standardized expectations.

Language learning before school age

During the 1920s it was argued that whatever difficulties children had on entering school, because they came from homes where a foreign language was spoken, would be eliminated by the third grade. The most significant attempt to refute this argument was a study of bilingual and monolingual children, in which the effects of a type of bilingualism associated with different contexts such as home, school, and play, were shown to be reflected in later school achievement. The design of this study has since come under criticism; there are still no definitive studies on the subject. However, from related fields, there have come some suggestive observations that should be considered.

Jakobson has assembled evidence to show that the way in which a language is learned by an initial dichotomizing of a large unstructured repertoire of sounds, which are then progressively elaborated into a structured system, can be found to be repeated in the loss of the mastery of speech that occurs in traumatic amnesia. This study suggests – and the suggestion is supported by observations in other fields – that children learn the phonemic structure of their language at a very early age. It may be hypothesized, although there is no evidence yet in support, that certain fundamental morphemic generalizations are also learned early, and that fundamental ways of viewing the world, with contrasts between durative and punctuated action and with an insistence upon sources of information and matters of this sort, are also learned within the first three or four years of life. At present, it seems probable that the ability of the child to learn other linguistic and thought patterns is not so much a question of the interference of the latter pattern by the earlier one, as it is of the conditions of learning the two patterns. If two or more languages are learned, either sequentially or simultaneously, but one is the language of play and the other the language of discipline; if one is taught within the intimate environment of the home and the other in the more demanding and impersonal environment of school; if one is a language that is spoken by all the members of the child's environment, and the other spoken only by servants, or only by parents, or only by teachers; then the learning of the two patterns will be affectively weighted, and the learning will be of a different sort.

When, for example, a Spanish-speaking child is taught English by a teacher whose mother tongue is Spanish, and who has only a classroom mastery of English, the situation is profoundly different from the case in which a child is taught English by a native English speaker with a good idiomatic knowledge of Spanish, or by a teacher who speaks no Spanish at all. It seems likely, but it has never been properly studied, that if the mother tongue is a dialect in which literacy is never attained, rather than a literate language in which literacy is first obtained, the results for the child's subsequent use of language will be very different. The success of the Colonial Dutch in teaching literacy and languages in Indonesia was based upon teaching literacy in the mother tongue, followed by literacy in Malay (the Indonesia *lingua franca* in the Netherlands Indies), followed by Dutch taught by native speakers, followed by English, French, or German taught as another formally mastered European language, by Dutch native speakers. Here a sequence of teaching had been developed that was severely mutilated when the school system was revised, and the Dutch dropped out. English teaching deteriorated markedly when the Dutch step was removed and Indonesian teachers were asked to go directly from Indonesian – a second language related to their own mother tongue – to English, a language that they had learned as a second European language from Dutch native speakers.

Experience of this sort suggests that it is most important to explore the relationship between different kinds of language learning and to identify breaks and continuities in the sequence within which different versions of the same language, or different languages, are learned. The most significant situations may well be those in which significant adults in the child's world do not share a knowledge of the different varieties of speech with which the young child has to cope; different degrees of identification of these versions may be most important. For example, children who speak a dialect, identified and labeled as a dialect, in a country such as France or Germany or Italy, may have parents who speak the dialect at home, but use the standard language in all formal and public situations. Such children may be far less handicapped than those who speak a version of the language that is treated not as a dialect with an identifiable style of its own but simply as class-typed, or regionally- or ethnically-typed, as in lower-class urban English in the United Kingdom, 'bad English' in the English-speaking Caribbean, or the typical Southern rural Negro Americans in the United States. If the mother tongue is treated as an inferior version of the standard language, rather than as a dialect, movement becomes much more difficult between the phonemic, morphemic, and cognitive structures of the two forms, the home language and the school language.

When, as is so often the case, the teacher has an inadequate grasp of the standard language and can only operate within a formal school context, the children with class-typed or race-typed speech are deprived of any formal grasp of the differences between the two forms. On the other hand, the teacher who is a native speaker of the standard language cannot recognize that the prevalent 'mistakes' in grammar or spelling or thought found among children whose home language is 'poor English' or 'bad English' are, in fact, intrusions into the standard speech from unrecognized dialect.

Experience therefore suggests the importance of making as articulate as possible the varieties of a language or of different languages that a child learns as an infant, as a toddler, in nursery and preschool, in elementary school, college and university. Such articulacy would include a detailed study of the various types of mother tongues, recognized dialects, recognized dialects associated with illiteracy and low prestige, unrecognized versions of the standard speech, standard expectations among the nonstandard speech speakers of what the standard language is like, divisions of experience that are learned in each language, counting, body parts, names for bodily functions, recitation of dreams, fantasy, disciplined logical thinking, authoritarian moral dicta, sacred scriptures, and poetry. Complementary to such an analysis, we will need the language style of the standard language and such contrasts as the

Dutch emphasis on learning to *speak* foreign languages rather than on learning to listen; the Chinese emphasis on learning to read a cross language script and to *hear* different languages while speaking them imperfectly, and the contrasts among ways of learning English, Spanish, Russian, and German spelling. Of particular interest would be the consequences of the older and later German experiences, in which a teacher was accustomed to correct for local dialects and still teach the children to spell as they spoke, and the postwar experience when (owing to the wartime dispersal of populations throughout Germany) this was no longer possible.

Similar interesting comparisons could be made of the ways that children progress in learning a standard language that is not their mother tongue – for example, between the Soviet Union where a Russian-speaking teacher may be faced with a group of children with a common foreign language, and the United States where, in cities like New York, the teacher may be faced with children speaking several mother tongues as well as unrecognized dialects of English.

Detailed analysis of some of these situations should yield a set of early childhood deutero-formulations of the order of: 'Real speech is how we speak at home; THEY speak and insist that I learn to speak in another way that has less reality.' 'Different people of the same kind speak different languages; it will be necessary to learn them all.' 'Different people of different kinds, some of higher or lower status, or greater or lesser warmth, speak different languages, learning these languages must include these extralinguistic differences.'

There are, of course, the much more extreme cases of children reared in foreign countries who learn to speak their nurses' language, but whose parents do not. When these children are removed to their country of origin, the original nurse-tongue may be completely suppressed, only appearing as grammatical or phonemic intrusions, or under conditions of extreme amnesic stress, while providing a background for unrecognized cognitive confusions. Even more extreme are the cases in which children, after having learned to speak, are adopted across a complete linguistic, cultural, and racial border, and are required to learn the new language from foster parents who know nothing of their mother tongues – as with Chinese, Korean, or Vietnamese war orphans adopted at the age of two or three in the United States.

Such deutero learning may be very potent in determining children's later ability to learn, to think in the abstract terms that are presented in the second, standard language. Access to their unconscious creativity is also affected. On the other hand, if these deutero learnings can be identified and articulated so that the mother tongue or the nurse tongue is treated with dignity as having equal reality standing with the standard language, much of the damage of such weighted compartmentalization can probably be avoided.

It will be particularly important to explore the later effects on the thinking ability of the coexistence of two languages: an infant or child language that remains rudimentary and undeveloped, unused since childhood, and a standard language that is reinforced with literacy, literature, and disciplined thought. The state of teaching the deaf in the United States is a case in point. American teaching of the deaf has until very recently repudiated the use of sign language, and insisted that deaf children be taught lip reading. The sign language, a language that uses many condensations for morphemes in addition to a manual alphabet, has continued to be used as a disapproved subversive form of communication among deaf children. Since it is not taught by competent and selfconscious teachers, as it is, for example, in the Soviet Union, dialects grow up; the deaf can easily recognize the great variety of divergent forms characteristic of sign language in the United States. But as the children do not connect the sign language with literacy, and no attempt is made to relate it systematically to standard English, it remains essentially the language of preliterate nursery years. In the Soviet Union, the use of a manual language coexists on formal terms with lip reading, reading, and writing, and very small children demonstrate an impressive mastery of thought and language.

But the situation of the deaf is only an extreme and dramatic example of what happens when any form of communication, including the modalities of touch, taste and smell, is developed in childhood and left unrecognized and undeveloped by later formal teaching. Many cultures, including the highly literate versions of our own, depend upon using such separations to dramatize the difference between intimate and informal and distant, impersonal, and formal relationships. As a result, the uncultivated, preliterate modes of early childhood become the modes of communication within marriage, often carrying with them as unrecognized baggage, the unbridled fears and hopes and fantasies of early childhood, so that records of the intimate life of highly cultivated people contrast astonishingly with their level of sophistication and humanization in less intimate contexts.

Remembrance of such earlier forms of once efficient and now disallowed communications has many repercussions in learning situations at the beginning of school. In establishing a nursery school in a South-eastern city in the early 1940s for White children who had had Black nurses, it was found necessary to bridge the gulf from home to school, by including in the nursery school staff, a warm

Black woman who fed the children to counterbalance the young White teachers who stood to the children for a different affective style.

It is probably impossible to overestimate the extent to which languages are the carriers of different kinds of thought. Quite aside from the resolution of the adequacy of the Whorfian hypothesis about the relationship between language and thought, the simple fact that more or less cognitively disciplined, socially hierarchical, or emotionally toned kinds of speech are used by the same individual, puts a burden on the transfer of learning. In the extreme case, the multilingual individual who has 'lost' his or her mother tongue through migration or adoption may experience extreme hiatuses in his thinking processes. Such an individual may be denied all access to poetry as a form, or be unable to move easily through different levels of consciousness, or through different kinds of imagery. The sorts of imagery associated with primary process thinking - the figures of speech of classical rhetoric - may become so disturbed that little or no congruence remains between image and word. This is the case of a great deal of American slang where the visual image is lost in favor of an inexplicit motor image.

Sex and temperament

Another conspicuous area of significant early childhood learning comes in the way a child experiences within the familial group cues to styles of intellectual behavior that are sex typed. Sex identity is imposed on children from birth; different terminology, different tones of voice, and different expectations all reinforce and elaborate underlying biological differences. Ways in which the world is to be perceived or represented may be so deep that when given pencils or crayons, children who have never drawn will nevertheless be sharply differentiated by the time they are five or six. Boys, for example, may draw scenes of activity from real life; girls draw patterns for cakes or clothing. Both style and content are conveyed to children very early, together with permission or prohibition about experimenting with styles of behavior culturally assigned to the other sex.

There is also great divergence in such cultural styles. In one culture, the small girls may be permitted to behave like boys, even in their stance and posture, as in Manus, where significantly the girls have taken to schooling as readily as the boys before puberty; their capacity to learn interrupted only by different expectations at puberty. In contrast, among the Iatmul, early childhood experience places the boys with the girls, with mothers as the first models; only in late childhood is a male model superimposed on a female model.

But in Bali each child is firmly assured of his or her sex identity, reared from earliest childhood to differentiated behavior, and individual children are given permission to experiment with the behavior of the other sex.

As a child learns its sex identity, it learns its appropriate cognitive style, and arrives in school with deeply ingrained expectations of what learning will be about. When the cultural style is rigid and extremely incongruent with the realities of human abilities, disturbances in the ability to learn are inevitable. This is so because of the child's already fixed sex identification and belief, such as that mechanics or mathematics are masculine and art is feminine, and because the teachers, as part of the same culture, reflect the same sex-typed expectations. Children whose abilities deviate sharply from normal expectation experience great difficulty in learning. This is exacerbated if, within the family, a child's proclivities for some sex-typed form of intellectual or artistic behavior is not only deviant from the cultural norm but also reinforced by temperamental similarities with the parent of the opposite sex. If a boy is both musical beyond the expectation for his class and region for male behavior, and has a musical mother with whom he identified, the complications are doubled. The school can help break down these very early, obdurate learnings, particularly if the school system presents at every stage both male and female models in sufficient profusion so that the child's earlier arbitrary learnings will be questioned rather than perpetuated. But small sensitive responses in early childhood to the cognitive style of the parents of the same and opposite sex can provide one of the often seemingly inexplicable blocks to learning, or a pathway of unusual facilitation, as when a certain high school provided an unusual number of good science students, all of whom went to the university from which the science teacher – also a first-class athlete – had come. As in other cases, knowledge of the cultural style, by class and region, can facilitate teaching in school. Where the learning capacities of a particular child are complicated by idiosyncratic learning, additional analysis is required.

Finally, it is important to recognize that preschool children may be learning ways of dealing with life that are radically opposed to the expectations on which the school system is built. The American school system is based upon the belief that children should and will accept more and better education than their parents had. (The parent who insists that what was good enough for him is good enough for his children has been treated as a gross reactionary.) Such institutions as the Parent-Teachers Association are postulated on the parents' enthusiastic support of this position, whether it is reflected in the pride with which the first report card is exhibited, or in the foresight with which the parents enroll a child at birth for a particular school or college. Each piece of infant learning, mastery of a new skill, learning to count, or reciting a nursery rhyme or the alphabet is greeted in this model American household as a precursor of achievement that will eventually outstrip that of the parent. The child's learning is never begrudged; the child who suffers is the child whose early achievements do not promise such later educational success.

This is the model – one based on the style set up by hopeful immigrants from older societies who emigrated of their own accord to find better opportunities for themselves, and particularly for their children. Our whole educational system has been postulated on this style. It was, therefore, with a terrible shock that Americans woke up, in the late 1950s, to a recognition that for some 30 million or more Americans there was no such expectation. The enthusiasm, bred of immigration to a wider and more open world, has died among those who failed generation after generation to make the grade. It had only a fitful life among those who had not been immigrants out of self-propelling hope, but who had been brought here as slaves, or pushed here by desperation and starvation within their own borders, or who were slowly reduced to despair as their traditional ways of life became less and less congruent with modern American life. In such families achievement is not rewarded. The child is not gazed upon as one who will go further than his father but instead is clutched or pitied, loved or rejected as part of the misery, poverty, deprivation, or grudgingly accepted low status that his parents, grandparents, and great grandparents have known, and from which they have no genuine hope of escape. This is the child who is a dropout from the first day of school. Deeper than the marks of a different intellectual style, of a failure to grasp the meaning of literacy as access to new experiences, and deeper than the learning that comes from the content of the home and from the cues given by sex and temperament, is the mark laid upon the small preschool child by his parents' expectations of his achievement. It is this cultural factor that we are just beginning to appreciate and allow for; it is this deep block to achievement with which programs such as Head Start are attempting to deal. Without seriously coming to grips with this discrepancy between a school system built for the first generation of aspiring immigrants and pupils who are the product of many generations of low expectation and despair, we will not be able to reconstruct our schools so as to provide the type of education that will be needed in the coming world.

But the reconstruction will need to provide ways through which children from whom little is expected may learn to expect much. It will also need to rescue those children – equally the victims of our one-way convictions of progress – from whom too much is expected and who are therefore branded as failures. Instead of a single-track notion of education from which those with the 'wrong' cultural backgrounds were automatically excluded, and within which those with the 'right' social backgrounds were often severely punished, we need to construct a system in which all sorts of lateral movements are possible, as some of the children of rural migrants become poets and physicists, and some of the children of lawyers and physicians and bankers become first-rate automobile mechanics or hospital orderlies. To accomplish this, the school needs to be more explicitly geared to compensate and balance, to take advantage of and when appropriate undo, the enormous strength of preschool experience.

The child in social time

Here our concern is not with the history of childhood but with the temporal passage of particular childhoods; the time span of individuals in social life. The idea of generational groupings relies upon the structuring of group allegiance in terms of expertise, specialization and responsibility; which is in turn contingent upon and itself fed by the dominant conception of time and mortality within the culture. Time becomes social through its being delineated by regular and successive symbolic indicators.

22 Eight ages of man
Erik Erikson

Basic trust *v.* basic mistrust

The first demonstration of social trust in the baby is the ease of his feeding, the depth of his sleep, the relaxation of his bowels. The experience of a mutual regulation of his increasingly receptive capacities with the maternal techniques of provision gradually helps him to balance the discomfort caused by the immaturity of homeostasis with which he was born. In his gradually increasing waking hours he finds that more and more adventures of the senses arouse a feeling of familiarity, of having coincided with a feeling of inner goodness. Forms of comfort, and people associated with them, become as familiar as the gnawing discomfort of the bowels. The infant's first social achievement, then, is his willingness to let the mother out of sight without undue anxiety or rage, because she has become an inner certainty as well as an outer predictability. Such consistency, continuity, and sameness of experience provide a rudimentary sense of ego identity which depends, I think, on the recognition that there is an inner population of remembered and anticipated sensations and images which are firmly correlated with the outer population of familiar and predictable things and people.

What we here call trust coincides with what Therese Benedek has called confidence. If I prefer the word 'trust', it is because there is more naiveté and more mutuality in it: an infant can be said to be trusting where it would go too far to say that he has confidence. The general state of trust, furthermore, implies not only that one has learned to rely on the sameness and continuity of the outer providers, but also that one may trust oneself and the capacity of one's own organs to cope with urges; and that one is able to consider oneself trustworthy enough so that the providers will not need to be on guard lest they be nipped.

Source: Erik Erikson, *Childhood and Society*, Hogarth Press (1950) reprinted Paladin (1977).

The constant tasting and testing of the relationship between inside and outside meets its crucial test during the rages of the biting stage, when the teeth cause pain from within and when outer friends either prove of no avail or withdraw from the only action which promises relief: biting. Not that teething itself seems to cause all the dire consequences sometimes ascribed to it. As outlined earlier, the infant now is driven to 'grasp' more, but he is apt to find desired presences elusive: nipple and breast, and the mother's focused attention and care. Teething seems to have a prototypal significance and may well be the model for the masochistic tendency to assure cruel comfort by enjoying one's hurt whenever one is unable to prevent a significant loss.

In psychopathology the absence of basic trust can best be studied in infantile schizophrenia, while lifelong underlying weakness of such trust is apparent in adult personalities in whom withdrawal into schizoid and depressive states is habitual. The re-establishment of a state of trust has been found to be the basic requirement for therapy in these cases. For no matter what conditions may have caused a psychotic break, the bizarreness and withdrawal in the behaviour of many very sick individuals hides an attempt to recover social mutuality by a testing of the borderlines between senses and physical reality, between words and social meanings.

Psychoanalysis assumes the early process of differentiation between inside and outside to be the origin of projection and introjection which remain some of our deepest and most dangerous defence mechanisms. In introjection we feel and act as if an outer goodness had become an inner certainty. In projection, we experience an inner harm as an outer one: we endow significant people with the evil which actually is in us. These two mechanisms, then, projection and introjection, are assumed to be modelled after whatever goes on in infants when they would like to externalize pain and internalize pleasure, an intent which must yield to the testimony of the maturing senses and ultimately of reason. These mechanisms are, more or less normally, reinstated in acute crises of love, trust, and faith in adulthood and can characterize irrational attitudes towards adversaries and enemies in masses of 'mature' individuals.

The firm establishment of enduring patterns for the solution of the nuclear conflict of basic trust versus basic mistrust in mere existence is the first task of the ego, and thus first of all a task for maternal care. But let it be said here that the amount of trust derived from earliest infantile experience does not seem to depend on absolute quantities of food or demonstrations of love, but rather on the quality of the maternal relationship. Mothers create a sense of trust in their children by that kind of administration which in its quality combines sensitive care of the baby's individual needs and a firm sense of personal trustworthiness within the trusted framework of their culture's life style. This forms the basis in the child for a sense of identity which will later combine a sense of being 'all right', of being oneself, and of becoming what other people trust one will become. There are, therefore (within certain limits previously defined as the 'musts' of child care), few frustrations in either this or the following stages which the growing child cannot endure if the frustration leads to the ever renewed experience of greater sameness and stronger continuity of development, towards a final integration of the individual life-cycle with some meaningful wider belongingness. Parents must not only have certain ways of guiding by prohibition and permission; they must also be able to represent to the child a deep, an almost somatic conviction that there is a meaning to what they are doing. Ultimately, children become neurotic not from frustrations, but from the lack or loss of societal meaning in these frustrations.

But, even under the most favourable circumstances, this stage seems to introduce into psychic life (and become prototypical for) a sense of inner division and universal nostalgia for a paradise forfeited. It is against this powerful combination of a sense of having been deprived, of having been divided, and of having been abandoned that basic trust must maintain itself throughout life.

Each successive stage and crisis has a special relation to one of the basic elements of society, and this for the simple reason that the human life-cycle and man's institutions have evolved together. In this chapter we can do little more than mention, after the description of each stage, what basic element of social organization is related to it. This relation is two-fold: man brings to these institutions the remnants of his infantile mentality and his youthful fervour, and he receives from them – as long as they manage to maintain their actuality – a reinforcement of his infantile gains.

The parental faith which supports the trust emerging in the newborn has throughout history sought its institutional safeguard (and, on occasion, found its greatest enemy) in organized religion. Trust born of care is, in fact, the touchstone of the *actuality* of a given religion. All religions have in common the periodical childlike surrender to a Provider or providers who dispense earthly fortune as well as spiritual health; some demonstration of man's smallness by way of reduced posture and humble gesture; the admission in prayer and song of misdeeds, of misthoughts, and of evil intentions; fervent appeal for inner unification by divine guidance; and finally, the insight that individual trust must become a common faith, individual mistrust a commonly formulated evil, while the individual's restoration must become part of the ritual practice of many, and must become a sign of trustworthiness in the community.

Each society and each age must find the institutionalized form of reverence which derives vitality from its world-image – from predestination to indeterminacy. The clinician can only observe that many are proud to be without religion whose children cannot afford their being without it. On the other hand, there are many who seem to derive a vital faith from social action or scientific pursuit. And again, there are many who profess faith, yet in practice breathe mistrust both of life and man.

Autonomy *v.* shame and doubt

In describing the growth and the crises of the human person as a series of alternative basic attitudes such as trust *v.* mistrust, we take recourse to the term a 'sense of', although, like a 'sense of health', or a 'sense of being unwell', such 'senses' pervade surface and depth, consciousness and the unconscious. They are, then, at the same time, ways of *experiencing* accessible to introspection; ways of *behaving*, observable by others; and unconscious *inner states* determinable by test and analysis. It is important to keep these three dimensions in mind, as we proceed.

Muscular maturation sets the stage for experimentation with two simultaneous sets of social modalities: holding on and letting go. As is the case with all of these modalities, their basic conflicts can lead in the end to either hostile or benign expectations and attitudes. Thus, to hold can become a destructive and cruel retaining or restraining, and it can become a pattern of care: to have and to hold. To let go, too, can turn into an inimical letting loose of destructive forces, or it can become a relaxed 'to let pass' and 'to let be'.

Outer control at this stage, therefore, must be firmly reassuring. The infant must come to feel that the basic faith in existence which is the lasting treasure saved from the rages of the oral stage, will not be jeopardized by this about-face of his, this sudden violent wish to have a choice, to appropriate demandingly, and to eliminate stubbornly. Firmness must protect him against the potential anarchy of his as yet untrained sense of discrimination, his inability to hold on and to let go with discretion. As his environment encourages him to 'stand on his own feet', it must protect him against meaningless and arbitrary experiences of shame and of early doubt.

The latter danger is the one best known to us. For if denied the gradual and well-guided experience of the autonomy of free choice (or if, indeed, weakened by an initial loss of trust) the child will turn against himself all his urge to discriminate and to manipulate. He will overmanipulate himself, he will develop a precocious conscience. Instead of taking possession of things in order to test them by purposeful repetition, he will become obsessed by his own repetitiveness. By such obsessiveness, of course, he then learns to repossess the environment and to gain power by stubborn and minute control, where he could not find large-scale mutual regulation. Such hollow victory is the infantile model for a compulsion neurosis. It is also the infantile source of later attempts in adult life to govern by the letter, rather than by the spirit.

Shame is an emotion insufficiently studied, because in our civilization it is so early and easily absorbed by guilt. Shame supposes that one is completely exposed and conscious of being looked at: in one word, self-conscious. One is visible and not ready to be visible; which is why we dream of shame as a situation in which we are stared at in a condition of incomplete dress, in night attire, 'with one's pants down'. Shame is early expressed in an impulse to bury one's face, or to sink, right then and there, into the ground. But this, I think, is essentially rage turned against the self. He who is ashamed would like to force the world not to look at him, not to notice his exposure. He would like to destroy the eyes of the world. Instead he must wish for his own invisibility. This potentiality is abundantly used in the educational method of 'shaming' used so exclusively by some primitive peoples. Visual shame precedes auditory guilt, which is a sense of badness to be had all by oneself when nobody watches and when everything is quiet – except the voice of the superego. Such shaming exploits an increasing sense of being small, which can develop only as the child stands up and as his awareness permits him to note the relative measures of size and power.

Too much shaming does not lead to genuine propriety but to a secret determination to try to get away with things, unseen – if, indeed, it does not result in defiant shamelessness. There is an impressive American ballad in which a murderer to be hanged on the gallows before the eyes of the community, instead of feeling duly chastened, begins to berate the onlookers, ending every salvo of defiance with the words. 'God damn your eyes.' Many a small child, shamed beyond endurance, may be in a chronic mood (although not in possession of either the courage or the words) to express defiance in similar terms. What I mean by this sinister reference is that there is a limit to a child's and an adult's endurance in the face of demands to consider himself, his body, and his wishes as evil and dirty, and to his belief in the infallibility of those who pass such judgement. He may be apt to turn things around, and to consider as evil only the fact that they exist: his chance will come when they are gone, or when he will go from them.

Doubt is the brother of shame. Where shame is dependent on the consciousness of being upright and exposed, doubt, so clinical observation leads me to believe, has much to do with a consciousness of having a front and a back – and especially a 'behind'. For this reverse area of the body, with its aggressive and libidinal focus in the sphincters and in the buttocks, cannot be seen by the child, and yet it can be dominated by the will of others. The 'behind' is the small being's dark continent, an area of the body which can be magically dominated and effectively invaded by those who would attack one's power of autonomy and who would designate as evil those products of the bowels which were felt to be all right when they were being passed. This basic sense of doubt in whatever one has left behind forms a substratum for later and more verbal forms of compulsive doubting; this finds its adult expression in paranoiac fears concerning hidden persecutors and secret persecutions threatening from behind (and from within the behind).

This stage, therefore, becomes decisive for the ratio of love and hate, cooperation and wilfulness, freedom of self-expression and its suppression. From a sense of self-control without loss of self-esteem comes a lasting sense of good will and pride; from a sense of loss of self-control and of foreign overcontrol comes a lasting propensity for doubt and shame.

We have related basic trust to the institution of religion. The lasting need of the individual to have his will reaffirmed and delineated within an adult order of things which at the same time reaffirms and delineates the will of others has an institutional safeguard in the *principle of law and order*. In daily life as well as in the high courts of law – domestic and international – this principle apportions to each his privileges and his limitations, his obligations and his rights. A sense of rightful dignity and lawful independence on the part of adults around him gives to the child of good will the confident expectation that the kind of autonomy fostered in childhood will not lead to undue doubt or shame in later life. Thus the sense of autonomy fostered in the child and modified as life progresses, serves (and is served by) the preservation in economic and political life of a sense of justice.

Initiative *v.* guilt

There is in every child at every stage a new miracle of vigorous unfolding, which constitutes a new hope and a new responsibility for all. Such is the sense and the pervading quality of initiative. The criteria for all these senses and qualities are the same: a crisis, more or less beset with fumbling and fear, is resolved, in that the child suddenly seems to 'grow together' both in his person and in his body. He appears 'more himself', more loving, relaxed and brighter in his judgement, more activated and activating. He is in free possession of a surplus of energy which permits him to forget failures quickly and to approach what seems desirable (even if it also seems uncertain and even dangerous) with undiminished and more accurate direction. Initiative adds to autonomy the quality of undertaking, planning and 'attacking' a task for the sake of being active and on the move, where before self-will, more often than not, inspired acts of defiance or, at any rate, protested independence.

I know that the very word 'initiative', to many, has an American, and industrial, connotation. Yet, initiative is a necessary part of every act, and man needs a sense of initiative for whatever he learns and does, from fruit-gathering to a system of enterprise.

The ambulatory stage and that of infantile genitality add to the inventory of basic social modalities that of 'making', first in the sense of 'being on the make'. There is no simpler, stronger word for it; it suggests pleasure in attack and conquest. In the boy, the emphasis remains on phallic-intrusive modes; in the girl it turns to modes of 'catching' in more aggressive forms of snatching or in the milder form of making oneself attractive and endearing.

The danger of this stage is a sense of guilt over the goals contemplated and the acts initiated in one's exuberant enjoyment of new locomotor and mental power: acts of aggressive manipulation and coercion which soon go far beyond the executive capacity of organism and mind and therefore call for an energetic halt to one's contemplated initiative. While autonomy concentrates on keeping potential rivals out, and therefore can lead to jealous rage most often directed against encroachments by younger siblings, initiative brings with it anticipatory rivalry with those who have been there first and may, therefore, occupy with their superior equipment the field towards which one's initiative is directed. Infantile jealousy and rivalry, those often embittered and yet essentially futile attempts at demarcating a sphere of unquestioned privilege, now come to a climax in a final contest for a favoured position with the mother; the usual failure leads to resignation, guilt, and anxiety. The child indulges in fantasies of being a giant and a tiger, but in his dreams he runs in terror for dear life. This, then, is the stage of the 'castration complex', the intensified fear of finding the (now energetically erotized) genitals harmed as a punishment for the fantasies attached to their excitement.

Infantile sexuality and incest taboo, castration complex and superego all unite here to bring about that specifically human crisis during which the child must turn from an exclusive, pregenital attachment to his parents to the slow process of becoming a parent, a carrier of tradition. Here the most fateful split and transformation in the emotional powerhouse occurs, a split between potential human glory and potential total destruction. For here the child becomes forever divided in himself. The instinct fragments which before had enhanced the growth of his infantile body and mind now become divided into an infantile set which perpetuates the exuberance of growth potentials, and a parental set which supports and increases self-observation, self-guidance, and self-punishment.

The problem, again, is one of mutual regulation. Where the child, now so ready to overmanipulate himself, can gradually develop a sense of moral responsibility, where he can gain some insight into the institutions, functions, and roles which will permit his responsible participation, he will find pleasurable accomplishment in wielding tools and weapons, in manipulating meaningful toys – and in caring for younger children.

Naturally, the parental set is at first infantile in nature: the fact that human conscience remains partially infantile throughout life is the core of human tragedy. For the superego of the child can be primitive, cruel, and uncompromising, as may be observed in instances where children overcontrol and overconstrict themselves to the point of self-obliteration; where they develop an over-obedience more literal than the one the parent has wished to exact; or where they develop deep regressions and lasting resentments because the parents themselves do not seem to live up to the new conscience. One of the deepest conflicts in life is the hate for a parent who served as the model and the executor of the superego, but who (in some form) was found trying to get away with the very transgressions which the child can no longer tolerate in himself. The suspiciousness and evasiveness which is thus mixed in with the all-or-nothing quality of the superego, this organ of moral tradition, makes moral (in the sense of moralistic) man a great potential danger to his own ego – and to that of his fellow men.

In view of the dangerous potentials of man's long childhood, it is well to look back at the blueprint of the life-stages and to the possibilities of guiding the young of the race while they are young. And here we note that according to the wisdom of the ground plan the child is at no time more ready to learn quickly and avidly, to become bigger in the sense of sharing obligation and performance, than during this period of his development. He is eager and able to make things cooperatively, to combine with other children for the purpose of constructing and planning, and he is willing to profit from teachers and to emulate ideal prototypes. He remains, of course, identified with the parent of the same sex, but for the present he looks for opportunities where work-identification seems to promise a field of initiative without too much infantile conflict or oedipal guilt and a more realistic identification based on a spirit of equality experienced in doing things together. At any rate, the 'oedipal' stage results not only in the oppressive establishment of a moral sense restricting the horizon of the permissible; it also sets the direction towards the possible and the tangible which permits the dreams of early childhood to be attached to the goals of an active adult life. Social institutions, therefore, offer children of this age an *economic ethos,* in the form of ideal adults recognizable by their uniforms and their functions, and fascinating enough to replace the heroes of picture book and fairy tale.

Industry *v.* inferiority

Thus the inner stage seems all set for 'entrance into life', except that life must first be school life, whether school is field or jungle or classroom. The child must forget past hopes and wishes, while his exuberant imagination is tamed and harnessed to the laws of impersonal things - even the three Rs. For before the child, psychologically already a rudimentary parent, can become a biological parent, he must begin to be a worker and potential provider. With the oncoming latency period, the normally advanced child forgets, or rather sublimates, the necessity to 'make' people by direct attack or to become papa and mama in a hurry: he now learns to win recognition by producing things. He has mastered the ambulatory field and the organ modes. He has experienced a sense of finality regarding the fact that there is no workable future within the womb of his family, and thus becomes ready to apply himself to given skills and tasks, which go far beyond the mere playful expression of his organ modes or the pleasure in the function of his limbs. He develops a sense of industry - i.e., he adjusts himself to the inorganic laws of the tool world. He can become an eager and absorbed unit of a productive situation. To bring a productive situation to completion is an aim which gradually supersedes the whims and wishes of play. His ego boundaries include his tools and skills: the work principle (Ives Hendrick) teaches him the pleasure of work completion by steady attention and persevering diligence. In all cultures, at this stage, children receive some *systematic instruction,* although it is by no means always in the kind of school which literate people must organize around special teachers who have learned how to teach literacy. In preliterate people and in nonliterate pursuits much is learned from adults who become teachers by dint of gift and inclination rather than by appointment, and perhaps the greatest amount is learned from older children. Thus the *fundamentals of technology* are developed, as the child becomes ready to handle the utensils, the tools, and the weapons used by the big people. Literate people, with more specialized careers, must prepare the child by teaching him things which first of all make him literate, the widest basic education for the greatest number of possible careers. The more confusing specialization becomes, however, the more indistinct are the eventual goals of initiative; and the more complicated social reality, the vaguer are the father's and mother's role in it. School seems to be a culture all by itself, with its own goals and limits, its achievements and disappointments.

The child's danger, at this stage, lies in a sense of inadequacy and inferiority. If he despairs of his tools and skills or of his status among his tool partners, he may be discouraged from identification with them and with a section of the tool world. To lose the hope of such 'industrial' association may pull him back to the more isolated, less tool-conscious familial rivalry of the oedipal time. The child despairs of his equipment in the tool world and in anatomy, and considers himself doomed to mediocrity or inadequacy. It is at this point that wider society becomes significant in its ways of admitting the child to an understanding of meaningful roles in its technology and economy. Many a child's development is disrupted when family life has failed to prepare him for school life, or when school life fails to sustain the promises of earlier stages.

On the other hand, this is socially a most decisive stage: since industry involves doing things beside and with others, a first sense of division of labour and of differential opportunity, that is, a sense of the *technological ethos* of a culture, develops at this time. We have pointed in the last section to the danger threatening individual and society where the schoolchild begins to feel that the colour of his skin, the background of his parents, or the fashion of his clothes rather than his wish and his will to learn will decide his worth as an apprentice, and thus his sense of *identity* – to which we must now turn. But there is another, more fundamental danger, namely man's restriction of himself and constriction of his horizons to include only his work to which, so the Book says, he has been sentenced after his expulsion from Paradise. If he accepts work as his only obligation, and 'what works' as his only criterion of worthwhileness, he may become the conformist and thoughtless slave of his technology and of those who are in a position to exploit it.

Identity *v.* role confusion

With the establishment of a good initial relationship to the world of skills and tools, and with the advent of puberty, childhood proper comes to an end. Youth begins. But in puberty and adolescence all samenesses and continuities relied on earlier are more or less questioned again, because of a rapidity of body growth which equals that of early childhood and because of the new addition of genital maturity. The growing and developing youths, faced with this physiological revolution within them, and with tangible adult tasks ahead of them are now primarily concerned with what they appear to be in the eyes of others as compared with what they feel they are, and with the question of how to connect the roles and skills cultivated earlier with the occupational prototypes of the day. In their search for a new sense of continuity and sameness, adolescents have to re-fight many of the battles of earlier years, even though to do so they must artificially appoint perfectly well-meaning people to play the roles of adversaries; and they are ever ready to install lasting idols and ideals as guardians of a final identity.

The integration now taking place in the form of ego identity is, as pointed out, more than the sum of the childhood identifications. It is the accrued experience of the ego's ability to integrate all identifications with the vicissitudes of the libido, with the aptitudes developed out of endowment, and with the opportunities offered in social roles. The sense of ego identity, then, is the accrued confidence that the inner sameness and continuity of one's meaning for others, as evidenced in the tangible promise of a 'career'.

The danger of this stage is role confusion. Where this is based on a strong previous doubt as to one's sexual identity, delinquent and outright psychotic episodes are not uncommon. If diagnosed and treated correctly, these incidents do not have the same fatal significance which they have at other ages. In most instances, however, it is the inability to settle on an occupational identity which disturbs individual young people. To keep themselves together they temporarily overidentify, to the point of apparent complete loss of identity, with the heroes of cliques and crowds. This initiates the stage of 'falling in love', which is by no means entirely, or even primarily, a sexual matter – except where the *mores* demand it. To a considerable extent adolescent love is an attempt to arrive at a definition of one's identity by projecting one's diffused ego-image on another and by seeing it thus reflected and gradually clarified. This is why so much of young love is conversation.

The adolescent mind is essentially a mind of the *moratorium*, a psychosocial stage between childhood and adulthood, and between the morality learned by the child, and the ethics to be developed by the adult. It is an ideological mind – and, indeed, it is the ideological outlook of a society that speaks most clearly to the adolescent who is eager to be affirmed by his peers, and is ready to be confirmed by rituals, creeds, and programmes which at the same time define what is evil, uncanny, and inimical. In searching for the social values which guide identity, one therefore confronts the problems of *ideology* and *aristocracy*, both in their widest possible sense which connotes that within a defined world image and a predestined course of history, the best people will come to rule and rule develops the best in people. In order not to become cynically or apathetically lost, young people must somehow be able to convince themselves that those who succeed in their anticipated adult world thereby shoulder the obligation of being the best. We will discuss later the dangers which emanate from human ideals harnessed to the management of super-machines, be they guided by nationalistic or international, communist or capitalist ideologies and the way in which the revolutions of our day attempt to solve and also to exploit the deep need of youth to re-define its identity in an industrialized world.

Intimacy *v.* isolation

The strength acquired at any stage is tested by the necessity to transcend it in such a way that the individual can take chances in the next stage with what was most vulnerably precious in the previous one. Thus, the young adult, emerging from the search for and the insistence on identity, is eager and willing to fuse his identity with that of others. He is ready for intimacy, that is, the capacity to commit himself to concrete affiliations and partnerships and to develop the ethical strength to abide by such commitments, even though they may call for significant sacrifices and compromises. Body and ego must now be masters of the organ modes and of the nuclear conflicts, in order to be able to face the fear of ego loss in situations which call for self-abandon: in the solidarity of close affiliations, in orgasms and sexual unions, in close friendships and in physical combat, in experiences of inspiration by teachers and of intuition from the recesses of the self. The avoidance of such experiences because of a fear of ego-loss may lead to a deep sense of isolation and consequent self-absorption.

The counterpart of intimacy is distantiation: the readiness to isolate and, if necessary, to destroy those forces and people whose essence seems dangerous to one's own, and whose 'territory' seems to encroach on the extent of one's intimate relations. Prejudices thus developed (and utilized and exploited in politics and in war) are a more mature outgrowth of the blinder repudiations which during the struggle for identity differentiate sharply and cruelly between the familiar and the foreign. The danger of this stage is that intimate, competitive, and combative relations are experienced with and against the selfsame people. But as the areas of adult duty are delineated, and as the competitive encounter, and the sexual embrace, are differentiated, they eventually become subject to that *ethical sense* which is the mark of the adult.

Strictly speaking, it is only now that *true genitality* can fully develop; for much of the sex life preceding these commitments is of the identity-searching kind, or is dominated by phallic or vaginal strivings which make of sex-life a kind of genital combat. On the other hand, genitality is all too often described as a permanent state of reciprocal sexual bliss.

The danger of this stage is isolation, that is, the avoidance of contacts which commit to intimacy. In psychopathology, this disturbance can lead to severe 'character-problems'. On the other hand, there are partnerships which amount to an isolation *à deux*, protecting both partners from the necessity to face the next critical development – that of generativity.

Generativity is primarily the concern in establishing and guiding the next generation, although there are individuals who, through misfortune or because of special and genuine gifts in other directions, do not apply this drive to their own offspring. And indeed, the concept generativity is meant to include such more popular synonyms as *productivity* and *creativity*, which, however, cannot replace it.

It has taken psychoanalysis some time to realize that the ability to lose oneself in the meeting of bodies and minds leads to a gradual expansion of ego-interests and to a libidinal investment in that which is being generated. Generativity thus is an essential stage on the psychosexual as well as on the psychosocial schedule. Where such enrichment fails altogether, regression to an obsessive need for pseudo-intimacy takes place, often with a pervading sense of stagnation and personal impoverishment. Individuals, then, often begin to indulge themselves as if they were their own – or one another's – one and only child; and where conditions favour it, early invalidism, physical or psychological, becomes the vehicle of self-concern. The mere fact of having or even wanting children, however, does not 'achieve' generativity. In fact, some young parents suffer, it seems, from the retardation of the ability to develop this stage. The reasons are often to be found in early childhood impressions; in excessive self-love based on a too strenuously self-made personality; and finally (and here we return to the beginnings) in the lack of some faith, some 'belief in the species', which would make a child appear to be a welcome trust of the community.

As to the institutions which safeguard and reinforce generativity, one can only say that all institutions codify the ethics of generative succession. Even where philosophical and spiritual tradition suggests the renunciation of the right to procreate or to produce, such early turn to 'ultimate concerns', wherever instituted in monastic movements, strives to settle at the same time the matter of its relationship to the Care for the creatures of this world and to the Charity which is felt to transcend it.

Ego integrity *v.* despair

Only in him who in some way has taken care of things and people and has adapted himself to the triumphs and disappointments adherent to being, the originator of others or the generator of products and ideas – only in him may gradually ripen the fruit of these seven stages. I know no better word for it than ego integrity. Lacking a clear definition, I shall point to a few constituents of this state of mind. It is the ego's accrued assurance of its proclivity for order and meaning. It is a postnarcissistic love of the human ego –not of the self – as an experience which conveys some world order and spiritual sense, no matter how dearly paid for. It is the acceptance of one's one and only life cycle as something that had to be and that, by necessity, permitted of no substitutions: it thus means a new, a different love of one's parents. It is a comradeship with the ordering ways of distant times and different pursuits, as expressed in the simple products and sayings of such times and pursuits. Although aware of the relativity of all the various life styles which have given meaning to human striving, the possessor of integrity is ready to defend the dignity of his own style against all physical and economic threats. For he knows that an individual life is the accidental coincidence of but one life cycle with but one segment of history; and that for him all human integrity stands or falls with the one style of integrity of which he partakes. The style of integrity developed by his culture or civilization thus becomes the 'patrimony of his soul', the seal of his moral paternity of himself (' . . . *pero el honor/Es patrimonio del alma':* Calderón). In such final consolidation, death loses its sting.

The lack or loss of this accrued ego integration is signified by fear of death: the one and only life cycle is not accepted as the ultimate of life. Despair expresses the feeling that the time is now short, too short for the attempt to start another life and to try out alternate roads to integrity. Disgust hides despair, if often only in the form of 'a thousand little disgusts' which do not add up to one big remorse: ' . . . *mille petits dégoûts de soi, dont le total ne fait pas un remords, mais un gêne obscur':* Rostand.

Each individual, to become a mature adult, must to a sufficient degree develop all the ego qualities mentioned, so that a wise Indian, a true gentleman, and a mature peasant share and recognize in one another the final stage of integrity. But each cultural entity, to develop the particular style of integrity suggested by its historical place, utilizes a particular combination of these conflicts, along with specific provocations and prohibitions of infantile sexuality. Infantile conflicts become creative only if sustained by the firm support of cultural institutions and of the special leader-classes representing them. In order to approach or experience integrity, the individual must know how to be a follower of image bearers in religion and in politics, in the economic order and in technology, in aristocratic living and in the arts and sciences. Ego integrity, therefore, implies an emotional integration which permits participation by followership as well as acceptance of the responsibility of leadership.

Webster's Dictionary is kind enough to help us complete this outline in a circular fashion. Trust (the first of our ego values) is here defined as 'the assured reliance on another's integrity', the last of our values. I suspect that Webster had business in mind rather than babies, credit rather than faith. But the formulation stands. And it seems possible to further paraphrase the relation of adult integrity and infantile trust by saying that healthy children will not fear life if their elders have integrity enough not to fear death.

23 The problem of generations

Karl Mannheim

The problem of generations is important enough to merit serious consideration. It is one of the indispensable guides to an understanding of the structure of social and intellectual movements. Its practical importance becomes clear as soon as one tries to obtain a more exact understanding of the accelerated pace of social change characteristic of our time. It would be regrettable if extra-scientific methods were permanently to conceal elements of the problem capable of immediate investigation.

It is clear from the foregoing survey of the problem as it stands today that a commonly accepted approach to it does not exist. The social sciences in various countries only sporadically take account of the achievements of their neighbours. In particular, German research into the problem of generations has ignored results obtained abroad. Moreover, the problem has been tackled by specialists in many different sciences in succession; thus, we possess a number of interesting sidelights on the problem as well as contributions to an overall solution, but no consciously directed research on the basis of a clear formulation of the problem as a whole.

The multiplicity of points of view, resulting both from the peculiarities of the intellectual traditions of various nations and from those of the individual sciences, is both attractive and fruitful; and there can be no doubt that such a wide problem can only be solved as a result of co-operation between the most diverse disciplines and nationalities. However, the co-operation must somehow be planned and directed from an organic centre. The present status of the problem of generations thus affords a striking illustration of the anarchy in the social and cultural sciences, where everyone starts out afresh from his own point of view (to a certain extent, of course, this is both necessary and fruitful), never pausing to consider the various aspects as part of a single general problem, so that the contributions

Source: Karl Mannheim *Essays in the Sociology of Knowledge*, Routledge and Kegan Paul (1927).

of the various disciplines to the collective solution could be planned.

Any attempt at over-organization of the social and cultural sciences is naturally undesirable: but it is at least worth considering whether there is not perhaps one discipline – according to the nature of the problem in question – which could act as the organizing centre for work on it by all the others. As far as generations are concerned, the task of sketching the layout of the problem undoubtedly falls to sociology. It seems to be the task of *Formal Sociology* to work out the simplest, but at the same time the most fundamental facts relating to the phenomenon of generations. Within the sphere of formal sociology, however, the problem lies on the borderline between the static and the dynamic types of investigation. Whereas formal sociology up to now has tended for the most part to study the social existence of man exclusively *statically,* this particular problem seems to be one of those which have to do with the ascertainment of the origin of social dynamism and of the laws governing the action of the dynamic components of the social process. Accordingly, this is the point where we have to make the transition from the formal static to the formal dynamic and from thence to applied historical sociology – all three together comprising the complete field of sociological research.

In the succeeding pages we shall attempt to work out in formal sociological terms all the most elementary facts regarding the phenomenon of generations, without the elucidation of which historical research into the problem cannot even begin. We shall try to incorporate any results of past investigations, which have proved themselves relevant, ignoring those which do not seem to be sufficiently well founded.

A. Concrete group – social location (Lagerung)

To obtain a clear idea of the basic structure of the phenomenon of generations, we must clarify the specific inter-relations of the individuals comprising a single generation-unit.

The unity of a generation does not consist primarily in a social bond of the kind that leads to the formation of a concrete group, although it may sometimes happen that a feeling for the unity of a generation is consciously developed into a basis for the formation of concrete groups, as in the case of the modern German Youth Movement. But in this case, the groups are most often mere cliques, with the one distinguishing characteristic that group-formation is based upon the consciousness of belonging to one generation, rather than upon definite objectives.

Apart from such a particular case, however, it is possible in general to draw a distinction between generations as mere collective facts on the one hand, and *concrete social groups* on the other.

Organizations for specific purposes, the family, tribe, sect, are all examples of such *concrete groups*. Their common characteristic is that the individuals of which they are composed do actually *in concrete* form a group, whether the entity is based on vital, existential ties of 'proximity' or on the conscious application of the rational will. All 'community' groups (*Gemeinschaftsgebilde*), such as the family and the tribe, come under the former heading, while the latter comprises 'association' groups (*Gesellschaftsgebilde*).

The generation is not a concrete group in the sense of a community, i.e. a group which cannot exist without its members having concrete knowledge of each other, and which ceases to exist as a mental and spiritual unit as soon as physical proximity is destroyed. On the other hand, it is in no way comparable to associations such as organizations formed for a specific purpose, for the latter are characterized by a deliberate act of foundation, written statutes, and a machinery for dissolving the organization – features serving to hold the group together, even though it lacks the ties of spatial proximity and of community of life.

By a concrete group, then, we mean the union of a number of individuals through naturally developed or consciously willed ties. Although the members of a generation are undoubtedly bound together in certain ways, the ties between them have not resulted in a concrete group. How, then, can we define and understand the nature of the generation as a social phenomenon?

An answer may perhaps be found if we reflect upon the character of a different sort of social category, materially quite unlike the generation but bearing a certain structural resemblance to it – namely, the class position (*Klassenlage*) of an individual in society.

In its wider sense class-position can be defined as the common 'location' *(Lagerung)* certain individuals hold in the economic and power structure of a given 'society as their 'lot'. One is proletarian, *entrepreneur,* or *rentier,* and he is what he is because he is constantly aware of the nature of his specific 'location' in the social structure, i.e. of the pressures or possibilities of gain resulting from that position. This place in society does not resemble membership of an organization terminable by a conscious act of will. Nor is it at all binding in the same way as membership of a community *(Gemeinschaft)* which means that a concrete group affects every aspect of an individual's existence.

It is possible to abandon one's class position through an individual or collective rise or fall in the social scale, irrespective for the moment whether this is due to personal merit, personal effort, social upheaval, or mere chance.

Membership of an organization lapses as soon as we give notice of our intention to leave it; the cohesion of the community group *ceases to exist* if the mental and spiritual dispositions on which its existence has been based cease to operate in us or in our partners; and our previous class position loses its relevance for us as soon as we acquire a new position as a result of a change in our economic and power status.

Class position is an objective fact, whether the individual in question knows his class position or not, and whether he acknowledges it or not.

Class-consciousness does not necessarily accompany a class position, although in certain social conditions the latter can give rise to the former, lending it certain features, and resulting in the formation of a 'conscious class'. At the moment, however, we are only interested in the general phenomenon of social *location* as such. Besides the concrete social group, there is also the phenomenon of similar location of a number of individuals in a social structure – under which heading both classes and generations fall.

We have now taken the first step towards an analysis of the 'location' phenomenon as distinct from the phenomenon *'concrete group'*, and this much at any rate is clear – *viz.* the unity of generations is constituted essentially by a similarity of location of a number of individuals within a social whole.

B. The biological and sociological formulation of the problem of generations

Similarity of location can be defined only by specifying the structure within which and through which location groups emerge in historical-social reality. Class-position was based upon the existence of a changing economic and power structure in society. Generation location is based on the existence of biological rhythm in human existence – the factors of life and death, a limited span of life, and ageing. Individuals who belong to the same generation, who share the same year of birth, are endowed, to that extent, with a common location in the historical dimension of the social process.

Now, one might assume that the sociological phenomenon of location can be explained by, and deduced from, these basic biological factors. But this would be to make the mistake of all naturalistic theories which try to deduce sociological phenomena directly from natural facts, or lose sight of the social phenomenon altogether in a mass of primarily anthropological data. Anthropology and biology only help us explain the phenomena of life and death, the limited span of life, and the mental, spiritual, and physical changes accompanying ageing as such; they offer no explanation of the relevance these primary factors have for the shaping of social interrelationships in their historic flux.

The sociological phenomenon of generations is ultimately based on the biological rhythm of birth and death. But to be *based* on a factor does not necessarily mean to be *deducible* from it, or to be implied in it. If a phenomenon is *based* on another, it could not exist without the latter; however, it possesses certain characteristics peculiar to itself, characteristics in no way borrowed from the basic phenomenon. Were it not for the existence of social interaction between human beings – were there no definable social structure, no history based on a particular sort of continuity, the generation would not exist as a social location phenomenon; there would merely be birth, ageing, and death. The *sociological* problem of generations therefore begins at that point where the sociological relevance of these biological factors is discovered. Starting with the elementary phenomenon itself, then, we must first of all try to understand the generation as a particular type of social location,

C. The tendency 'inherent in' a social location

The fact of belonging to the same class, and that of belonging to the same generation or age group, have this in common, that both endow the individuals sharing in them with a common location in the social and historical process, and thereby limit them to a specific range of potential experience, predisposing them for a certain characteristic mode of thought and experience, and a characteristic type of historically relevant action. Any given location, then, excludes a large number of possible modes of thought, experience, feeling, and action, and restricts the range of self-expression open to the individual to certain circumscribed possibilities. This *negative* delimitation, however, does not exhaust the matter. Inherent in a *positive* sense in every location is a tendency pointing towards certain definite modes of behaviour, feeling, and thought.

We shall therefore speak in this sense of a tendency 'inherent in' every social location; a tendency which can be determined from the particular nature of the location as such.

For any group of individuals sharing the same class position, society always appears under the same aspect, familiarized by constantly repeated experience. It may be said in general that the experiential, intellectual, and emotional data which are available to the members of a certain society are not uniformly 'given' to all of them; the fact is rather that each class has access to only one set of those data, restricted to one particular 'aspect'. Thus, the proletarian most probably appropriates only a fraction of the cultural heritage of his society, and that in the manner of his group. Even a mental climate as rigorously uniform as that of the Catholic Middle Ages presented itself differently according to whether one were a theologizing cleric, a knight, or a monk. But even where the intellectual material is more or less uniform or at least uniformly accessible to all, the *approach* to the material, the way in which it is assimilated and applied, is determined in its direction by social factors. We usually say in such cases that the approach is determined by the special traditions of the social stratum concerned. But these traditions themselves are explicable and understandable not only in terms of the history of the stratum but above all in terms of the location relationships of its members within the society. Traditions bearing in a particular direction only persist so long as the location relationships of the group acknowledging them remain more or less unchanged. The concrete form of an existing behaviour pattern or of a cultural product does not derive from the history of a particular tradition but ultimately from the history of the location relationships in which it originally arose and hardened itself into a tradition.

D. Fundamental facts in relation to generations

According to what we have said so far, the social phenomenon 'generation' represents nothing more than a particular kind of identity of location, embracing related 'age groups' embedded in a historical-social process. While the nature of class location can be explained in terms of economic and social conditions, generation location is determined by the way in which certain patterns of experience and thought tend to be brought into existence by the *natural data* of the transition from one generation to another.

The best way to appreciate which features of social life result from the existence of generations is to make the experiment of imagining what the social life of man would be like if one generation lived on for ever and none followed to replace it. In contrast to such a utopian, imaginary society, our own has the following characteristics:

(a) new participants in the cultural process are emerging, whilst
(b) former participants in that process are continually disappearing;
(c) members of any one generation can participate only in a temporally limited section of the historical process, and
(d) it is therefore necessary continually to transmit the accumulated cultural heritage;

(e) the transition from generation to generation is a continuous process.

These are the basic phenomena implied by the mere fact of the existence of generations, apart from one specific phenomenon we choose to ignore for the moment, that of physical and mental ageing. With this as a beginning, let us then investigate the bearing of these elementary facts upon formal sociology.

(a) *The continuous emergence of new participants in the cultural process*

In contrast to the imaginary society with no generations, our own – in which generation follows generation – is principally characterized by the fact that cultural creation and cultural accumulation are not accomplished by the same individuals – instead, we have the continuous emergence of new age groups.

This means, in the first place, that our culture is developed by individuals who come into contact anew with the accumulated heritage. In the nature of our psychical make-up, a fresh contact (meeting something anew) always means a changed relationship of distance from the object and a novel approach in assimilating, using, and developing the proffered material. The phenomenon of 'fresh contact' is, incidentally, of great significance in many social contexts; the problem of generations is only one among those upon which it has a bearing. Fresh contacts play an important part in the life of the individual when he is forced by events to leave his own social group and enter a new one – when, for example, an adolescent leaves home, or a peasant the countryside for the town, or when an emigrant changes his home, or a social climber his social status or class. It is well known that in all these cases a quite visible and striking transformation of the consciousness of the individual in question takes place: a change, not merely in the content of experience, but in the individual's mental and spiritual adjustment to it. In all these cases, however, the fresh contact is an event in one individual biography, whereas in the case of generations, we may speak of 'fresh contacts' in the sense of the addition of new psychophysical units who are in the literal sense beginning a 'new life'. Whereas the adolescent, peasant, emigrant, and social climber can only in a more or less restricted sense be said to begin a 'new life', in the case of generations, the 'fresh contact' with the social and cultural heritage is determined not by mere social change, but by fundamental biological factors. We can accordingly differentiate between two types of 'fresh contact': one based on a shift in social relations, and the other on vital factors (the change from one generation to another). The latter type is *potentially* much more radical, since with the advent of the new participant in the process of culture, the change of attitude takes place in a different individual whose attitude towards the heritage handed down by his predecessors is a novel one.

Were there no change of generation, there would be no 'fresh contact' of this biological type. If the cultural process were always carried on and developed by the same individuals, then, to be sure, 'fresh contacts' might still result from shifts in social relationships, but the more radical form of 'fresh contact' would be missing. Once established, any fundamental social pattern (attitude or intellectual trend) would probably be perpetuated – in itself an advantage, but not if we consider the dangers resulting from onesidedness. There might be a certain compensation for the loss of fresh generations in such a utopian society only if the people living in it were possessed, as befits the denizens of a Utopia, of perfectly universal minds – minds capable of experiencing all that there was to experience and of knowing all there was to know, and enjoying an elasticity such as to make it possible at any time to start afresh. 'Fresh contacts' resulting from shifts in the historical and social situation could suffice to bring about the changes in thought and practice necessitated by changed conditions only if the individuals experiencing these fresh contacts had such a perfect 'elasticity of mind'. Thus the continuous emergence of new human beings in our own society acts as compensation for the restricted and partial nature of the individual consciousness. The continuous emergence of new human beings certainly results in some loss of accumulated cultural possessions; but, on the other hand, it alone makes a fresh selection possible when it becomes necessary; it facilitates reevaluation of our inventory and teaches us both to forget that which is no longer useful and to covet that which has yet to be won.

(b) *The continuous withdrawal of previous participants in the process of culture*
The function of this second factor is implied in what has already been said. It serves the necessary social purpose of enabling us to forget. If society is to continue, social remembering is just as important as forgetting and action starting from scratch.

At this point we must make clear in what social form remembering manifests itself and how the cultural heritage is actually accumulated. All psychic and cultural data only really exist in so far as they are produced and reproduced in the present: hence past experience is only relevant when it exists concretely incorporated in the present. In our present context, we have to consider two ways in which past experience can be incorporated in the present:

(i) as consciously recognized models on which men pattern their behaviour (for example, the majority of subsequent revolutions tended to model themselves more or less consciously on the French Revolution); or

(ii) as unconsciously 'condensed', merely 'implicit' or 'virtual' patterns; consider, for instance, how past experiences are 'virtually' contained in such specific manifestations as that of sentimentality. Every present performance operates a certain selection among handed-down data, for the most part unconsciously. That is, the traditional material is transformed to fit a prevailing new situation, or hitherto unnoticed or neglected potentialities inherent in that material are discovered in the course of developing new patterns of action.

At the more primitive levels of social life, we mostly encounter unconscious selection. There the past tends to be present in a 'condensed', 'implicit', and 'virtual' form only. Even at the present level of social reality, we see this unconscious selection at work in the deeper regions of our intellectual and spiritual lives, where the tempo of transformation is of less significance. A conscious and reflective selection becomes necessary only when a semi-conscious transformation, such as can be effected by the traditionalist mind, is no longer sufficent. In general, rational elucidation and reflectiveness invade only those realms of experience which become problematic as a result of a change in the historical and social situation; where that is the case, the necessary transformation can no longer be effected without conscious reflection and its technique of de-stabilization.

We are directly aware primarily of those aspects of our culture which have become subject to reflection; and these contain only those elements which in the course of development have somehow, at some point, become problematical. This is not to say, however, that once having become conscious and reflective, they cannot again sink back into the a-problematical, untouched region of vegetative life. In any case, that form of memory which contains the past in the form of reflection is much less significant - e.g. it extends over a much more restricted range of experience - than that in which the past is only 'implicitly', 'virtually' present; and reflective elements are more often dependent on unreflective elements than *vice versa*.

Here we must make a fundamental distinction between *appropriated* memories and *personally acquired* memories (a distinction applicable both to reflective and unreflective elements). It makes a great difference whether I acquire memories for myself in the process of personal development, or whether I simply take them over from someone else. I only really possess those 'memories' which I have created directly for myself, only that 'knowledge' I have personally gained in real situations. This is the only sort of knowledge which really 'sticks' and it alone has real binding power. Hence, although it would appear desirable that man's spiritual and intellectual possessions should consist of nothing but individually acquired memories, this would also involve the danger that the earlier ways of possession and acquisition will inhibit the new acquisition of knowledge. That experience goes with age is in many ways an advantage. That, on the other hand, youth lacks experience means a lightening of the ballast for the young; it facilitates their living on in a changing world. One is old primarily in so far as he comes to live within a specific, individually acquired, framework of useable past experience, so that every new experience has its form and its place largely marked out for it in advance. In youth, on the other hand, where life is new, formative forces are just coming into being, and basic attitudes in the process of development can take advantage of the moulding power of new situations. Thus a human race living on for ever would have to learn to forget to compensate for the lack of new generations.

(c) *Members of any one generation can only participate in a temporally limited section of the historical process.*
The implications of this basic fact can also be worked out in the light of what has been said so far. The first two factors, (a) and (b), were only concerned with the aspects of constant 'rejuvenation' of society. To be able to start afresh with a new life, to build a new destiny, a new framework of anticipations, upon a new set of experiences, are things which can come into the world only through the fact of new birth. All this is implied by the factor of social rejuvenation. The factor we are dealing with now, however, can be adequately analysed only in terms of the category of 'similarity of location' which we have mentioned but not discussed in detail above.

Members of a generation are 'similarly located', first of all, in so far as they all are exposed to the same phase of the collective process. This, however, is a merely mechanical and external criterion of the phenomenon of 'similar location'. For a deeper understanding, we must turn to the phenomenon of the 'stratification' of experience *(Erlebnisschichtung)*, just as before we turned to 'memory'. The fact that people are born at the same time, or that their youth, adulthood, and old age coincide, does not in itself involve similarity of location; what does create a similar location is that they are in a position to experience the same events and data, etc., and especially that these experiences impinge upon a similarly 'stratified' consciousness. It is not difficult to see why mere chronological contemporaneity cannot of itself produce a common generation location. No one, for example, would assert that there was community of location between the young people of China and Germany about 1800. Only where contemporaries definitely are in a position to participate as an integrated group in certain common experiences can we rightly speak of community of location of a generation. Mere contemporaneity becomes sociologically significant only when it also involves participation in the same historical and social circumstances. Further, we have to take into consideration at this point the phenomenon of 'stratification', mentioned above. Some older generation groups experience certain historical processes together with the young generation and yet we cannot say that they have the same generation location. The fact that their location is a different one, however, can be explained primarily by the different 'stratification' of their lives. The human consciousness, structurally speaking, is characterized by a particular inner 'dialectic'. It is of considerable importance for the formation of the consciousness which experiences happen to make those all-important 'first impressions', 'childhood experiences' – and which follow to form the second, third, and other 'strata'. Conversely, in estimating the biographical significance of a particular experience, it is important to know whether it is undergone by an individual as a decisive childhood experience, or later in life, superimposed upon other basic and early impressions. Early impressions tend to coalesce into a *natural view* of the world. All later experiences then tend to receive their meaning from this original set, whether they appear as that set's verification and fulfilment or as its negation and antithesis. Experiences are not accumulated in the course of a lifetime through a process of summation or agglomeration, but are 'dialectically' articulated in the way described. We cannot here analyse the specific forms of this dialectical articulation, which is potentially present whenever we act, think, or feel, in more detail (the relationship of 'antithesis' is only one way in which new experiences may graft themselves upon old ones). This much, however, is certain, that even if the rest of one's life consisted in one long process of negation and destruction of the natural world view acquired in youth, the determining influence of these early impressions would still be predominant. For even in negation our orientation is fundamentally centred upon that which is being negated, and we are thus still unwittingly determined by it. If we bear in mind that every concrete experience acquires its particular face and form from its relation to this primary stratum of experiences from which all others receive their meaning, we can appreciate its importance for the further development of the human consciousness. Another fact, closely related to the phenomenon just described, is that any two generations following one another always fight different opponents, both within and without. While the older people may still be combating something in themselves or in the external world in such fashion that all their feelings and efforts and even their concepts and categories of thought are determined by that adversary, for the younger people this adversary may be simply non-existent: their primary orientation is an entirely different one. That historical development does not proceed in a straight line – a feature frequently observed particularly in the cultural sphere – is largely attributed to this shifting of the 'polar' components of life, that is, to the fact that internal or external adversaries constantly disappear and are replaced by others. Now this particular dialectic, of changing generations, would be absent from our imaginary society. The only dialectical features of such a society would be those which would arise from social polarities – provided such polarities were present. The primary experiential stratum of the members of this imaginary society would simply consist of the earliest experiences of mankind; all later experience would receive its meaning from that stratum.

(d) *The necessity for constant transmission of the cultural heritage*
Some structural facts which follow from this must at least be indicated here. To mention one problem only: a utopian, immortal society would not have to face this necessity of cultural transmission, the most important aspect of which is the automatic passing on to the new generations of the traditional ways of life, feelings, and attitudes. The data transmitted by conscious teaching are of more limited importance, both quantitatively and qualitatively. All those attitudes and ideas which go on functioning satisfactorily in the new situation and serve as the basic inventory of group life are unconsciously and unwittingly handed on and transmitted: they seep in without either the teacher or pupil knowing anything about it. What is consciously learned or inculcated belongs to those things which in the course of time have somehow, somewhere, become problematic and therefore invited conscious reflection. This is why that inventory of experience which is absorbed by infiltration from the environment in early youth often becomes the historically oldest stratum of consciousness, which tends to stabilize itself as the natural view of the world.

But in early childhood even many reflective elements are assimilated in the same 'a-problematical' fashion as those elements of the basic inventory had been. The new germ of an original intellectual and spiritual life which is latent in the new human being has by no means as yet come into its own. The possibility of really questioning and reflecting on things only emerges at the point where personal experimentation with life begins – round about the age of 17, sometimes a little earlier and sometimes a little later. It is only then that life's problems begin to be located in a 'present' and are experienced as such. That level of data and attitudes which social change has rendered problematical, and which therefore requires reflection, has now been reached; for the first time, one lives 'in the present'. Combative juvenile groups struggle to clarify these issues, but never realise that, however radical they are, they are merely out to transform the uppermost stratum of consciousness which is open to conscious reflection. For it seems that the deeper strata are not easily destabilized and that when this becomes necessary, the process must start out from the level of reflection and work down to the stratum of habits. The 'up-to-dateness' of youth therefore consists in their being closer to the 'present' problems (as a result of their 'potentially fresh contact'), and in the fact that they are dramatically aware of a process of de-stabilization and take sides in it. All this while, the older generation cling to the re-orientation that had been the drama of *their* youth.

From this angle, we can see that an adequate education or instruction of the young (in the sense of the complete transmission of all experiential stimuli which underlie pragmatic knowledge) would encounter a formidable difficulty in the fact that the experiential problems of the young are defined by a different set of adversaries from those of their teachers. Thus (apart from the exact sciences), the teacher-pupil relationship is not as between one representative of 'consciousness in general' and another, but as between one possible subjective centre of vital orientation and another subsequent one. This tension appears incapable of solution except for one compensating factor: not only does the teacher educate his pupil, but the pupil educates his teacher too. Generations are in a state of constant interaction.

This leads us to our next point:

(e) *The uninterrupted generation series.*
The fact that the transition from one generation to another takes place continuously tends to render this interaction smoother; in the process of this interaction, it is not the oldest who meet the youngest at once; the first contacts are made by other 'intermediary' generations, less removed from each other.

Fortunately, it is not as most students of the generation problem suggest – the thirty-year interval is not solely decisive. Actually, all intermediary groups play their part; although they cannot wipe out the biological difference between generations, they can at least mitigate its consequences. The extent to which the problems of younger generations are reflected back upon the older one becomes greater in the measure that the dynamism of society increases. Static conditions make for attitudes of piety – the younger generation tends to adapt itself to the older, even to the point of making itself appear older. With the strengthening of the social dynamic, however, the older generation becomes increasingly receptive to influences from the younger. This process can be so intensified that, with an elasticity of mind won in the course of experience, the older generation may even achieve greater adaptability in certain spheres than the intermediary generations, who may not yet be in a position to relinquish their original approach.

Thus, the continuous shift in objective conditions has its counterpart in a continuous shift in the oncoming new generations which are first to incorporate the changes in their behaviour system. As the tempo of change becomes faster, smaller and smaller modifications are experienced by young people as significant ones, and more and more intermediary shades of novel impulses become interpolated between the oldest and newest re-orientation systems. The underlying inventory of vital responses, which remains unaffected by the change, acts in itself as a unifying factor; constant interaction, on the other hand, mitigates the differences in the top layer where the change takes place, while the continuous nature of the transition in normal times lessens the frictions involved. To sum up: if the social process involved no change of generations, the new impulses that can originate only in new organisms could not be reflected back upon the representatives of the tradition; and if the transition between generations were not continuous, this reciprocal action could not take place without friction.

24 Historical development of the multiplicity of times and implications for the analysis of ageing

C. Davis Hendricks and Jon Hendricks

Although time is a basic component of man's existence as well as an essential concept in scientific constructions, it is ambiguously defined, generally relegated to an implicit role in the social sciences. The definition of time proffered depends in large measure on the differential emphasis characteristic of each discipline. Clearly, time has many faces, be they biological, physical or psychological. The model representing time may be linear and nonrepetitive or cyclical and recurrent. However, the major point of contention in the available literature rests with the determination of the source of time.

Is time merely a human construct, measured at will, or is our perception of it founded on a categorical reality, external to human consciousness, yet appropriated by it? Too often in scientific research the nature of time is presumed without examination. This is particularly true in the field of gerontology, whose central variable, age, is predicated on a uniform temporal flow.

A norm governing scientific research requires the clear, cogent and precise definition of concepts, especially crucial in attempts at empirical verification of theoretical propositions. Concepts represent reality, abstractions intended to convey the same idea to a number of people. The concepts comprising man's thoughts are both predictive and prescriptive. In everyday use a concept delimits the present and any possible future cognitions. It circumscribes the boundaries of reality, determining what is experientially possible; it delineates the essential characteristics that must be perceivable in any entity before that entity can enter our experience.

Conceptualizations of time clearly illustrate this position. The model of time most often utilized in science, including gerontology, is chronological, physical, 'objective'. Time is often equated with its measure, which lends itself to easy operationalization, as time then

Source: *The Human Context* (1975), VII, 1.

becomes simply a mechanical construction.

The problems arising from this singular definition of time become apparent in gerontology. If time exists external to human existence, independent of human intervention, then man's perception of time, a subjective action, is potentially distorted. The emphasis on the 'objective', quantitative nature of time presupposes externally real facts autonomous from the consciousness of the observer. The processes of aging, encompassing individual requirements and interpretations, are conditioned by a reified view of time. Time has become an object, not a process, capable of being accumulated, wasted, invested. This conceptualization is normative, imposing particular patterns on our study of old age. Our questions revolve around the disposition of time (an object), perceptions of its speed and reactions to its passage. Time has become a coercive concept.

It is the thesis of this paper that such a stance significantly affects the future of and obscures potentially rewarding theoretical contributions to gerontology. The historical dichotomy of a mechanistic, 'objective' model of time based on quantitative measurement, reflected in writings of Aristotle and Newton, and a qualitative, multiple, subjective time, defined by Augustine, Bergson, Husserl, Mannheim, Sorokin and Gurvitch, clouds the problem. Both views of time can be seen as components of a larger sphere of temporality that is constituted by the consciousness of the actor. As with previous considerations of time, the image of temporality and the nature of man involve *a priori* assumptions which condition the investigative process and subsequent conclusions. This position is itself the expression of an assumption about the nature of science as a world perspective.

Schutz, Berger and Luckmann, Blumer and others maintain the sociologist or social scientist interferes with existing patterns of relations and interactions wherever he operates. The scientist actively creates knowledge in his identification of symbols, his choice of topic and research instruments and his interpretation of data. Objectivity then is associated with a particular paradigm which depicts a specific world view. Each paradigm structures the area of reality on which it concentrates, narrowing the focus of its concepts and limiting the questions that can be asked. Thus the model of time utilized by the scientist reflects his perception of reality. It follows that social scientists, gerontologists specifically, should be aware of the implications attendant with the models of time characterizing their disciplines.

In addressing the primary role of time in gerontology and the tacit assumptions involved, we must consider the historical development of concepts of time. How did we reach our present state (implying, of course, progressive evolution of the scientific enterprise)? To anticipate our conclusions, what are the advantages of the orientation assumed in this paper? What are the divergent implications resulting from the image of man as a reactive being, currently favored in gerontological literature, as opposed to man as the active constructor of his life world?

Classical conceptions of time

We must look to Plato and Aristotle for the first detailed descriptions of time, though such writers as Democritus, Pythagoras and Zeno had earlier attempted to isolate the nature of time in formulating links between time, its measure and physical bodies. Recurrent problems are highlighted; namely, the interaction of time with its measure, and the nature of reality as eternal, unchanging, and thus nontemporal.

Plato was the first to devote an extensive passage to the nature of time. In the *Timaeus* he contrasts time with eternity to illustrate the changing character of time. In Plato's view God took the unchanging eternal as his model to bring order out of disorder and create the universe. Yet the universe is only an image of the eternal, for nothing can be the perfect eternal except eternity itself. God made the universe a moving image of eternity which, according to Plato, is time.

Time is an image which proceeds according to number and must be measurable. Plato's interest in time is focused on the manner in which it reflects eternity; it is an imperfect image, as is man, but only through the analyses of images is one able to approach the truth that resides in eternity. He concentrates on the concept of time to the extent to which it allows him to further his search for truth.

Aristotle's definition of time differs from Plato's as do his orienting questions. Aristotle does not address the origin of the universe, but the principles of nature. As motion and change are both principles of nature and motion seems to involve time, time must be analyzed within the framework of motion. Time is not motion because motion and change are in the object which is moving and time is present to all things. Aristotle defines time as 'the number of motion according to the before and after'. To recognize time there must be perception not only of motion, but of motion with a before and after on which a numbering process is based. Anything that is moved travels a certain magnitude and since magnitude is continuous, motion too must be continuous. Hence the time of the motion must be continuous in so far as the length of time corresponds to the amount of motion. Time is the *number* of motion rather than the measure of it, since motion is determined by successive nows, discrete, which possess order as does number. Aristotle defined number as divisible into discrete parts and magnitude as measurable by division into continuous parts like a line or surface. Time becomes objectively real, a matter of the inherent motion of the universe; regardless of how one counts, the time is not affected.

Aristotle does not dwell on whether or not time would exist if there were no numberer; we have souls, and our investigation of the nature of time makes consideration of no soul irrelevant. It would appear that there would be only motion, no time, if there were no soul which would number the before and after in motion.

Augustine, writing several centuries later, alters the neo-Platonic model in his discussions of time in *Confessions*. He begins with a clear statement: 'What, then, is time? If no one asks me, I know; but if I want to explain to him who asks, I know not'. Augustine asserts that time is inferior to eternity; eternity, wherein God resides, is changeless while time is dependent on motion or change. Time is not a part of God's nature, therefore the world and change must exist if time is to exist. Augustine echoed Plato when he stated the world and time came into being simultaneously. Time is not the motion of anything, but that by which we measure the motion of a body.

For Augustine the present is without extension, else it could be divided into past and future. By definition past and future do not exist and cannot be measured, neither can the present as it has no extension. Yet it is common to think of long and short periods of time. With this introduction Augustine presents his case for the most subjectively oriented view of time up to that point in history.

Past and future, in Augustine's view, must exist as present or else they do not and cannot exist. Thus, whatever exists is present, and if it appears to be past, it is not the event itself that exists but the image of it in the memory of what he termed the soul. When we predict the future we perceive not the future events but the causes of fore-shadowings of them in the present. He maintains that nothing is perceived unless it is present in the soul. Thus in the soul are a present memory of past events, a present attention to present events and a present anticipation of future events.

The soul of man measures intervals of time, and motion by means of time. Although Aristotle regarded the soul as necessary for the existence of time, the soul for Augustine was of primary importance in any consideration of time. For Aristotle time is an aspect of motion, it exists in so far as it is perceived by the mind, but it can be considered in relation to motion without explicit references to the perceiving mind. For Augustine the mind is independent of external motions, time is present in the mind and an absolute in relation to which motions proceed. The soul is not in time since its attention never becomes memory. Time is in the soul, yet the universe of changing things is in time. Time demands a universe in succession and a mind apart from the universe able to grasp phases of this motion and measure its duration.

Even though he clearly specified the relation of time to mind, the measurement of time presents a difficult problem for Augustine. The soul is an absolute, the standard by which motions are measured. 'We cannot measure past and future time, because they do not exist; present time, because it is indivisible; passing time, because it is not complete'. To resolve this dilemma he feels we do not measure things themselves, but something which remains fixed in our memory. Thus we measure the present impression that passing events leave in the soul. One measures a distension of the soul itself.

Augustine represents a departure in the conceptualization of time. For him time is a matter of the soul and consciousness; it is an activity of the soul by which man measures motion. Outside the soul only the present phase of time exists; in consciousness there is memory, attention and anticipation. Time is that which in passing characterizes consciousness. Physical motion might cease but the three acts of consciousness would still remain and so would time.

These two streams of thought set the stage for subsequent considerations of the nature of time. It is a variable which permeates man's existence and influences every realm, not merely the limited one of scientific inquiry. New factors came into play with the rise of science and the mechanization of man and the universe which altered the basic conceptions of time. However, the earlier definitions were not eclipsed; the Platonic model was expanded as natural science explained the universe and the Augustinian model was refined a the subjective came to the fore in the phenomenological school of inquiry.

The rise of science

With the Copernican revolution and the development of theories about the relativity of motion came new conceptions of time. If there is no absolutely regular motion and time is dependent on motion, then there can be no absolute measure of time. Kepler demonstrated that for any scientific knowledge of the world there must be recognition of quantitative relations. Galileo recognized the existence of quantitative relations in nature; he and Newton reduced reality to an external, objective mechanism wherein number, magnitude and motion were real and qualities usually associated with the self or subjectivity were of a lower order of reality, if not illusionary. Objective reality was external to man, existing apart from his consciousness of it.

Newton's theories proposed an absolute and relative space and time. Absolute time flows without regard for external events, being continuous and subjective. Relative time is the commonly used measure of duration by motion. Duration as used by Newton differs from that defined later by Bergson in the lack of reference to its direction or cumulative effect in passng. These latter aspects would apply specifically to events in time rather than time itself. In Newton's view, events are dependent on time, simultaneity is determined by existence in the same moment of time; later, in the relative view developed by Einstein, time is derived from events whose simultaneity does not require the presence of an entity of time.

Anticipating the twentieth century, the conception of time introduced by Newton was vastly altered by the theories of Einstein. He departed from the mechanical model of Newton, locating the basic data for science in energy rather than matter. Concepts of space and time lost their stability with the relativity theories; as a consequence the number of times corresponds to the frames of reference. Similarly, the speed of movement is relative to the point of view of the observer. Space and time lost their objective status and had no existence apart from the events by which the actor perceived and measured them. Einstein clearly realized that the time for macrophysics was not the same as that applicable to microphysics. The multiplicity of times had correspondingly different measures; only past, present and future were thought of as measures differentially applied to diverse times.

Writers in fields other than physics also addressed themselves to the problem of time. Descartes, couching his discussion in a philosophical perspective, made the distinction between time and duration; duration being a mode of extension and time a mode of thought about extension. It is possible for substance to be conceived without time but not vice versa. Kant's formulation of time, in contrast to Descartes', emphasizes time as a pure form of sensible intuition; a universal condition for the possibility of knowing anything. Intuition is that through which knowledge is related to objects and time is a subjective condition under which intuition occurs. It has objective validity with respect to appearances, the objects of our senses. All things are in time, including change and motion; thus there would be no empirical world without forms of sensibility. Substance is permanent and objectivity rests on permanence which in turn is found in the time order of events.

For Kant, time is a function of the mind, making possible perception; that is, we do not reflect on it as it is an *a priori* condition for all experience. It has empirical reality because all things, as objects of sensible intuition, are in time. Time does not inhere in objects, merely in the intuiting subject. Kant does not identify the perceiving subject as an object of analysis, merely that time is a condition for perception.

Throughout the course of the nineteenth century the spirit of Newtonian physics imbued most spheres of intellectual endeavor. Neutral objectivity and analytic reduction, two aspects of the scientific process espoused by Newton, became primary elements in the mechanistic model of the universe. Saint-Simon presents a clear example of the Newtonian influence on the social sciences. He had a vision of society in which everything was under scientific management, totally predictable and technically rational. There existed an objective reason which was impersonal, detached from individual men, toward which society would gradually evolve. In his development of a 'scientific religion', Saint-Simon followed the popular tendency to define a single principle as underlying all of reality.

Darwin and organic evolution fell naturally into the scheme of reality that flowered from Newton's model. The image of man as a creature of involuntary behavior was the base not only for Darwin, but for widely differing theories about society. One held that human society was an aggregate of individuals unresponsive to political control. Another subordinated the individual to the functionings of a larger group or society. Common elements could none the less be found in many of the theories which reflected the mechanistic model, man as spectator and the perceived rationality of nature.

Subsequent conceptions of time were not exempt from the influence of Newton's physics; indeed, they were more closely bound to it than many other theories. As noted in the discussion above, by the end of the classical period, two streams of thought existed. One flows directly from Newtonian physics, positing two senses of time: time as experienced, an object of consciousness, and time which is independent of consciousness or objective time. With this view time *per se* ontologically precedes consciousness. Time arises from physical processes that are not dependent upon the perceiving subject. In this conception, mind-dependent time, or time as experienced, is a relatively unimportant facet of an indispensible variable.

This accentuation of a unidirectional, objective, mechanistic model of time had its greatest impact during the industrialization of Western societies. Time is inextricably related to production and profit in the economic arena. Eventually this model becomes predominant in the social sciences, clearly illustrated in sociology by evolutionists such as Comte and Spencer. Much of the gerontological focus can be traced to this conceptualization. The implications of time external to man, with one face, and man as the subject rather than the author of his world will be explored at a later point.

The second stream flows in opposition to the objective and mechanical view of the world and time. It runs directly from Augustine through Einstein and Henri Bergson to the writers currently labelled phenomenologists. In general, this view emphasizes the subjective basis for time, its multiple nature and the special origin of objective time.

Phenomenological conceptions of time

Flowing from the second model for conceiving time, many writers sought alternatives for the quantitative, physical model of time. The criticism was often voiced that objective clock time was coercive in the study of men and that, being external, it was hardly the most relevant to their lives.

Henri Bergson sought the reality of time in inner experience. Real time for him was found in pure duration and experience, a totally subjective view. He considered Kant's description of time as a homogeneous entity erroneous; real time is heterogeneous and in-divisible, constantly unfolding. 'Time is identical with the flow of the continuity of our inner life.... Duration is continuation of what no longer exists into what does exist. This is real time, perceived and lived'. Bergson also conceived of time that is homogeneous or spatialized, time that is quantitative.

Pure duration flows, while measured time is composed of instants. Through the intermediary of motion simultaneous moments are marked off in duration to create the measure of time; hence it is only by conversion to spatial models that time can be quantified. Bergson did not reconcile these opposing times; he presented a strong case for experienced, qualitative time, but did not base scientific and quantitative time on this inner experience which he considered fundamental and *real*.

Husserl and Merleau-Ponty expanded the concept of time as pres-ented by Bergson to arrive, in Husserl's case, at the inner constitution of objective time and, in Merleau-Ponty's, at an emphasis on the subjectivity-in-the-world which constitutes time. For these writers the objective, physical model of time is only one of several types derived from the qualitative inner experience of time.

Husserl found the roots of knowledge in the consciousness of the knowing subject for whom things appear. Any phenomenon must be studied with the subjective, intending (noetic) and the objective, intended (noematic) linked together; in fact they are inseparable. All forms of objectivity have their origin in the subjective consciousness and the essences are constituted by conscious intention based on the perception of particulars.

The transcendental ego is the *a priori* source of objectivity in so far as experience is the source of subjectivity. An object becomes known only through knowing the subjective act that intends it. Likewise, the world becomes known when the individual begins constituting it. The world is the totality of objectivity but is only objective as the subjectivity focuses on it. The transcendental ego constitutes time and other intentional objectivity; as with Kant, it is the temporality of consciousness that enables us to perceive. Objective time arises as we focus on the objects of consciousness that endure, and the constancy becomes attached to the objects themselves, creating temporal accessibility. Memory, the possibility of returning to an object over and over and comparing it temporally with others, is the source of objective time. It establishes the objective in the before and after relationship providing permanent identifiability.

While Husserl traces the roots of the life world back to the subject, grounding all knowledge in the subjectivity, Merleau-Ponty contends:

The world is there before any possible analysis.... The real has to be described, not constructed or formed.... Truth does not inhabit only the inner man ... there is no inner man, man is in the world and only in the world does he know himself.

For Merleau-Ponty the subjective and objective, internal and external are inseparable. All our experiences orient themselves in terms of before and after; the individual lives time and is involved and permeated with it. Man is a temporal being by virtue of inner necessity and in analyzing time we gain access to the concrete structure of subjectivity.

In the past and future are dimensions of subjectivity appearing in the field of the present time consciousness. What is past and future for an individual is present for the world. 'Time is not a real process, not an actual succession which I record. It arises from *my* relation to things'. Time is not a series of successive events because events are shaped by an observer from the spatio-temporal totality of the objective world. 'Change presupposes a certain position which I take up and from which I see things in procession before me: there are no events without someone to whom they happen and whose finite perspective is the basis of their individuality'.

Time is always in the process of constituting itself(from consciousness); hence true time is characterized by flux and transience, a synthetic relationship among before, present and after which is a dimension of the being. The past and future exist only when there is a subjectivity which introduces a perspective.

Merleau-Ponty emphasizes the role of the world over that of Husserl's subjectivity in the perception of time. Objects exist in the world in a present sense and only as we introduce consciousness do succession and time appear. Both rejected the foundation of time on motion, focusing instead on the perception of the actor and his role in creating his world.

Heidegger presents a similar analysis. He sees temporality as basic to the structure of knowledge; time becomes the center of all cognitional syntheses. The temporality of consciousness is proposed as the unifier of thought processes and the objects of reflection. The consciousness of time arises from the temporal modes expressed in the synthetic process fundamental to any cognition. The modes involved in the synthesis and cognition are: what is as having been, what is as can be, what is as presenting itself. Clearly these elements are reminiscent of Augustine's formulation of awareness of time. Time is not a thing; it cannot appear as the object of sensory perception; instead it permeates the knower, knowing and known. It is indispensible to intelligibility. This presupposed temporal framework is necessary in order for man to know, act, think and relate to the world. Temporality is a function; it is the human mode of constituting general experience. The human mind is in some senses a free causal agent, making an essential contribution to its own knowledge.

Sociologists who have investigated the nature of time have drawn on the foregoing conceptualizations presenting their own versions of the mechanical and qualitative orientations. Few sociologists have directed prolonged attention to the subject of time, perhaps reflecting the security of its implicit status. Mannheim, Sorokin and Gurvitch have been forerunners in proposing a specific time for sociology, objecting to the ties to the mechanistic model as well as its assumed objectivity.

Sociological conceptions of time

Durkheim reflects the first stream of thought regarding conceptions of time; he viewed space and time as neither *a priori* nor empirical in the traditional sense. Both concepts were provided by society or culture, taken from the 'social life' to become the abstract and impersonal framework that surrounds all of personal life and humanity. There is private experience in the flow of time, but it is far from enough to constitute the category of time itself. For Durkheim man is not primarily one who imposes his order on nature; he is to a greater degree produced by the cultural system. The individual's private experience of time is systematized and ordered by the culture which, in addition, provides the abstract and universal nature of time. It is through the coercive power of the collective memory that the flow of an individual's past experience is stabilized. The function of time is pragmatic, determined by the rhythmic ordering of cultural life.

More recently Karl Mannheim searched for an alternative to the objective time posited by classical physics. He rejected the positivist formulations of historical development, mechanical divisions of generational length and time because they were based solely on the 'biological law of limited life-span of man'. Mannheim, following Dilthey, postulated the generation as his unit over quantitative temporal units; generation as determined not merely by chronological data, but by the experience of common influences. 'The time interval separating generations becomes subjectively experienceable time; and contemporaneity becomes a subjective condition of having been submitted to the same determining influences'. The generational style and rhythm is conditioned by the social and cultural processes as in a manner reminiscent of Durkheim.

Sorokin also distinguished a definite sociocultural time which has characteristics differing from those of physical, biological or psychological times. The periodization and rhythms of social life have purely social origin and little in common with natural phenomena as such. He sees mathematical time as a subset of sociocultural time made possible only under certain sociocultural circumstances. Sociocultural time therefore cannot be replaced with quantitative time without a loss of orientation in the time process, a homogenizing of time, the division of indivisible durations into identical units, or the equivalence of unequal phenomena.

The qualitative and discontinuous flow of sociocultural time specified by Sorokin is further explicated in the work of Georges Gurvitch. Gurvitch is one of several writers offering a dialectical model of the world wherein man creates the social order which in turn acts upon him to alter his nature. Though the role of the actor in the formation of the social world is of prime importance. The reality that arises from his interaction is the usual subject of sociological study.

From this vantage point Gurvitch presented his theory of social time. Earlier writers approached a view of the multiple nature of time, but until Einstein it had not been made explicit. For Gurvitch each social system with its particular components has its own time which varies in duration, rhythm and orientation. Time is conditioned by the social framework and reciprocally affects it. The multiple manifestations of time are not unified; any attempts to do so represent man's struggle to re-master his created world.

Different times exist for physical and social life as well as in the particular definitions used by scientific disciplines. Gurvitch declined treatment of the subjective – objective dichotomy or the ontological status of time. He proposed to cull relevant factors from the two streams of thought such that: 'From Aristotle I retain the idea that time is movement (rather a plurality of movements), and from his opponents the idea that time possesses a qualitative element, it is not always measurable and even more not always quantifiable'. Gurvitch defined time as 'convergent and divergent movements which persist in a discontinuous succession and change in a continuity of heterogeneous movements'. The important aspect of time is its dialectical nature, which is the source of its multiplicity.

Gurvitch distinguished different times for different spheres of reality; for example, micro- and macro-physical, astronomical, mechanical, chemical, geological, biological, psychological, historical and social. Social time marks the dialectical movements of total social phenomena of whatever level is the subject of analysis. Social time is more complex than physical time and is harder to unify; taking one of eight possible forms, it exhibits more discontinuity than any other manifestation of time. The eight social times that Gurvitch constructed for sociological analysis are: Enduring (time of slowed down long duration), Deceptive, Erratic (time of irregular pulsation between the appearance and disappearance of rhythms), Cyclical, Retarded, Alternating, Time in Advance of Itself (time pushing forward) and Explosive.

Sociologists have recognized the importance of time in the social world; for the most part, however, they have not acknowledged the complexity Gurvitch specified. Durkheim felt conceptions of time were determined by societal conditions; Sorokin saw time as a social necessity; Gurvitch believed that time, a product of inner experience, had qualitatively distinct faces corresponding to specific social contexts.

Is it possible to reconcile these divergent streams? Are there common themes to be found in the Greek conception of time as secondary to the eternal or timeless and that of time as a linear progression of instants reflected in human existence by the meaning that man gives to each unit (clearly characterized by ancient Hebrews)? Where do phenomenologists and others enter the scene with their firm assertions of the temporality of human consciousness and the constitution of time by human action? Finally, what roles do these conceptions play in the study of aging?

The insistence on a linear conception of temporality restricts our vision of the world, obscuring possible alternative temporal experiences and interpretations. Scientists often presuppose that time was first defined by religious or philosophical men focusing on the nature of humanity. Eventually time was pressed into the service of social institutions to demarcate religious, economic or political activities. By the medieval era time assumed value as an objective entity, generally with respect to God and man's purpose in worldly life. The final stage was set by the rise of the scientific perspective and industrialism in the sixteenth century. Time was secularized, accorded a commodity-like status, and gradually gained ascendancy over man's affairs.

Time and aging

In a number of contemporary views temporal flow is seen as destructive; men focus on the world of external phenomena which are continually passing away, such that the momentarily present provides the base for temporal reality in science. The objective character of time, measured by arbitrary devices, overshadows the role of the actor - man - in the creation of this convention.

The unique problems associated with this orientation are apparent in the analysis of aging. Aging is predicated on the passage of time or awareness of change. The unilinear conception of time, externalized and beyond control of the actor, curtails his freedom. Life satisfaction is dependent upon social conditions defined by mechanistic models of causality which establish norms for the judgement of time passage and individual progression. On one hand research in gerontology focuses on the estimation of time intervals, measured by clock or calendar time, and the degree to which the elderly refer to past or future time. The model of time is constructed from subjectively external, quantitative, linear dimensions. Time is analogous to points on a line, in both direction and order. Often in the same literature, seemingly contradictory, gerontologists assert that perception and experience of the speed and duration of time varies greatly among individuals. Aging is a relative process; the labels 'aged, elderly or old' are differentially applied to individuals of the same chronological age. The necessary groundwork has been laid for a dynamic conception of the multiplicity of times constituted by actors. Yet we insist on couching our investigations in restrictive, no-alternative definitions of the central component of aging - time.

The identification of aging processes with the linear flow of time negates individual contributions to or modifications of this uniform measure. A cursory review of the literature reveals the prevalence of this orientation. Birren states 'chronological age is one of the most useful single items of information about an individual if not the *most* useful'. Aging has many definitions, but the crucial factor revolves around a change in the properties of an organism over time. The very nature of science presupposes causal ordering in aging processes, such that time flows linearly.

Man's brain resembles a registering instrument for Reichenbach and Mathers. This ability to record the objective properties of time, specifically emphasizing temporal direction which reflects the increasing entropy of a system, provides the essential link with subjective determinations of time direction. The idea of unidirectional time is basic to the analysis of aging within this perspective. Man perceives an objective time that exists apart from himself only subjectively. Thus, objective time is measured by physical properties (movement of earth, pendulum and so forth) whose relations are defined by an instrument (calendar, clock) dependent upon those periodic relations among physical phenomena. Nevertheless there remains an objective time external to man which determines the objective criteria of aging.

The strict linear model of time is utilized in several studies exploring the time *perspective* of the elderly. Eson and Greenfield found that adults in their sixties were as likely to have thoughts of or to speak of future time as were adolescents and young adults. Individuals over sixty-five do not differ significantly from youth in their ability to use future time as a hypothetical abstract concept. Expectations of and reactions to specific future activities are found to differ by chronological age. It is assumed that individuals of similar chronological age will perceive and interpret time sequence and importance in a like manner.

Additional research has been done in the area of subjective estimations of clock time. Wallach and Green found that subjective judgements of the speed of time were influenced more directly by the value placed on time, than by the activity level of the judges. Thus the oldest members of the sample preferred dynamic, swift descriptions of time, while younger members selected static metaphors. A study by Feifel indicated that positive attitudes to time are highly correlated with accurate estimates of clock time. Tejmar, reporting on an elderly sample, and Surwillo on institutionalized older people, found a tendency for both groups to underestimate time intervals to a greater degree than their younger counterparts.

What assumptions are involved in this type of age-related research? Time is cast into the role of an object, a concrete phenomenon everywhere the same, while individual perspectives differ on the perception of this object. Time is depicted as a line on which the present is the dividing point between past and future. As the individual ages, the amount of future time decreases, thus increasing past time. The resulting implications rest on the objective nature of aging processes to which man must adjust. The qualities identified with the experience of time are reduced to mechanical measurement. Quantitative time determines the essence of qualitative temporal experience. This overriding theme denies the possibility of creative action, as time does not truly belong to the individual.

Conclusion

Jean-Paul Sartre suggests a viable avenue for the modification of the unilinear, mechanical definition of time intrinsic in most gerontological research. Sartre sees man engaged in projects creatively acting and determining temporal flow. The linear model of time denies alternatives potentially available to the actor. Sartre recognizes man's projects are defined in terms of past (memories) and future (imaginations) times, plus personal and social spheres. It is only through the construction of projects that man's time becomes his own.

'As time gives us the world so with the same motion it takes it from us'. Man does not experience completed periods of time; Husserl maintains memory allows us to continually return to objects, Augustine that imagination structures the future. Man differs in his experience of temporal speed and duration. It is this that we admit to commonsense knowledge – chronological age is not the best indicator of man's feelings of age – that now provides the impetus for consideration of the multiplicity of times.

Linear, clock time is but one of the relevant dimensions of the temporal experience. Societal views of time influence the actor's orientation in his life world. The typifications constructed to make sense of the social may in turn assume an objective status in the actor's experience. Objective, physical time routinely used in technological societies determines the value of man's experience. Biological rhythms, durations associated with emotions, social times are all presumed inferior to this objective time. Cross-cultural investigations have revealed differing statuses accorded the elderly. The value of experience (by extension), the depth of temporal experience, is more highly valued in traditional, often agrarian-based societies than in industrialized countries. The impact of science in technological societies fostered the adoption of a restricted definition of time which tended to denigrate individual temporal experience.

Initially the use of the natural science conception of time by social scientists may have reflected the search for neutrality and objective truth. As physical scientists realized the limited nature of their concept, social scientists looked the other way, continuing to base their search on abstract, quantitative time. 'But if the multiplicity of time forces itself on the natural sciences, how can we take exception to it in the social sciences where the conflicts of time are much sharper and much more striking?'.

Since Einstein and Bohr, natural scientists have recognized the plurality of time and the involvement of the scientist with his observations. Total neutrality presupposes a position of omniscient observation rejected by natural scientists, but still assumed possible by some social scientists. Physicists now concede the likelihood of times other than one-directional time, but lack the tools to identify them. When the perspectival character of knowledge and the multiplicity of times are ignored, man becomes a reactive object rather than an active subject. This focus on monolinear time often leads to conclusions of inevitability concerning the status of social situations.

The convenience of a mechanical model of time in research is clear; quantitative measures have ease of application and high reliability, however far-reaching are the implications of such models in social research. The mechanical model of time possesses a normative character within which human action is explained. The historicity of social objects is discarded in favor of the replicability of human events. Social life in general, and aging in particular, are represented by discrete data exhibiting repetitive patterns linked with theoretical language which rarely admits references to time. This limited approach to temporal experience in aging conceals a holistic view of man's development.

Gerontology, owing to its interdisciplinary parentage, is ready to consider new descriptions of time. To do so we must explore the possibility of returning control of temporal construction to the actor in our analysis of his experiences. Not all will be able to transcend the limited view of time now prevalent; others will readily assume a central role in defining different measures of temporality in human experience. Times are qualitatively different; emotional moments are uneven; some times feel like no time at all, that is we do not experience duration, while others seem of unending duration. An examination of our implicit assumptions and restructuring of our research instruments will lead to new theoretical and practical orientations in the study of aging.

If we posit man in dialectical relation to his social world, actively constructing temporal experience, many issues could be redefined in gerontology. Presently the economic institutions of society are seen to convey to the retiring individual that he has outlived his usefulness, and is now embarking on the last phase of his existence destined to be marked by work-like activities. Time appears to be 'running out' for the aged; thus many refuse to actively appropriate time, focusing instead on past experiences. The routines of everyday life are disrupted by retirement; hence individuals feel incapable of creating new schedules.

These problems might profit from new considerations of time and aging. The individual could establish legitimacy for differential measures of time, emphasizing those that allow him greatest freedom of choice. He can never escape the experience of time, and thus should clearly establish his relation to objective time. Man is only able to live in objectified mechanical time in a secondary fashion. This time is created in the reflective consciousness of man after he has lived and experienced time. Merleau-Ponty has clearly specified the relation of the knower to his intentional world; a knower must recognize his ties to the intentional world before constructing knowledge. The world extends in time and space, which are first experienced by the knower, then mathematically formulated. Objective clock-time is known but not lived as an entity present in the world; it is instead a particular order of signification.

The knowledge of objective clock-time and its units presupposes structures in the social world that are grounded in the temporal modes of human existence. Objective time may be based on measures of sequences in nature, but its origin is found in a sociocultural milieu and lived experience. Merleau-Ponty states:

It is of the essence of time to be in process of self production, and not to be; never, that is, to be completely constituted. Constituted time, the series of possible relations in terms of before and after, is not time itself, but the ultimate recording of time, the result of its passage which objective thinking always presupposes yet never manages to fasten on to.

When time is seen as a process, continually becoming, man is free to attribute a variety of meanings to his temporal experience. The imposition of quantitative measures on temporal flow exerts a restrictive force on man's experience. Unfortunately the latter approach does not take cognizance of man's active participation in the construction of his temporal world. Students of aging, regardless of their discipline, would increase the scope of description and explanation if they adopted a more flexible conceptualization of time in aging processes. It does not require an astute observer to suggest the interactive nature of the biological, psychological and social aspects of aging; therefore, more innovative conceptual frameworks are required for an appreciation of man's holistic nature and the temporally determined dynamics of aging.

Select Bibliography

Bandoin, L. C., *The Mind of the Child*, Allen & Unwin, 1933.

Beck J., Jenks, C. et al., *Worlds Apart. Readings for a Sociology of Education*, Collier-Macmillan, 1976.

Bernstein, B., *Class, Codes and Control*, vol. 1, Routledge, 1971.

Bettelheim, B., *The Children of the Dream*, NY, Macmillan, 1969.

Boas, G., *The Cult of Childhood*, London, Warburg Institute Press, 1966.

Bossard, J., and Ball, E., *The Sociology of Child Development*, NY, Harper, 1948.

Bowlby, J., *Child Care and the Growth of Love*, Penguin, 1965.

Bronfenbrenner, U., *Two worlds of Childhood: US and USSR*, NY, Russell Sage Foundation, 1970.

Brown, C., *Man Child in the Promised Land*, Penguin, 1965.

Chamboredon, J. C. and Prevot, J., 'Changes in the Social Definition of early Childhood and the New Forms of Symbolic Violence' in *Theory and Society*, vol. II, no. 3.

Chomsky, N., *Aspects of a Theory of Syntax*, Cambridge, MIT Press, 1965.

Chomsky, N., *Language and Mind*, NY, Harcourt, Brace & World, 1968.

Cicourel, A., 'The Acquisition of Social Structure' in Douglas, J. (ed) *Understanding Everyday Life*, Routledge, 1970.

Cicourel, A., et al, *Language Use and School Performance*, NY, Academic Press, 1974.

Clausden, J., *Socialization and Society*, Boston, Little, Brown & Co, 1968.

Cohen, Y., *The Transition from Childhood to Adolescence*, Chicago, Aldine, 1964.

Collins, P., *Dickens and Education*, Macmillan, 1963.

Cooper, D., *The Death of the Family*, NY, Vintage Books, 1971.

Danzinger, K., *Socialization*, Baltimore, Penguin, 1971.

Deardon, R. F., *The Philosophy of Primary Education*, Routledge, 1968.

Denison, G., *Lives of Children*, NY, Random House, 1969.

Dreitzel, H. P., *Recent Sociology No. 5: Childhood and Socialization*, NY, Macmillan, 1973.

Durkheim, E., *Moral Education*, NY, Free Press, 1961.

Durkheim, E., *Education and Sociology*, NY, Free Press, 1956.

Erikson, E., *Identity and the Life Cycle*, NY, International Universities Press, 1959.

Freud, S., *Collected Papers*, vols. II and III, Hogarth, 1924, 1925.

Freud, S., *New Introductory Lectures in Psycho-Analysis*, Hogarth, 1957.

Gil, D. A., *Violence against Children*, Cambridge, Harvard U. P., 1970.

Holt, J., *How Children Fail*, NY, Putnam, 1964.

Isaacs, S., *Social Development in Young Children*, Routledge, 1933.

Jung, C., *Collected Works*, vols. 9, 12, 13, Routledge, 1967, 1968.

Keddie, N., *Tinker, Tailor ... The Myth of Cultural Deprivation*, Penguin, 1973.

Kozol, J., *Death at an Early Age*, Boston, Houghton Mifflin, 1969.

Lacan, J., *Ecrits, A selection,* Tavistock, 1978.

Laye, C., *The African Child,* Fontana, 1959.

Mead, M., and Wolfenstein, M., *Childhood in Contemporary Cultures,* Chicago U. P., 1955.

Middleton, J., *From Child to Adult: Studies in the Anthropology of Education,* NY, Natural History Press, 1970.

Musgrove, F., *Youth and the Social Order,* Routledge, 1964.

Opie, I. and Opie, P., *Children's Games in Street and Playground,* Oxford U. P., 1959.

Parsons, T. and Bales, R. F., *Family, Socialization and Interaction Process,* NY, Free Press, 1955.

Piaget, J., *Genetic Epistemology,* NY, W. W. Norton, 1970.

Piaget, J., *The Language and Thought of the Child,* Routledge, 1926.

Piaget, J., *The Child's Conception of the World,* Routledge, 1929.

Piaget, J., *The Psychology of Intelligence,* Routledge, 1950.

Pinchbeck, I. and Hewitt, M., *Children in English Society,* vols. I and II, Routledge, 1969, 1974.

Plato, *Protagoras and Meno,* Penguin, 1956.

Richards, M., *The Integration of the Child into the Social World,* Cambridge U. P., 1973.

Rogers, C., *On Becoming a Person,* Boston, 1961.

Talbot, T., *The World of the Child,* NY, Anchor, 1978.

Ward, M. C., *Them Children,* NY, Holt, Rinehart, Winston, 1971.

White, B. L., and Watts, J. C. et al, *Major Influences on the Development of Young Children,* New Jersey, Prentice-Hall, 1972.

Wishey, B., *The Child and the Republic,* Pennsylvania U. P., 1968.

Acknowledgements

Grateful acknowledgement is made to the following sources for permission to reproduce material used in this Reader:

Ariés, Philippe (1973) *Centuries of Childhood*, trans. Robert Baldick, Jonathan Cape; Coveney, Peter (1957) *Poor Monkey*, Hutchinson, reprinted 1967 as *The Image of Childhood*, Penguin; De Mause, Lloyd (1974) *The History of Childhood*, Souvenir Press; Merleau-Ponty, Maurice (1964) *The Primacy of Perception*, Editions Gallimard; O'Neill, John (1973) 'Embodiment and child development: a phenomenological approach' in Dreitzel, H P (ed.) *Recent Sociology* No 5, Macmillan Publishing Co., Inc; Winter, Gibson (1966) *Elements for a Social Ethic*, Macmillan Publishing Co., Inc; Hillman, James (1975) *Loose Ends*, Spring Publications; Bachelard, Gaston (1969) *The Poetics of Reverie* trans. Daniel Russell, translation copyright © 1969 by Grossman Publishers Inc., reprinted by permission of Viking Penguin Inc.; Morano, Donald V. (1973) *Existential Guilt: a phenomenological study*, Van Gorcum Publishers; Barthes, Roland (1972) *Mythologies*, copyright © the Estate of Roland Barthes, trans. Annette Lavers, Jonathan Cape, first published in French 1957 by du Seuil; Parsons, Talcott (1951) *The Social System*, Routledge and Kegan Paul; Durkheim, Emile (1979) 'Childhood' in Pickering, W. F. F. (ed.) *Durkheim: Essays on Morals and Education*, Routledge and Kegan Paul; Platt, Anthony (1969) 'The rise of the child-saving movement' in *The Annals*, January, The American Academy of Political and Social Science; Foucault, Michel (1967) *Madness and Civilization*, trans. Richard Howard, Tavistock; Opie, Iona and Opie, Peter (1959) *The Lore and Language of School-children*, copyright © 1959 Iona and Peter Opie, reprinted by permission of Oxford University Press; Speier, Matthew (1970) 'The everyday world of the child' in Douglas, Jack (ed.) *Everyday Life*, Routledge and Kegan Paul; Denzin, Norman K. (1971) 'The work of little children' in *New Society*, January, IPC Magazines; Stone, Gregory P. (1965) 'The play of little children' in *Quest* Vol 4 Human Kinetics Publishers; Piaget, Jean (1972) *Psychology and Epistemology* trans. P. A. Wells, Penguin; Mead, Margaret (1971) 'Early childhood experience and later education in complex cultures' in Wax, M. et al (eds.) *Anthropological Perspectives on Education*, Basic Books; Erikson, Erik (1950) *Childhood and Society*, Hogarth Press; Mannheim, Karl (1927) *Essays in the Sociology of Knowledge*, Routledge and Kegan Paul; Hendricks, C. Davis and Hendricks, Jon (1975) 'Historical development of the multiplicity of times and implications for the analysis of aging' in *The Human Context*, Vol. VII, Martinus Nijhoff Publishers.

Index